POCO

A

MICHELE
MORRIS

outskirts
press

For Greg

And for our children,
Chris, Jon, and Jenny

Throughout the world, the dragonfly symbolizes transformation.

This is my spirit animal.

TABLE OF CONTENTS

CHAPTER ONE

THE COLLAPSE

I RECALL NOTHING about the Madrid airport. I don't remember getting off the plane, going through passport control, or walking through the airport. As we exited the crowded restrooms in the baggage claim area, Greg bumped me from behind. I assumed he was tired from the long flight, not watching where he was going. I thought nothing of it, until I heard a man yell, "He's going down!"

Jolted, I turned. Greg was struggling to stand, his legs rubbery. Two men helped me as I tried to get him to his feet. He could speak and understand us, but he seemed confused by what was happening with his legs. He kept fighting it, trying to get back up. "I'm okay," he said. "I don't know what's wrong."

But he was unable to stand. The two strangers and I dragged him to a row of hard plastic chairs to the side of the baggage claim area. Greg and I searched for an explanation, discussing how little water he'd had during the flights. Greg was always convinced most ailments could be handled by drinking water. "I'm sure that's it," he said. "I must be dehydrated."

The rest of our flight had deplaned, and we were surrounded by a crowd of passengers staring at us while they waited for their luggage. I hated the fishbowl feeling of strangers gawking at us, and I knew Greg hated being the center of this kind of attention. Several people tried to hand me their half-drunk water bottles. Some pushed wadded-up tissues at me. I didn't have a hand free to take anything.

An English-speaking man approached and said he was a doctor. A Spanish man said his wife had called for the airport ambulance. The doctor asked Greg if his chest hurt. Greg said he wasn't in pain, but he still couldn't control his body. As the doctor assessed Greg's condition, another man interrupted, "Do you think he's having a heart attack? Should you give him a shot of adrenaline?"

"Well if it's a heart attack, that'll kill him," the doctor said. Only later did I realize how absurd the suggestion had been, as if the man had been recalling the scene from *Pulp Fiction* when John Travolta rams the syringe full of adrenaline into Uma Thurman's heart to revive her from a heroin overdose.

The EMTs arrived quickly because we were in the airport of what I learned later was the third largest city in Europe. Had this happened in any of the other places we had planned to be on our trip, Greg would have likely died in that moment. They laid him across the dirty plastic chairs while passengers from our flight exited the airport with their luggage, still staring. The EMTs ran an EKG to assess for a heart attack. Then they ran a second one. The feeds came back normal. Greg repeated that he had no pain in his chest, arms, or stomach, but he began sweating profusely, soaking through his clothing, his sweat pooling on the plastic chairs beneath him. He was squeezing his eyes shut, and he said his head hurt. I mopped the sweat from his face with the tissues someone had tossed at me, small flecks of white paper sticking to his wet forehead and the stubble on his chin. He began grimacing—I could see he was in pain, but I kept hoping he was just massively dehydrated.

The EMTs confirmed that he wasn't having a heart attack and prepared to transport him to the hospital for further evaluation. When they sat him up, though, he began to have what I understood later was a massive seizure. His crimson face looked like it was going to explode, he clenched his jaw tightly, the veins in his neck bulged, he had stopped breathing, and in that moment, I suspected not only that something bad was happening, but, from his repeated comments about how much his head hurt, that something serious could be wrong with his brain. He looked like he was dying.

"Do something!" I screamed at the EMTs, my own heart-rate dangerously high.

"Wait a second," one of the EMTs said, sticking his arm out to hold me back. "He just sat up too quickly."

But as I watched Greg, still not breathing, I knew better—I knew he hadn't passed out from sitting up. For those few moments, I thought I would lose him right then and there.

I waited for what seemed like an hour but was probably fifteen seconds for Greg to gasp for air. When he finally took a single, labored breath, the EMTs swept him onto the gurney and strapped him in. I was told I couldn't ride in the ambulance, and to follow in a taxi. I thought these were Spanish rules, but I now know it was because Greg was in such bad shape that there was a very good chance he was going to die in that ambulance. They needed to be free of me and my hysteria, so they could do their job of trying to save him.

Before the EMTs started running toward the ambulance, I kissed Greg and said, "Just breathe. I love you." It would be the first of hundreds of times over the coming months that I would say "I love you" to his sleeping, inert body. I turned around to gather our bags and saw Greg's lone suitcase next to the luggage conveyor, the baggage claim area now empty, all the passengers from our flight already off to their families, their vacations, their lives. I grabbed our bags and ran outside to find a taxi.

"Hospital Ramón y Cajal emergency room," I said in a panic to the cab driver. I had spent ten years avoiding learning Spanish so it wouldn't confuse my Italian. Now, as I struggled to explain myself to the driver, I cursed that decision.

Our friends Cindy and Peter had arrived in Madrid from Philadelphia earlier in the day for our vacation together, a driving trip starting in Madrid and continuing through Spain and Portugal. As the cab exited the airport, I turned on my phone, frantically trying to contact them, but their cell phones went straight to voicemail. I sent a quick text, "Greg collapsed at the airport," but neither one responded. I ripped my printed itinerary from my carry-on tote and scanned for the hotel information.

An asphyxiating mix of fear, adrenaline, and jetlag was washing over me. I felt like I was going to pass out. Outside the window, there was no sign of Madrid, only sweeping countryside next to the highway. Where was the city? I didn't know where we were going, nor how far it was to the hospital. It felt like the cab driver was taking a leisurely Sunday drive. Did he not understand when I said *"Mi esposo?"* My husband.

I found the hotel number on my notes and tried calling.

Every attempt gave me a disconcerting message in Spanish that I took to mean "this number is out of service." I traveled internationally a lot and was comfortable traveling alone, but under the strain, I couldn't remember how to call Spain from my cell phone. Did I dial 011 first? Should I use the country code? What *was* the country code? Should I drop the leading 0? Should I just call the local number with no prefix?

I tossed the paper onto the seat, opened a browser window on my phone, and searched for the hotel. As soon as the page came up, I discovered that the phone number listed on my itinerary was missing a digit. The mistake had cost precious minutes. My heart was still racing, and my head was pounding.

When the front desk clerk at the hotel answered, I explained what was happening, desperately hoping he understood English. He transferred my call, and Peter picked up on the first ring. I choked out a quick sentence: "Greg collapsed in the airport and he's on his way to the hospital in an ambulance—I'm following behind in a cab." As I heard myself telling Peter, as if watching myself from above, I cracked and began to cry. "Can you come to the hospital right away? It's bad. I need Cindy."

"Okay, okay—we're on our way," he said, and hung up.

Cindy and I had been sorority sisters at Bucknell and had lived together for three years of college. She had been dating Peter, captain of the soccer team, and I had been dating Greg, captain of the wrestling team. We had shared the most formative years of our lives. While both of us had started out as premed students, only she had followed through. Over the past thirty years, she had built a reputation as a world-renowned pediatrician. I had a technical college degree and an unexplainable aptitude for understanding medical terms, but I needed someone with real medical training, I knew, to help me now.

Just as my taxi driver pulled up in front of the Ramón y Cajal Urgencias door, the ambulance opened up its doors to unload Greg. They had stripped off his clothes and he was connected to IVs and machines. *"Mi esposo,"* I told the cab driver again. He had been so calm on the drive, I realized, because he had not understood that my husband was fighting for his life. Now, seeing the severity of the situation, he swept me into the hospital with my luggage before hugging me and wishing me, *"Suerte."* Good luck.

I dragged our suitcases to the Urgencias desk to register Greg but remembered I had removed my insurance card from my wallet to save space while traveling. So stupid. Had I thought we were immune from needing medical treatment on vacation? The language barrier prevented much discussion with the admissions clerk, but I gave her a few key pieces of information before turning to enter the room where they were working on Greg. The nurses pushed me away, leaving me standing in the hallway of this dingy-looking hospital, in a foreign country, jet-lagged and scared, waiting for my friends. I heard the doctors and nurses urgently calling Greg—*"Gregorio! Gregor!"*—as they worked to control his seizures and sedate him.

Gregor was what his mom called him as a child; she had died four years before. No, I thought, don't call him that. He's not ready to join her. He's only fifty-nine. I can't lose him.

It had barely been an hour since we had deplaned in Madrid. I stood chilled and shaking in the hallway when Cindy and Peter came rushing through the front door. Cindy stopped the first doctor she saw. *"Soy doctora,"* she said. I am a doctor. *"Inglés?"* English?

"Si," he told her as she quickly tried to assess what kind of

hospital we were in and what sort of care Greg would receive here. Ramón y Cajal was massive, and everything looked old, dirty, and dated, the surroundings at odds with what we'd think of as a hospital capable of providing world class medical care.

Cindy started to explain the U.S. system, which ranks hospitals by levels of care, but the Urgencias doctor stopped her mid-sentence. "We're the same here. This is a tertiary hospital, and this is where he can receive the best care," he said.

Then he began to explain the extent of Greg's trauma, confirming my worst fears: Greg had suffered a massive hemorrhage in his brain. There was so much bleeding, in fact, that they couldn't tell where it was coming from. Blood kills brain tissue, he explained, and they needed to start draining the blood right away before his entire brain died.

They wheeled Greg to the operating room to insert the drain and left us to wait.

Cindy and Peter and I sat on uncomfortable plastic chairs in the cramped, dirty waiting room filled with Spanish families. A small TV spewed out Spanish news. I knew Greg's condition was grave, but I was in shock and unable to cry. It sounded like his brain had exploded. The doctor's explanation echoed in my head: massive hemorrhage, too much blood, brain damage. How could this be happening? We were supposed to be on vacation.

I don't know how long we sat there, how long it took for them to successfully place the drain and sedate Greg. *"Familia de Morris,"* someone finally called into the waiting room. The doctor suspected the bleeding in the right frontal lobe had been caused by a ruptured aneurysm, but Greg's right carotid artery was also collapsed; they didn't know why. I couldn't understand how he was even alive without one of his carotid arteries, the major source of blood to the brain.

Peter waited with the luggage while Cindy and I followed the medical team, with Greg on the gurney, from the Urgencias wing on the ground floor through the maze of hallways and corridors to the UCI Medica wing (what would be ICU in the states) on the first floor (what would be the second floor in the states). My head was spinning as I tried to keep up with both the nomenclature and the gurney.

After they settled Greg into bay number ten, right by the front door of the UCI, the nurse said to go home and return to the hospital at twelve-thirty the next day, the set family visitation time, when the doctors would give us an update on Greg's condition and let us see him again. It seemed wrong to leave him. At home, wouldn't the patient's family gather at the hospital in a crisis and camp out to be sure he made it through the first critical night? Wouldn't we show up first thing in the morning for doctors' rounds instead of waiting until twelve-thirty?

I stared at his sedated, sleeping form, naked except for a small sheet across his groin, his head wrapped in gauze with a drain now in place. I had trouble registering what was happening. When Cindy said, "Talk to him," I struggled to find any words. I didn't know if he could hear me. I didn't know if he was going to make it through the night. I was only able to choke out, "I love you. I'm here."

We had been left alone with Greg, and as Cindy and I attempted to find our way back to Peter in the waiting room, we became lost in the massive hospital complex. Nobody understood English and we couldn't figure out how to get from the UCI on the first floor of the right wing to the Urgencias on the ground floor of the middle wing. After arriving at the front desk, I said, "Let's just go out the front door and walk around the building," thinking it would be less disorienting.

As we started walking, I saw Cindy was in bad shape. She was dry-heaving all the way around the building and was having trouble standing and walking, and she told me she had been fighting a racing heartbeat—tachycardia—ever since she had arrived at the hospital. I panicked. Was she going to have a heart attack out here in the cold night air and die in front of me? "Should I get a doctor?" I asked, thinking: how silly, she *was* a doctor, the one I was relying on to help me through this. What would happen if she collapsed too?

I finally got her around the building and in through the Urgencias door, and she immediately said, "Mic, go get Peter." As I turned left towards the waiting room she went straight to the desk and said, "*Mi corazón.*" My heart. They whisked her into a room.

Peter and I waited for the doctors to tell us what was wrong with Cindy, luggage at our feet. My heart and head pounded, and I kept thinking, is this really happening? Are Peter and I both going to become widowed tonight? I couldn't talk. I couldn't cry. I was numb.

Sometime later they called us to the room where they had been treating Cindy. Her heart rate had been stuck at 220 beats per minute, dangerously high, for probably an hour or more as we had worked to get Greg admitted. The combination of jet lag, a stomach bug, and Greg's medical crisis, had left her drained and unable to break the tachycardia, so they had administered medicine to bring her heart rate back to normal.

By the time they released her and we piled into a taxi, it was after eleven at night. I hadn't slept on the overnight flight to Frankfurt and had only briefly napped on the short flight to Madrid. Although I had been up for twenty-four hours and was exhausted, I was wide awake from so much adrenaline. Peter checked me into the hotel and helped me to my room. Cindy went straight to bed, wiped out. Peter and I ordered room service. I opened a small bottle of cava from the minibar, hoping a drink would sedate me. I had never been so disoriented in my life.

After Peter left my room, I lay in my hotel bed trying to grasp what was happening. I feared Greg would die overnight, alone in a Spanish hospital. How would I get him home to Denver? How would our family cope? How would I live without him?

Throughout the night, I stared at the time on my cell phone. The minutes ticked by slowly, sleep elusive. I Googled "right frontal lobe hemorrhage" on my iPad. Motor function. Problem solving. Spontaneity. Memory. Language initiation. Judgement. Impulse control. Sexual behavior. These were all controlled by the part of the brain the doctors had told me was damaged. The iPad glared at me in the dark hotel room, and I kept looking for information to ease my worries, instead finding only more things to fear. One website suggested that sexual deviancy could result from damage to this part of the brain. I knew only one person who'd had a ruptured aneurysm—one of Greg's roommates after college—he had died instantly. It was like those ridiculous "would you rather" games the kids used to play in which neither choice was one you wanted. But this wasn't a game. This was my husband's life; it was my life and our life together.

Saturday morning, I pulled myself out of bed, shaking and chilled, in a state of shock and disbelief. I'd had little sleep, and

I was haunted by what I had read on the Internet. Madrid is west of London, but it shares a time zone with Rome, a thousand miles to the east. That meant the sun rose much later than I was expecting. It was pitch-black at eight-thirty in the morning and I thought I must have misread the time.

When Cindy, Peter, Greg, and I had graduated from Bucknell, we had all gone our separate ways: Peter to work in the northwest, Cindy to medical school, Greg to work for P&G outside of Philadelphia, and I to work for IBM an hour north of Greg. We saw each other frequently in those early years, meeting for weekends or catching up at friends' weddings. In 1985, right after Cindy and Peter's wedding, Greg and I, newlyweds ourselves, moved to Colorado to start our life together. We stayed in touch with calls and notes, exchanged ornaments every Christmas, and went to a few college reunions together.

More recently, as empty nesters, we had begun traveling together internationally—to Salzburg, Prague, and Bellagio in 2012, and then Burgundy and Paris in 2014. On each trip, we had picked up right where we'd left off as teenagers at Bucknell thirty years earlier, reminiscing and laughing. Peter enjoyed planning travel as much as I did—perhaps he shared my need for control—and we jockeyed over who would choose hotels and restaurants and itineraries.

When Cindy and Peter came to gather me from my hotel room the morning after Greg's collapse, I was in no shape to choose anything. Peter led us to breakfast, and I followed in a trance. Relinquishing control gave me an unexpected, unfamiliar sense of relief. Cindy told me what to bring to the hospital. Peter picked a place to eat breakfast. He said he'd pay for everything while we were here and we'd figure it out later. They said we had a couple of hours to fill since we weren't allowed back at the hospital until twelve-thirty. Cindy urged me to eat something. I nodded.

Greg and I would have considered this a perfect breakfast café—cute, foreign, strong coffee, great people watching, a view of the city. We were supposed to be on vacation. The four of us were supposed to be wandering around Madrid this morning, getting caught up. We were young—Greg was fifty-nine and I was fifty-seven—and had been looking forward to the coming years with great anticipation, with our three kids launched and happy, Greg nearing retirement, and the time and money to travel. Instead, here I sat, with our oldest friends, without Greg, trying to drink my coffee, struggling to take even a couple of bites of a croissant, for fear I would vomit.

I had no idea what to do.

The night before, I had suggested to Cindy and Peter that they should go on with their planned vacation while I stayed behind with Greg. I had even thought—or hoped—I might get to the hospital and they'd tell me Greg was going to be fine. I was a strong and independent woman, I thought, so maybe I didn't need Cindy and Peter's help. I now understood how absurd that would have been. Since we had planned to be traveling in Spain and Portugal for ten days, they said they would stay in Madrid until their scheduled return date. What I heard them say was, Greg wasn't going to get better any time soon.

We arrived at the hospital a little before the scheduled visiting time. The Spanish families in the UCI waiting area began waving at us and pointing to the doctors. How do they know who I am, I wondered? Do Americans look so obviously American? And if the doctors needed us why hadn't they called?

From outside the UCI door, we saw a large group of doctors and nurses working frantically on Greg. We stood in the hall with an unobstructed view of them hovering over him while the on-call doctor explained what was happening. She talked to Cindy, knowing Cindy was a doctor, but I understood everything she said. The aneurysm was still bleeding. All that blood inside Greg's skull was causing dangerous pressure on his brain. His kidneys were shutting down. They were losing him.

As the three of us stood listening to the doctor, Cindy saw the terror on my face. "Mic, are you okay?"

"No!" I blurted out, breaking the trance, tears finally flowing. It suddenly hit me—the odds were not good, Greg was in bad shape, and my husband of thirty-two years might die. Greg and I had two friends our age who had recently passed away, leaving their wives widowed far too young. This could not be happening to me. "I'm not ready to be a widow!" I cried while Cindy and Peter hugged me.

We were sent to the waiting room. Soon afterward, a team of four neurosurgeons approached us. It was Saturday, and I knew nothing happened in most hospitals on a weekend—not in the United States, and surely not in Spain either—unless it was critical, so nothing screamed emergency more to me than being approached by a team of four neurosurgeons in scrubs and caps, filled with a sense of urgency and ready to operate on Saturday afternoon. The youngest doctor explained that Greg's brain was still bleeding. He urgently needed surgery to clip the source of the bleeding, likely a ruptured aneurysm in his right frontal lobe. "There is a less invasive procedure using coils to repair the bleed, but that can't be done until the radiologist arrives on Monday, and we don't think Gregory will survive until Monday."

I authorized the surgery blindly, not understanding what would be done, just knowing Greg would die if they didn't act quickly.

They took him to the operating room on the sixth floor and we followed to the adjacent waiting room. It was marginally cleaner and fresher looking than the first-floor waiting room, but still sparse, and we sat in hard-plastic chairs for hours. Around eight o'clock, Peter went searching for food, realizing we had eaten nothing since breakfast. He knew if he veered too far from our location in this labyrinth of a building, he might not find his way back, so he limited his search to the vending machines on the floors directly below us and returned with some pretzels. Not really food, but we were starving. As we waited, Cindy said something that made me laugh, catching me off guard, and I was surprised I could laugh during a crisis. Over the coming months I learned not only that I *could* laugh, but also that I *needed* to laugh to preserve my sanity.

The long day of waiting was the start of my education about socialized medicine and public hospitals in Spain. On the plus side, a world-class team of neurosurgeons was working to save Greg's life, in a facility with state-of-the-art equipment at their disposal. The downside was that the socialized system provided few amenities for patients' families. The waiting areas were old and dirty; the chairs were hard, uncomfortable, and worn; and the vending machines contained scary-looking food like shrimp salad sandwiches with expiration dates three weeks out. As a chef, I couldn't imagine how you could safely preserve shrimp for three weeks. The restrooms were barely usable: the toilets were dirty, the door locks were broken, and there was no toilet paper. While there were paper towels, the dispenser was falling off the wall and there wasn't any soap. There were no gift shops, no magazines, no concierge, no valet parking. The window in the waiting room looked out over the ugly and deteriorating roof of the floor below. That it was gray and raining and foggy only added to the dreary atmosphere, and it seemed like punishment to be agonizing over a loved one while waiting in such miserable conditions. The lights were kept turned off, presumably to save money, so we waited in the dark waiting room, in the dark about Greg's prognosis.

Late in the evening, the surgeons emerged; they had successfully clipped the aneurysm and had stopped the bleeding. I exhaled a small breath of relief. Greg was moved back to the UCI to recover, and I was allowed to see him for a few minutes. I stared at his lifeless body, hooked up to fifteen different machines. There was an intubation tube down his throat and a ventilator provided life support, pumping oxygen into his lungs with a steady swish. His bay had no privacy curtain or door. Cindy, before stepping away to allow me to be alone with Greg, again told me to talk to him. Again, I stumbled on my words. "It's Michele. I'm here. I love you. I won't leave you."

Around eleven o'clock, a taxi returned us to our boutique hotel on Plaza St. Ana, the pretty square in the historic center where tourists gather. We were surprised and relieved to find restaurants open late. As a chef and cooking teacher, I usually spent considerable time researching restaurants before our trips, never wanting to waste a single meal on something forgettable. Tonight, we collapsed into the first chairs we saw open, then ordered a disgusting amount of quite mediocre Spanish comfort food—patatas bravas, Spanish tortilla, Manchego cheese, jamón. We ate blindly. Sitting in that plaza, with Madrileños and tourists enjoying a warm fall evening of outdoor dining, it still didn't seem possible that Greg wasn't with us, sipping a beer and enjoying the people watching. Nobody said it, but we all were thinking the same thing: Greg might never travel with us again. Greg might not survive the night.

It was now a full day since Greg's collapse, but I hadn't called anyone. I had badly wanted to call my kids, but after much discussion Cindy and Peter had convinced me there wasn't anything definitive to say yet. Our oldest son, Chris, who would soon turn thirty, and his new wife, Katie, would be busy with Chris's new food truck business. Our twenty-eight-year-old son Jon and his girlfriend, Keely, were at a friend's wedding in Sonoma. Our twenty-six-year-old daughter, Jenny, had recently moved into a new house on Lake Dillon with her boyfriend, Ben, and I knew she was working this weekend. Cindy suggested we return to the hospital on Sunday to see if the surgery was successful—to see, frankly, if Greg was still alive—before I called anybody. I knew what the call would do to the kids, but I also feared I might be making another call soon to share worse news.

Alone in my hotel room, I lay awake for the third night in a row. I didn't turn on my iPad. Cindy had gently told me, for my own self-preservation, to get off the Internet. Instead, I spent the night crying, worrying, analyzing, debating, bargaining, and everything else people do in the scary hours of sleeplessness during a long night of a crisis.

The next morning, Cindy and Peter helped me gather my things. Peter, in an effort to provide a bit of distraction, picked

POCO A POCO

a different small café for breakfast, and as we settled into the table by the front window, we saw a parade coming down the street. Life continued around us. Flamenco dancers twirled by, and it wasn't lost on us that since we wouldn't be making it to Sevilla as planned, this would be the only flamenco show we would see on this trip. The parade included a herd of sheep that stopped long enough in front of the window for the males to get bored and start humping the females. That bit of comic relief forced a laugh from all of us, forced us to take a breath.

We arrived at the hospital for the scheduled visiting time and waited to be called. I was learning it would take hours each day to get just a few minutes with the doctors and a few minutes with Greg. In these first few days, I didn't know what to ask the doctors, so short consults were perfectly sufficient. Later, I came prepared, writing down questions I had discussed with Cindy or doctors back in Denver, to be sure I understood Greg's progress, to ensure he was getting the best care, and to advocate to get him home to Colorado. The challenge of communicating in different languages was ever present. I desperately wanted to speak with the older and more experienced doctors because I felt they were better equipped to treat Greg, but only the younger and inexperienced residents spoke English with ease. As they translated, I tried to read the expressions on the senior doctors' faces. Had she translated that correctly? Was he leaving something out? What was I missing?

The doctors called the families from the waiting room sequentially for consults. When it was our turn, a doctor called, *"Familia de Gregorio,"* and in two short minutes gave us the day's report: Greg had stabilized after the successful surgery to clip the aneurysm; he was still in critical, although for now stable, condition. There was a risk of re-bleeding which would likely result in death, a risk of vasospasm which would cause strokes resulting in more brain damage, and a risk of increased cranial pressure because of the blood from the hemorrhage that had pooled in his brain.

The surgeons had left off a piece of Greg's skull after the surgery to provide a release for some of that pressure, and one of the doctors told us the piece was stored in his abdomen.

I interrupted the doctor. "Wait, what? A piece of his skull is in his stomach?" I asked, slightly nauseated by the thought.

"Not exactly his stomach," the surgeon said. Because Greg would likely end up traveling home before the piece of skull could be replaced, he explained, the safest place to store it—so they wouldn't lose it in this massive hospital—was between the skin and the fat layer of his stomach.

Greg had wrestled on the varsity team for four years at Bucknell and was incredibly disciplined about his weight, so Cindy said what Peter and I were thinking: "Greg doesn't really have a 'fat layer.'"

"Tell me about it," replied the doctor with a gentle smile. "That wasn't easy." We all laughed, and I was again surprised I could laugh.

After my allowed three minutes with Greg, during which I repeated, "It's Michele. I'm here. I love you. I won't leave you," Cindy and Peter and I returned to the hotel to start calling family and friends. During the past two nights, I had fought the urge to call the kids in the middle of the night, wanting to share the burden with my family. But now, faced with the responsibility of telling them about Greg's collapse, I was terrified.

Greg and I were each the middle child in families with three kids, and we had both assumed we would also have three. Having dated for seven years by the time we were married, I was anxious to get pregnant, and within five years we had three children.

We had wanted our kids close together, figuring we could get the baby phase with diapers out of the way more quickly, and thinking vacationing with kids would be easier if they were similar in age. We hadn't thought through how tough it might be to have three teenagers at the same time.

Our oldest son, Chris, had struggled during his early years of school. When he was diagnosed with Type 1 diabetes at the age of fourteen, we were told his diabetes had likely contributed to his difficulties in school. In hindsight, he had undiagnosed learning disabilities, and at age seventeen, he dropped out of high school, something a parent is never prepared for. He had struggled through his teen years and early twenties, Greg and I cringing every time the phone rang for fear more bad news was coming. But by twenty-five, he had gotten his life on track. He had worked his way up from a bus boy to a waiter to a head waiter before becoming a manager of a successful restaurant in Denver.

Katie had been a waitress in the same restaurant. They'd met shortly after Chris had started working there, had married in 2015, and had moved into a new home together after their honeymoon. Right before we left for Spain—just three months before his thirtieth birthday—Chris had left the restaurant to take over a food truck operation. He was excited about the new opportunity, and we were thrilled to see him thriving.

Jon was born only twenty months after Chris. During his early years, he felt the pinch of being the middle child, sandwiched between his big brother, who picked on him endlessly, and his baby sister, who seemed to always side with Chris. Jon rarely shared the same interests as Chris, but after watching Chris play lacrosse, Jon decided to attend a lacrosse camp. He tried out for the team his sophomore year and was devastated not to make the cut, then surprised us by going to camp again the next summer and trying out for the team again his junior year. He made varsity, and although he didn't play much, he was given the sportsmanship award for his enthusiasm. Greg and I had joked that he only wanted to be on the team for the uniform—Jon didn't disagree.

Jon's miserable 2.3 GPA in high school wasn't going to earn him a spot at Harvard, but his letter about persisting to make the lacrosse team impressed Colorado State University enough to get him into the business school. His grades were equally bad there; he graduated with a 2.4 GPA after taking calculus four times before eventually passing the class. Greg had been a terrible student as well yet had gone on to be a successful businessman. That made it hard to stress the importance of grades with Jon. Like his dad, he had found leadership roles in college that proved more important developmentally than any class he could have taken.

Within months of graduating, Jon took a transfer with his company to open a new office in Manhattan, surprising us with his decision to move so far from his Colorado home. The past six years in New York had been good for him, giving him some distance from his siblings, which, in the end, had brought them closer. He'd met his girlfriend, Keely, during his early months in New York, and they'd been sharing an apartment—and a ninety-pound black lab—for the past few years. We hated that Jon was so far away but had agreed that if we had to pick some place to visit a kid, New York was pretty spectacular.

Jenny was the baby of the family and the only girl. From an early age, she was both smart and fiercely independent. I came into the kitchen once when she was about two to find she had pulled a chair up to the counter and was making her own toast. In second grade, she finished her own work so rapidly that she graded other students' papers for her teacher. She clearly needed more challenge, so they placed her in an accelerated math program; in grade school, she was doing middle school math, by middle school she was traveling to the high school for math, and by high school she was taking college classes.

Because of her affinity for math, Jenny's counselors pushed her to study engineering, and she got accepted into the Engineering School at the University of British Columbia, but at the last minute she changed direction. She enrolled instead in the Business School at the University of Colorado. While she was good at math and science, she explained, she hated them. She eventually switched to the Journalism School to pursue an advertising degree, but halfway through her studies decided she wanted to go to culinary school. We were amazed and proud that she understood her passions at such a young age, though we joked that she was working her way down the pay scale, from engineering to business to advertising to cooking.

I had begun aggressively pursuing my own culinary education when Jenny was about ten, and she had watched everything I did and learned quickly. One Saturday, I found her making crepes for her friend after a sleepover. She was only twelve, but she already had a passion for cooking. Within a year, she asked me for weekly cooking lessons; she was a natural.

Jenny finished her undergrad degree at the University of

Colorado, graduating a semester early, before applying to culinary school, where her success blew me away. She was far more creative and skilled as a young chef than I had been at that age, and I was tickled to see her lead her class as executive chef for their graduation dinner. She went to New York for her externship, working at a Michelin-starred restaurant for two months, before returning to Colorado and continuing as a chef at a prestigious restaurant in Vail. Although she was talented, she never loved the work environment of restaurant kitchens, and eventually left for a job at Whole Foods, hoping to use both her culinary and undergraduate degrees in a less volatile environment.

She had reunited with her high school boyfriend, Ben, shortly after culinary school. They had remained friends over the five years since their breakup, and once they began dating again, it was clear they were soulmates. In high school, they had been avid skiers and snowboarders; now they were both serious rock climbers. They had moved in together after just a few months of dating, and the month before Greg and I left for Spain, they had purchased their first home together, a condo on Lake Dillon, about an hour from Denver.

Our kids were adults. We had done the hard work of raising them and were watching them all thrive in their careers and relationships. Yet as I prepared to call each of them, I couldn't stop thinking of them as my babies. I didn't want to lose it on the phone. Maybe, if they heard strength in my voice, they would stay hopeful. For the first time, I discovered that it was going to be easier to speak to them on the phone than to face them in person, when delivering difficult news. I was too nervous to wing it and told Cindy I needed to write down what I would say. Together we crafted a script:

Dad collapsed shortly after getting off the plane in Madrid
He was rushed to the hospital

*An anterior cerebral artery aneurysm in his brain rup-
tured, causing a large subarachnoid hemorrhage (level 4)
in his right frontal lobe—the cause is not known, we could
not have predicted it*

*He had brain surgery 24 hours later to clip the aneu-
rysm and stop the bleeding—it was 4 hours long and was
successful with no complications—it went as well as the
surgeons could have hoped for*

*Dad is stable now but in very delicate condition. He's
heavily sedated, in ICU. This will be a long road with
many unknowns. Hope he will progress and move out of
ICU in 3-7 days*

*We are likely to be here at least a few weeks, possibly
a month or two—Cindy and Peter are with me here for
the week*

I looked back on these notes months later, when Greg was
still lying in ICU, and wondered how the hell I ever thought he
would be out of ICU in a week. Much later I asked Cindy why
we had included that in the script, and she told me she knew
it wasn't going to be the case, but the burden and my fear were
already so great that she didn't have the heart to correct me.
Maybe in hindsight that was for the best, allowing everyone,
starting with me, to slowly come to terms with how long and
difficult Greg's journey would be.

I was still in shock myself, and I know the kids reeled from
the news, even though I have only vague recollections of my
individual conversations with each of them. I called Jon first
to make sure I reached him before he and Keely got on a plane

back to New York after their friend's wedding. I remember asking him if Keely was with him, and I remember hearing him sniffling as he said yes.

I called Chris next and could tell by his groggy voice that he was still in bed. I heard him also crying, and I asked if Katie was with him. While I knew she would be a comfort to him, I was also worried about her. Greg was an important father figure in her life, and she would be as scared and heartbroken as any of my own kids.

I hated having to call Jenny at work. Despite all of her independence and accomplishments and world travels, she could be emotional, and I knew she would shatter when she heard the news. She was out of town to open a new store for work, and she picked up her phone from inside the walk-in refrigerator. As I talked, she cried, unable to speak. I was worried sick about how she would get home to Colorado in that condition, so I texted Ben's mom to ask for her help.

All of the kids said they would fly to Spain to be with me. I told them all no. We were only allowed a few minutes each day to see Greg, I explained, and he was in a coma. I had Cindy and Peter to help me, I reassured them, and I had other friends who could come. None of the kids could afford extended time off from their jobs, and I wanted them to stay put. I assured them I would welcome their help when we got home. "As soon as I get an update from the doctors and have a chance to see Dad each day, I'll either send a text or call you."

The time difference meant they'd get the update first thing when they got up each day, which I hoped would ease their worries as they tried to go on with their lives.

I had created a list of other people to contact, and began trudging through those calls, exhausted from sleep deprivation, terrified of what was happening, and sad to report such horrible news to people I knew loved Greg.

I first called Don Kortz, who had been the president of Greg's commercial real estate firm, Fuller & Company, when we moved to Denver in 1985. When Don left the company in 1995 to head up the Rose Foundation, he tapped Greg to take over as President and CEO. Don and Greg been friends and colleagues for over thirty years. Also, I suspected Don's work with the Rose Foundation and subsequent hospital boards he had served on would be an asset. I asked him to help me find a doctor in Colorado who could help me communicate with the team in Spain, and within an hour he had contacted the CEO of Craig Hospital, a world-class facility specializing in traumatic brain injury, to arrange a call with me.

I emailed Greg's operations executive, knowing the burden of keeping things running at work would fall to her. The company had recently been acquired and was going through the difficult process of merging operations at the same time that they were building out new office space. These two projects had been consuming most of Greg's time and energy before we left for Spain, and although he had told me during the flight about all the progress he had made recently on both fronts, now others would need to step in to cover for him.

I made the difficult calls to Greg's brothers and their wives, and to my sister, whom I feared might collapse from the news after having suffered so many other losses over the past few years—our parents, our brother, her son's father, and her best friend. I asked her to be strong for me and to take care of my kids, thinking if she had an important mission she would be better equipped to soldier through the sadness.

We had moved the furniture out of our house before leaving Denver in order to have our wood floors refinished while we were away, and the thought of dealing with that from Spain was overwhelming. I didn't know where this journey would take us. I could be returning to Denver very soon with Greg's ashes, to a house that was ripped apart with no bed to cry myself to sleep in. Or I could be staying in Spain for a long time, without any way to deal with everything at home. Both scenarios seemed impossible.

"Which one of your friends can get everything done without needing help from you?" Cindy asked.

That was easy: Susan, my good friend of thirty years. Susan had grown up on the east coast and had maintained that edge—she didn't take crap from anyone. She had worked for IBM in Manhattan before moving to Colorado shortly after we had, and having watched her raise three kids, I knew she was good at giving orders. I tried her cell, then her husband Scott's, and then hers again, hanging up each time the calls went to voicemail, not wanting to leave news of this magnitude in a message.

It was Sunday morning in Denver. Probably they were taking a walk or bike ride together. I figured I'd call again later—but Susan quickly called back. She knew, she told me, something must be wrong for me to call her from my vacation in Spain. I read her the script I had prepared, then gave her the contacts for the flooring company, the movers, and the AV installer. I asked her to handle other things like cancelling my upcoming hand surgery and Greg's dental appointments. Letting go of these responsibilities, letting Susan take control, lightened my burden; I was incredibly grateful for our friendship.

I called some of our closest friends—Rob and Lee, Rod and Melanie—and told them what had happened, hoping they could help with anything the kids might need. The conversations were short and stilted, everyone grappling to comprehend the horrible news. I started emailing people. I postponed my writing coach, cancelled my hair appointment, cancelled our massage appointments, asked our bank to keep an eye on our accounts, gave people Susan's phone number, and cancelled social commitments we had made. Before we had departed, I had cleared my work calendar for three months in order to recover from hand surgery, so luckily, I had no business commitments to reschedule.

Although it was a massive relief to shed my responsibilities, it felt out of character to abdicate. Things I had previously cared so much about, that I'd had such a strong need to micromanage, seemed unimportant now. I would normally supervise the fall cleanup in my yard, picky about how every single perennial was trimmed, yet I asked another friend to handle it, telling her I didn't care what they did.

I texted Ben's mom and asked her to find Ben and make sure he would be there to help Jenny. I knew from our call that Jenny was fragile. She was going to need Ben's calm support now more than ever.

I contacted the dog trainer to see if he could keep the dogs longer than planned since Susan needed time to get the house back together after the floors were finished.

I addressed all the things that I could handle, everything I could control. But what I cared most about, whether Greg would live or die, was completely out of my control.

By the time I finished, it was late into the evening. I had

spent three nights with almost no sleep, and I was drained. I let family and friends know I needed to sleep, told them they would hear from me the next day, and gave my cell phone to Cindy and Peter in case the hospital called. Then I took a sleeping pill and collapsed into a much needed deep, deep sleep.

CHAPTER TWO

SURREAL CHAOS

WHEN I WOKE on Monday, I had a fleeting sense of calm that lasted only as long as it took my brain to engage, those few seconds before I remembered what was happening. As the memories came flooding back, my body instantly felt heavy. My head felt disconnected—a hangover of sorts from the sleeping pill I had taken, the drug still working to make me sleepy while I was working to wake up. A shower would help, but as I started the water, the hotel phone rang, piercing the quiet in my room. A chill came over me, not unlike when our kids were teenagers and the phone rang in the middle of the night. No. Please let this not be bad news. The person was speaking English, but it was choppy and difficult to grasp. I understood the hospital needed us to come right away, but I couldn't understand why.

Wrapped only in a robe, the panic rising in my chest, I frantically threw open my door and pounded on Cindy and

Peter's door to tell them we had to leave now. They saw the terror on my face and started throwing on clothes as I went back to my room to do the same.

In less than five minutes we were down the stairs, rushing past the hotel front desk to find a taxi to take us to the hospital, not knowing if Greg was alive or dead.

Peter and I had chosen the boutique hotel we were staying in for its location in the historic center of the city and had convinced each other to splurge for nicer rooms with balconies. Our kids were now "off the payroll," as Greg liked to say, and we could afford a bit of luxury. We should have been sipping wine and laughing on those balconies, not fleeing this hotel to navigate rush hour to attend to a medical emergency.

Madrid traffic is heavy and chaotic, punctuated by a steady stream of tourists crossing wide boulevards and massive traffic circles, and the drive to the hospital on the northern perimeter of the city was painfully slow. I was crammed between Cindy and Peter in the back of a taxi smelling of stale cigarette smoke, anxiously fretting. Why were we so far from the hospital? Why was there so much traffic? Why didn't I know what was happening? Had Greg died?

When we finally arrived, an hour later, Cindy and I jumped out of the taxi before Peter even paid the driver. We pushed our way through the throngs of patients, doctors, nurses, and visitors who stood smoking on the front steps. We ran up the stairs to the UCI waiting area and burst through the door, where the doctors were waiting for us, anxious looks on their faces. The surgeons, they explained, were confident they had stopped the bleeding, but because there had been so much blood blocking their view as they operated, they had missed a small portion of the aneurysm. If left untreated, Greg could have a second, likely fatal, hemorrhage. They wanted to do another procedure, to place coils inside this bubble so it wouldn't rupture again.

The radiologist was pacing, ready to start the procedure. But first he needed to review the risks with me. I was desperate for him to get started, for him to fix Greg. I grabbed a pen to sign the release, attempting to wave off his explanation, but, in broken English, he kept going, covering everything about the procedure and the risks—more bleeding, infection, cardiac arrest, or death. I contemplated the worst-case risk—Greg could die from the procedure—and wondered why we were continuing to discuss this. I didn't need to hear the risks because I had heard "likely fatal" if he had another bleed. The doctor finally finished and allowed me to sign the form.

We followed the team and, two floors up, took our seats in creaky white plastic chairs in the narrow hallway outside of the interventional-radiology portion of the hospital. A construction crew was working on a small room to our left. It seemed absurd there wasn't anything to separate the construction dust and mayhem from the patients. The piercing sounds of the power tools made it impossible to calm myself.

Waiting had never been easy for me—my impatience a flaw I readily admitted to. Cindy and Peter tried to keep me distracted by showing me pictures on their phones—their girls, travel shots, food photos from dining out—and telling me stories. It's a special gift to share a forty-year friendship, and I was relieved I didn't have to wait alone.

Several hours later, when the radiologist had completed the procedure, he called us into his office to show us the before and after images of Greg's arteries in his brain. He wanted us to see that the small bubble they had been worried about had been closed off, mitigating the risk of another deadly hemorrhage.

We crowded into the tiny room with the other doctors, our gazes drawn to the computer screens, and the images were so clear that even I could read them, despite having no medical training.

Cindy saw Greg's brain scans—images showing where Greg's brain tissue was healthy or dead—on an adjacent computer screen and asked if she could look at them. She had promised to be completely honest with me about Greg's case, and to do that, she needed to assess the extent of Greg's brain damage. The doctors bristled at her request, not understanding how a pediatrician could make sense of those images. They didn't know Cindy was the head of a child abuse program at a renowned children's hospital, or that she traveled worldwide to educate about child abuse and to testify in child abuse cases. They didn't know that her work for the past twenty-five years had required her to review, sadly, thousands of brain scans. But I did. And I needed to hear the assessment from her, from someone I trusted.

We were less than three days into Greg's journey, but already I was concerned I was doing the wrong thing, scared we were keeping him alive when the brain damage was too great. Only a month before our trip, we had revised our wills, so his living will—with his preference not to be kept alive artificially—was fresh in my mind. While I was terrified Greg was going to die, I had a stronger, pervasive fear that he would survive and never forgive me.

"He's going to hate me for saving his life!" I said to Cindy when we were out of earshot of the doctors.

"Mic, there hasn't been any point where there was any other choice for you to make."

It was true. Everything had happened so quickly that I'd

had no information to act on other than the recommendations from the doctors. But the possibility was looming that Greg would not recover well, that his life—and therefore my life and our life together—would be forever changed.

Cindy tried to reassure me: she had seen plenty of healthy tissue on the brain scans. I was still inconsolable. She returned to the neurosurgeons and radiologists, who had remained standing in the hallway to discuss Greg's case. "Yes, it was a very bad bleed," they told her. "But there will be an opportunity, with much rehabilitation, for him to recover and have a good quality of life." Perhaps it was my complete lack of understanding of what rehabilitation would be like that made this so hard to grasp. What exactly would they do to rehab his brain? He was lying in a coma, paralyzed. I couldn't picture the steps that would move him from this point to any meaningful recovery.

This would be the first of countless times I questioned whether I was doing the right thing authorizing treatments for Greg. And it would be the first of countless times when physicians explained to me that, with time and rehabilitation, people with brain damage can and do recover. I had been told we wouldn't know the outcome though, wouldn't know to what extent Greg could recover, for probably a year or more. That meant I wouldn't know until then if he would be happy to be alive and glad the medical team had worked so hard to save his life, or if he would be miserable living with the deficits I had read about three nights before.

My mind spun with imagined scenarios. He might recover, or he might still die. He might walk with a limp, or he might never walk again. He might be able to return to work, but not in the same job. He might know us, or he might not. He might speak and understand, or he might be childlike. He might come home to live with me, or he might live in a nursing home. We might pick up our marriage where we left off, or he might become a sexual deviant and need to be institutionalized. I became acutely aware of the tremendous burden of uncertainty, a burden I carried during our entire journey.

We returned to the hotel, exhausted from the mad rush to get to the hospital that morning and drained from worry. The young staff at the front desk had been shocked by our crisis and wanted to help us, but I dreaded facing them as we entered the lobby. I needed to sit calmly, without feeling the need to explain anything, so Peter updated them. The hotel kept an iced bottle of cava on the counter, and Cindy and I each poured ourselves a glass and sat down. Not until much later did we realize that the bottle was meant to be a welcome drink at check in, not a salve for people in crisis.

As we sat in silence, I looked around at the tall flower vases in the lobby. While we had been at the hospital, the flowers had been replaced with gorgeous cut orchids. A mass of twisted wire coils had been inserted into each vase to anchor the stalks of the flowers, something I'd never seen in a floral arrangement. It was a sign, I thought, sipping my cava—it symbolized the success of Greg's coil procedure that day, which I found oddly comforting.

Prior to Greg's collapse, I don't recall taking much note of things like this. I had been a "do-er," a person with a full and busy life. I wasn't religious, so traditional symbols like the Christian cross held no meaning for me. I didn't believe in God, at least not in the way many of my friends did. During the first days after the collapse, the mere suggestion that a friend was praying for us made me prickly with annoyance. I didn't need someone's futile prayer to a God I didn't believe in. I needed a medical team that could use modern technology to provide real miracles through their skills and actions. I needed science, not religion.

I was getting texts of encouragement and support from a small group of sorority sisters that Cindy and I had taken a reunion trip with just three months before. Cindy had updated each of them when Greg collapsed. Although I didn't notice this at the time, none of them said a thing about praying. Later, I learned that Cindy had cautioned them about my sensitivity in an effort to protect me in any small way she could.

I was surprised that I made peace with the concept of prayer within a few days. We're all human, just doing what we think we can, to get the outcome we want, I thought one night. Some were praying, some sending healing thoughts, some crossing their fingers, some wishing, some carrying around good luck charms, and some bartering with their gods. In the end, everyone wanted what I wanted: for Greg to recover.

On Tuesday, four days after Greg's collapse, the doctors began using the word "stable" in their daily reports. The bleeding was under control, the pressure was being managed, he had been placed in a medically induced coma, heavily sedated and paralyzed to protect his brain—at least for now, there was no imminent crisis. This would be a waiting game; I was being challenged to take things one day at a time, which was not at all easy for me.

I had always been a planner—planning my career, planning our wedding, planning to have a family, planning our move to Colorado, planning vacations, planning, planning, planning every detail of our lives well in advance. All of that planning might have seemed exhausting and tedious to others, but it had been my way to attempt to control my life, and until this point, if I had put enough energy into most challenges, I had been relatively successful in achieving the outcomes I wanted. Now, the future was completely uncertain and completely out of my control. For what felt like the first time in my life, I was unable to make any plan at all. That terrified me.

After my brief bedside time with Greg in the UCI, and after a long lunch to calm ourselves, Cindy and Peter began helping me figure out what needed to be addressed while we waited it out. All the reservations we had for our trip needed to be cancelled—Peter handled that with the help of the young hotel staff, who amazingly, helped secure a refund for every "nonrefundable" payment we had made. I was grateful for the kindness of these strangers and couldn't know then how many more times over the coming months I would experience such generosity and kindness.

I contacted our health insurance provider, thinking how fortunate we were not to have a financial crisis along with Greg's medical crisis. We had great benefits as a perk of Greg's position in his company. Our membership in YPO—an international business organization Greg had joined years before—provided repatriation insurance to fly Greg home on an air ambulance if needed. Even if they didn't approve the request, we had the means to cover the cost ourselves. The expense of living in a hotel in Spain while Greg was hospitalized was not catastrophic for me. I knew many families of patients in Ramón y Cajal were not so lucky. If this tragedy had happened to others, it might have saddled them with a devastating financial loss.

Susan's daughter and son-in-law, who were anxious to help,

picked up our dogs from the trainer and moved in to our house. They were newlyweds who had just set up house together, yet said they would stay as long as needed, not having any idea how long that might be. I was grateful for their flexibility. I was grateful to Chris and Katie, too; they picked up my car from the airport garage in Denver, and Greg's car from his office, and took both cars home for us.

I continued to work through the long list of things needing my attention. Most of my bills were on auto pay. The mail was on a vacation hold. I put the newspaper on permanent hold, not knowing if Greg would ever read again. I had discussed with Cindy and Peter the need for another friend to come to Madrid when they had to leave; I considered whether I needed anything sent to me right away or could wait for someone else to come. Doing something, anything, naturally gave me a feeling of progress, though I knew none of this had anything to do with Greg's recovery.

Our connected world, with cell phones, email, text, and social media, enabled the news of Greg's collapse to spread rapidly. Within a few days, not just our immediate friends, family, and colleagues in Denver, but also friends from the east coast, college friends, friends of mine in Italy, and even Greg's oldest high school friends had heard about our situation. Every hour someone new asked to be added to the list of people I was updating.

Although I had been sending a daily email to this growing list of people, and although the support of all these people who clearly cared about us was comforting, I quickly became overwhelmed. Too many people kept trying to reach me by text or phone, and I couldn't respond. I needed a better way, especially with the time zone difference, to share Greg's progress with the world, and I made a note to start using an online journaling tool called CaringBridge.

I had been delaying the most important task of the day because it was the most difficult: in-depth discussions with the kids about what to expect. I practiced first with Cindy, then called each of the kids in turn.

Chris and Jenny were on mountain time in Colorado, and Jon was on eastern time in New York, and I had to think where they each would be at the moment I called, not wanting to interrupt them at work or upset them in a public place. Jon often worked from home, so I sent him a text asking, "Can you talk for a minute?" He called my cell instantly, and I scolded myself for not prefacing the text by letting him know that Greg was okay.

"Hey, Jon. Dad's okay," I started. Then I forced myself to say out loud the words that Cindy had helped me practice. "The outcome can't be predicted. The next ten days will be a very dangerous time because he's at risk for vasospasm. It could damage his brain further and kill him." I could feel Jon's tension through the phone. He was my optimistic child; this must be torture for him. Did I hear him crying softly?

I pressed on. "And then, even if—I mean when—he makes it through that," I said, still working on speaking in positive tones, "the road to recovery will be very long. We don't when he will recover, or what deficits he will be left with." I hated saying that word out loud: deficits.

"Okay," was all Jon said. What was he trying to say? That he was okay? That he believed his dad would be okay? Or just okay he had heard me? I wanted to stay on the phone with him to make sure he really was okay.

"I need to call Chris and Jenny, so let's hang up for now,

okay?" I said. "I love you so much."

I called Chris next, hoping his shift on the food truck was finished. "What's happening? Is everything okay with Dad? Are you okay?" he asked in rapid fire.

I couldn't possibly tell him how terrified I was for fear it would scare the shit out of him. Instead I said, "Dad is stable and I'm okay, just tired. Cindy and Peter are taking care of me." Then I relayed the same practiced speech I had gone through with Jon.

Chris's life to this point hadn't always been easy. He had battled some demons during those tough teenage years, and all too often he had learned things the hard way. As a result, he was a realist, and he wanted the truth. "I understand what you're saying, but what do *you* think it's going to take? How long do *you* think until he recovers?" he asked.

I had no idea, but knowing he needed an answer, I put a stake in the ground. "It'll probably take at least six months for Dad to make any meaningful recovery." I wasn't sure if I believed this or not. I wasn't sure Greg was ever going to recover, but Chris needed a goal, something against which to track his dad's progress, so I had given him one.

"What do you mean by deficits?" he asked. Chris and I were close, very connected after the many challenges he had faced, and I could feel him trying to work this out. I owed him honesty, so I said his dad might have difficulty walking or require a wheelchair. But I didn't want to terrify him, so I didn't mention that Greg might not know us and might be forced to live in a nursing home. Chris was a lot like his dad. He would understand how Greg would feel about living in a nursing home. He didn't say it, but he knew: his dad would rather die than live with severe deficits.

I was drained, but I still needed to call Jenny. She asked fewer questions—not because she didn't have questions; she just couldn't stop crying long enough to ask them. She was Greg's only daughter, and though I didn't think Greg was as aware of it as I was, they shared a special father-daughter bond. She was highly competent and independent, but she still relied on her dad to guide her in career changes, relationships, and other important life decisions. The night before we had left for Spain, I had gone to bed, and the two of them had stayed up for hours playing pool and talking. She later told me she had known they should go to bed, but she had just wanted to be with her dad.

I knew how much she needed him in her life, and I knew how scared she was that he was so sick. I was grateful to be having the conversation over the phone rather than in person. It was hard enough listening to her cry while I talked, imagining her face contorted in grief, imagining her slumped in her car in the parking lot at work. If she had been in front of me, it would have crushed me.

With everything needing my attention handled for the day, I leaned back on my bed.

"I have something to share with you guys," I told Cindy and Peter.

In the summer of 1986, a year after our marriages, Cindy and Peter had come to Colorado to visit us. Video cameras were new and trendy, and Greg had taped much of our week together as we traveled through the Colorado mountains.

Greg and I had watched the old home video a few weeks

before our trip. Thinking it was hysterical, he had asked me to load it onto my iPad so we could watch it with Cindy and Peter while we were traveling together.

I felt a need to honor his request, so the three of us poured a glass of wine, toasted Greg, and crowded together on the small bed in my hotel room. Greg was an introvert, often only loosening up after a couple of drinks, so he was behind the camera for most of the video. But you could hear his voice, teasing out conversation by questioning the three of us. There was so much laughter—including Greg's chuckle from behind the camera—and it reminded me of our early days as friends: those early years of dating when life was so carefree. Those mornings in Cindy's and my apartment at Bucknell when the guys would stick their heads out of their girlfriends' bedroom windows to say good morning to each other. How Peter would tease Greg for sneaking out the back door near my basement bedroom as if nobody would notice he had come over to sleep with me. The early years of our friendship had been so easy and fun-filled; we had been so innocent about how our lives would unfold.

We watched the video, laughing as hard as we cried, and though none of us said it, we hoped one day we would again be laughing together with Greg.

I had just about fallen asleep that night, something that was nearly impossible during those early days, when Cindy and Peter pounded on my door. The front desk had accidentally connected a call from the hospital to their room instead of mine. Peter couldn't understand what they were saying—even though he had studied Spanish—so we hurried down to the reception desk for help.

The UCI doctor on call didn't understand how the concierge had gotten the number of her mobile phone. Annoyed, she was stonewalling; she wouldn't tell him anything. It was grueling—we envisioned a life or death crisis unfolding as we watched someone speak on our behalf in a language we couldn't comprehend. The clerk continued to press her. "Mrs. Morris is a guest at our hotel. She doesn't understand Spanish, but she is standing right here," he said, glancing at me.

The doctor finally relented, explaining we needed to arrive earlier than planned in the morning to sign a release for a procedure. It didn't occur to me to ask what the procedure was. All I understood was that if they were performing a procedure tomorrow it meant Greg hadn't died and they expected him to be alive tomorrow.

Back in my room I tried to calm my racing heart and clear the adrenaline once again pulsing through my body. Never in my life had I been so unable to communicate with people. I was extroverted, social, and well-spoken. I was a perceptive person, known for my ability to get to the heart of an issue quickly. So why was I struggling so much to understand? Was it the language barrier? Or was I simply too tired and scared to handle this?

I had considered starting the CaringBridge journal later, as a way to let people know how Greg's rehab was going once we were back in Denver, but the overwhelming outpouring of support from friends convinced me to start it on day five. I hoped it would relieve me of the daily burden I felt to update everyone. Months later, I re-read my first entry. It sounded so clinical and detached, completely void of any emotion. I hadn't mentioned any of my fears or heartbreak, only the facts about what had happened to Greg:

Greg and I arrived in Madrid on Friday night, 10/21, where he collapsed at the airport from a ruptured cerebral aneurysm. He was rushed to Hospital Ramón y Cajal where he was diagnosed with a level four subarachnoid hemorrhage and they put in a drain to prevent pressure on the brain. By Saturday morning he was still bleeding in the brain, so they proceeded to surgery to clip the aneurysm—that was successful, and he became stable after the surgery. By Sunday night the CT scan showed that while the bleeding had stopped, some of the aneurysm still remained, so on Monday morning they performed the procedure to place coils inside the aneurysm to prevent a secondary rupture—that was successful, and he remained stable.

Months later I understood: I wasn't ready to let the world see I was vulnerable. I wasn't ready to ask for help. I had always been the person who got things done, not the person needing help. I was the person so many friends thought of as accomplished and successful. I couldn't stomach their pity now. I was the caregiver—not only for aging parents, but for many friends and family members. I wasn't in any way comfortable being the one who needed to be taken care of. To be vulnerable and needy felt like I was failing, and I hated to fail.

Without consciously thinking it, I was also protecting

Greg. He was well known in the Denver business community and, after thirty-two years in commercial real estate, was considered a strong leader, well liked and respected by his employees and colleagues. He had served on the Chamber board of directors and had been involved in various charities. It was hard to imagine his career might be stopped short, and it pained me to think people in the community were speculating about his future—or lack of one. I didn't want his many friends and colleagues to know he would likely have deficits. Our friends had access to the same Internet data I did, and I pictured people at dinner parties talking about us, horrified to think they might be discussing Greg's brain damage. Greg, who cared deeply about his privacy and image, would hate that.

Not soon after that first CaringBridge post, my phone and email exploded with concern and offers of help. Colleagues wanted to send things. Friends were ready to fly to Madrid. People wanted—and I would understand later, needed—to help. But I didn't want anyone to break into what now felt like our private bubble in Spain. The entire experience was so surreal, still like some weird out-of-body experience. Deep down I worried that the more people got involved, the more they saw of the situation, the more real it was going to feel. I wasn't ready for that. In the five days that had passed, I had only begun to digest the enormity of the tragedy. If I let anyone into my nightmare, I might discover it wasn't a nightmare at all, but a horrible reality. If that happened, I feared I would snap; I had already felt how sympathy and caring from both friends and strangers in an unexplainable way intensified my searing pain. I couldn't afford a breakdown. I had so much work to do. Moreover, I worried that involving others would be more work than help—that I would feel some misplaced obligation to take care of anyone who came to help me. If the kids came, I worried my energy would be diverted from Greg's care to theirs.

It was different with Cindy and Peter. They were our oldest friends, and they were already in Madrid and part of the nightmare. Cindy could not only help me interpret the medical landscape, but also help me relax—and even laugh. I knew Peter would handle everything else. They were inside the bubble; I trusted them.

I couldn't ascertain, at least not from so far away, who could be trusted at home. I later understood I could have trusted everyone—they all loved us and had only our best interests at heart. But in those early days, I wasn't ready to reveal how bad things were. So I pushed back hard. I explained the socialized hospital system meant we weren't equipped to receive cards, flowers, or visitors. I asked Greg's many friends to use CaringBridge instead to express their support, promising to share their messages with him. It wasn't lost on me that if we hadn't had so many wonderful friends, if Greg had not been so successful, if he had been a "nobody," none of this self-protection would have been necessary. But that wasn't the case. He meant so much to so many people—over the coming months I learned just how much—and he was loved. Despite never wanting the role, I had become the public face to Greg's private tragedy.

During the remainder of Cindy and Peter's time with me, we developed a routine. We always ate breakfast, never sure what might happen during the day and knowing we'd feel better with food in our stomachs. We'd make our way to the hospital with a tote bag holding snacks, water, change for the vending machine, and notes about Greg's care. We carried tissues, knowing there would be no toilet paper in the bathrooms. Time passed at a snail's pace as we waited, and we distracted ourselves by looking at pictures on our phones and sharing stories. We were never brave enough to eat any of the vending machine food, but I discovered the coffee machine dispensed a decent *cortado* that helped clear some of the cobwebs in my mind.

Each day, by the time we had our doctor consult and I saw Greg, it was mid-afternoon. We'd leave the hospital, holding our breath as we stepped over smoldering cigarette butts, get in a taxi, and find a nice restaurant where we settled in for a long, Spanish-style lunch, not finishing until late in the afternoon.

It wasn't just that we needed to eat—we also needed to escape and decompress. We needed to be together, to smile, and to laugh. We needed a drink. We needed to pretend, for at least a couple of hours, that the nightmare wasn't happening. In many ways, being in Madrid made it easier, even if friends at home didn't understand this. There were no distractions from my life at home, and because the city was gorgeous and the food delicious, I entered a fantasy world each time we left the hospital: we were simply old friends on vacation.

I didn't photograph anything and wouldn't allow Cindy or Peter to take my picture. I didn't want evidence of this fantasy, inwardly ashamed of enjoying myself in any small way while Greg suffered.

Since we had plenty of time to fill and fall in Madrid was pleasant, we walked through the city every day. In the Retiro, the public park in the center of Madrid, the older evergreen trees on the lower quadrant had been trimmed in a topiary style resembling giant, green brains. Every time I walked through that park, I was drawn to them. They somehow symbolized Greg's brain healing.

When we'd been planning our trip, Peter's cousin had suggested we look up a law school friend in Madrid. Peter had taken the information, even though our planned itinerary wouldn't really allow time for a meeting. But soon after Greg's collapse, Peter decided a friend in Madrid might be helpful. I didn't yet want help, but Peter wanted me to have someone on call after he and Cindy left, so he contacted Pedro. Coincidentally, only two days later I needed a lawyer to execute a legal document; Pedro was quick to offer his help.

Because I was in Spain, the agreements were far more complex than a simple notarized power of attorney would have been in Denver. We met at Pedro's sister's law office in the high-end Salamanca neighborhood, where professional offices, luxury shops, and expensive restaurants shared space on the tree-lined streets. I sat numb and mute, and Pedro, Cindy, and Peter made small talk while the documents were executed. During my two months in Madrid, Pedro became a friend as well as a much-needed advocate in my navigation of the Spanish medical system. Although I asked him several times to send me a bill for the legal work, he never did: the kindness and generosity of strangers.

During those first ten days, Greg fought to survive despite the setbacks and odds against him. Because of the severity of the injury to his brain, the doctors had warned he could have brain spasms that could cause strokes. They handled the first round of these spasms with a minimally invasive drug treatment. The blood from the hemorrhage was lodged in his brain as clots, which they treated with medication. Each day I struggled to keep up with the challenges Greg faced. Each day, Cindy reminded me, as she would for Greg's entire journey, that the road to recovery would not be straightforward. He was going to have setbacks; I needed to get comfortable with that trajectory.

For the entire week, of course, I had known that Cindy and Peter would be leaving, but I had been trying not to dwell on it. I couldn't imagine how I was going to continue without Cindy's medical guidance, without my oldest and best friend to help me smile in the face of such sadness, to make me laugh despite my fears. She assured me she was only a text or a phone call away, day or night. Still, I had to start taking care of myself in Madrid, instead of allowing Peter to make every decision. Each day as we'd driven to the hospital, he'd been looking for a closer hotel, and when we found one, the young assistant manager from our first hotel negotiated a great setup at the new hotel: two large connecting rooms (one for me and one for friends who might come to Spain to help me) at a bargain price that included breakfast. The new hotel was only ten minutes from the hospital, so I wouldn't need to battle rush hour traffic to reach Greg. The new hotel would be an improvement, but the pain of saying goodbye to Cindy and Peter overshadowed those feelings.

As we checked out of the first hotel, I was choking back sobs and couldn't say goodbye to the assistant manager. He had been so solicitous throughout the week, had bent over backwards to help us, and had even brought his mother to the hospital to help, yet I didn't have the strength to thank him. I couldn't look at the young clerk who had told Peter a few days before that she'd spent her two days off praying for Greg, or the manager who had cancelled our remaining reservations in Spain and Portugal. If I let myself think about the kindness of these strangers, tried to articulate how much it meant to me, I would break. I couldn't let that happen. Instead, I let Peter say what I couldn't to these generous people while I waited outside for a cab in the fresh morning air.

Our friends Rod and Melanie had lived in Spain for three years, and during those years had spent considerable time in hospitals after their son suffered a bad burn. Experience with the Spanish medical system would be helpful, so I had asked Melanie to come to Madrid when Cindy and Peter left. Unfortunately, her flight to Madrid had been diverted the night before because of storms, and she wouldn't be arriving until Tuesday. So as I prepared to say goodbye to Cindy and Peter, I also prepared to be on my own for at least a day.

The taxi, before taking Cindy and Peter to the airport, dropped me at the new hotel. I felt childlike and small, like when you're dropped at school for the first day all alone, tears streaming down my cheeks. The new hotel was enormous, catering to business people, conventions, and flight crews from the nearby airport. Cindy, Peter, and I huddled amidst the chaos. The doormen were helping with luggage as people were exiting taxis and carelessly tossing cigarette butts on the ground. We hugged briefly. Cindy and Peter promised to call when they landed. They jumped back in the cab and drove away from the hotel. It had been ten days; I was alone for the first time since Greg's collapse.

I hurried to check in, wanting to escape the crowded lobby. Once in my room, I unpacked my suitcase for the first time. I had kept the bag packed, I realized, thinking we might be going home soon, thinking Greg might not make it. He was stable, now; it was time to unpack.

I had only brought enough toiletries for our ten-day trip. Before stowing Greg's suitcase, I raided his dopp kit for anything I could use: razor blades, deodorant, Excedrin, Claritin. As an afterthought, I took out one of his t-shirts to sleep in. Or maybe I just wanted to smell him, something I had never before understood. The room was spacious and comfortable. I looked around and pulled open the curtains to crack the window and saw the sunrise.

It was too early to see Greg, so I investigated the hotel breakfast room. It was huge, with stations for breads and sweets, eggs and hot dishes, cheese and meats, and yogurt and fruits. A line cook in the back made eggs or churros on request. There were self-serve coffee machines that dispensed an *espresso*, a *café con leche*, a *cappuccino*, or a *cortado*. A new morning ritual developed: I sat down where the dining captain indicated there was space and had a cappuccino to fire up my brain, not even taking the time to remove my purse from across my body. Next, I circled the food-filled tables, sat down with my food, removed my purse, and ate my breakfast. I finished with a second cappuccino for good measure. I ate well—Spanish tortilla, crusty bread with pureed tomato and Spanish olive oil, Manchego cheese, and roasted tomatoes on some days; scrambled eggs, fresh ricotta on toast, or an omelet on others. On that first morning, I studied the business travelers and families around me, wondering why they were there, wondering if any of them could see the sadness on my face or guess the crisis I faced every day.

I retreated to my room after breakfast to wait until it was time to see Greg. When the hotel phone rang, echoing loudly, it startled me. It was Clodagh, a friend of one of my friends in Denver, married to a Spanish man and living in Madrid. My friend in Denver had asked her to call me. Clodagh had been reaching out through emails and text messages for days, making it clear she was there to help—lunch, driving, laundry, company, whatever I needed. I hadn't been ready and had been avoiding her, but as we finally spoke, I softened, and we made plans. Melanie was now scheduled to arrive the next day; after our visit with Greg, Clodagh would pick us up for lunch. I was both looking forward to meeting her and dreading it.

The families in the UCI waiting room had begun to recognize each other. They all knew I was the American with the sick husband, so when I arrived at the hospital at the scheduled time that morning, they began frantically signaling to me— with urgent hand gestures and Spanish I didn't understand. If they had needed me urgently, why hadn't the medical staff called? There was a reason I had a pit in my stomach every time the cab pulled up in front of the building: I never knew what crisis I would encounter, and I didn't have confidence the medical staff knew how to reach me.

The doctors believed Greg was having more spasms, this time more severe. Every time he suffered more of these spasms, more vessels shut off delivery of blood and oxygen to his brain, causing more brain damage, resulting in more deficits. In the first week, the radiologist had drawn the quadrants of the brain on a piece of paper for me to reference, crossing out a large circle near his right frontal lobe, explaining that part of the brain was dead from the initial hemorrhage. It was okay, both he and Cindy had explained, because other healthy parts of his brain could be trained to take over functions normally handled by this part of his brain.

But now, with each new round of spasms, he was crossing out more areas on the drawing to reflect new areas of dead brain tissue. I was terrified every time I pulled out the diagram for an update. Would Greg be able to recover? Was I doing the right thing authorizing another treatment? Would he hate me for prolonging his life?

I sat on the same white plastic chairs in the same narrow hall where I'd sat with Cindy and Peter just days before. The doctor who had shown me the damaged areas of Greg's brain said, "We will do an angiogram, and if we find anything, we will treat it."

I sent a text to Melanie: "Fuck—radiologist just reviewed with me that there is more brain damage now than they saw before—going in now for angiogram. Trying to breathe and not freak out. Not telling any of this to anyone yet until I see where we are later today."

After the first hour, when nobody had returned with an update, I knew they had moved beyond diagnosis and into treatment. If the vasospasm was severe enough, it would require not just an injection of drugs, but a riskier treatment with angioplasty balloons. The doctor had cautioned that the balloons could explode when being inserted, which would cause a massive bleed that would likely kill Greg. But if his brain didn't get the oxygen it needed, he was going to die anyway. So I had signed the authorization, impatient for the doctor to begin.

Why did this have to happen on the first day I was alone? I couldn't reach Cindy to review what was happening because she was already on the long flight home. Melanie was about to board her own flight. She suggested I call her husband Rod to talk, but I sent them both a text explaining I was afraid I would fall apart crying if I tried to speak. Instead, I sat alone on those uncomfortable white plastic chairs, fidgeting, crying, and worrying.

Over three hours later, the radiologist called me into his office, and seeing Cindy wasn't there, said, "I know you are not the doctor, but I think you understand." I nodded. He proceeded to show me before and after views of the collapsed arteries in Greg's brain. Two places were severe enough that he had inserted balloons to open up the arteries. More medication had been inserted into other smaller arteries at the back of his brain to open up the blood flow there. The radiologist looked exhausted, and as I sensed how difficult this procedure must have been, how hard he must have worked to save Greg, I was overcome with gratitude for his efforts.

After they transported Greg back to his bay in the UCI, I stood at his bedside talking to him, reciting my daily mantra. "It's Michele. I'm here. I love you." They had not been able to remove the drain yet as I had hoped—the pressure on his brain was still dangerously high. So high, I would later learn, that had they not left the piece of skull off after Greg's brain surgery the first day, he would have died by now from the pressure.

The nurse signaled it was time for me to go. Before leaving, I asked why nobody had called me given the urgency of the situation that morning. "We aren't allowed to call your cell phone," one of the younger residents explained. "We can't make toll calls." In their socialized medical system long-distance fees were forbidden. "Can you purchase a Spanish phone with a local phone number?" she asked.

Because of the long wait for Greg's treatment, it was late in the day when I returned to the hotel. I quickly dropped my things in my room before asking the concierge where to purchase a phone and then took off. Over the coming days I discovered just how perfect the location of my new hotel was. Everything I might need—a department store, a grocery store, the Vodaphone store, an ATM that didn't charge me a fee, a metro stop to get to the city center cheaply, several good restaurants, and even Pedro's office—were nestled right in this two-block area of Madrid.

By the time I had purchased the phone, it was seven o'clock. I hadn't eaten lunch, so I popped into the Alimentari store across the street from the phone store and bought a bag of potato chips and a cheap bottle of cava. Ten years before, when I'd left my twenty-five-year career at IBM to launch my business as a cooking teacher, many clients had asked me what I made for my family for dinner, inspiring me to start my first food blog. For one full year I'd posted what I had for dinner every day, whether it was a gourmet multi-course meal paired with wines, which I did occasionally for friends, or something simple like a pasta dish or meatloaf. Later, when that year of blogging was over, I was embarrassed to count how many times I settled for my comfort food of choice: potato chips and sparkling wine. Alone in Spain it was no different. Thankfully both were readily available and surprisingly cheap.

Back at the hotel, I retreated to my room where I could binge in private. I sent the kids a text and updated the rest of the world through CaringBridge. In that post, perhaps because being alone all day had given me more time to reflect,

I shared something personal for the first time, something that revealed how tortuous my own thoughts had become.

I had a revelation today: I am not "keeping Greg alive."
He's beaten the odds, so clearly, he's fighting to stay alive.
It will be a very long journey, but he seems intent on it.

The difficult day had shown me I could do this on my own if I had to. It had also convinced me I didn't want to. Melanie would arrive in the morning and stay for the next ten days, but I had no plans beyond that, and it seemed certain at this point we would be staying in Spain for much longer. I was finally ready to ask for help, so before I collapsed into my bed, entirely spent, I sent an email to Susan. "Do you think you could come to Madrid after Melanie? I don't think I can do this alone."

CHAPTER THREE

BLACK MONDAY

OVER THE NEXT week, as Greg stabilized, my CaringBridge posts reflected the relative calm. *Greg is stable, no news is good news.* Still, I struggled with the snail's pace of his recovery. When would they remove the drain? When would he be past the risk of more strokes? When would it be safe to travel?

Greg and I had met Melanie and her husband Rod when we had joined YPO in 1997. We had walked into the room of an event and the first YPO members we noticed were Melanie and Rod—tall, extremely good looking, and more than a little intimidating. The four of us had laughed about this over the years as Rod and Melanie became some of our closest friends. Melanie had cleared her calendar immediately when I asked her to come. Rod had been crushed his buddy was in lying in a coma in critical condition. They had played in a golf tournament together only a month before, and Rod had been texting me pictures from that fun weekend, a big grin on Greg's face in every photo.

Melanie and I quickly settled into a routine. We'd have breakfast at the hotel before taking a taxi to the hospital around eleven. Then we'd wait for what felt like hours for the doctor's report. Every day I would remind Greg: "It's Michele. I'm here. I love you. I won't leave you." And then, after my allotted few short minutes with him, we'd leave the hospital for the day.

At the time, I didn't think about the contrast to what this would have been like in the states. There were obvious things: patients and doctors and nurses wouldn't have been smoking on the front steps. But there was more. I wouldn't have needed to use a language translator to make sure the doctors understood me. I would have been able to camp out in Greg's room to wait for the doctors to make rounds and pepper them with questions. I would have been able to stay with Greg all day and night if I had chosen to.

Here I wasn't given that choice. It almost felt like being released from the tragedy for the rest of the day. I kept my new Spanish cell phone with me day and night, but Greg was stable, and the hospital never called. Instead of camping out at the hospital, Melanie and I would go enjoy a long lunch; I don't remember a single day I didn't have a glass of cava. Was I drinking at lunch because that's what everyone around me in the restaurant was doing? Was I trying to numb myself from the deep fear I carried every day? Or was I fantasizing I was on vacation, drinking wine at lunch as Greg and I surely would be doing if he were with me?

After lunch each day, we walked around the city, ran errands, and picked up supplies before retreating to the hotel for the night. Each evening I washed laundry in the tiny hotel sink, using the small bottles of bath gel the cleaning staff left, then hung my clothes in the bathroom to dry. I made sure to update the kids first before posting a CaringBridge update for the rest of the world. I tried to decompress.

I was skilled at packing light, always carrying my luggage onboard, whether I was traveling for a weekend or a month, and had only a limited selection of clothes with me. I hadn't planned on lounging around in a hotel room, so I dragged Melanie to the H&M store across the street to buy something comfortable to wear at night. "Is that what you were looking for?" she asked when I exited the dressing room to model the sweat suit for her. The fabric was an ugly gray tweed, the crotch of the pants hung inches too low on my petite frame, the top was far too large, and the pants were pleated in front, making them look like some MC Hammer outfit from the 1980s. Melanie was a former Miss Colorado who had used her pageant money to put herself through college; she had more sense of style then I could ever pull off. I was sure she would never have been caught dead in something so unflattering. "I don't mind shopping while you try on some other things," she said.

But I didn't want to try on more outfits. I didn't care how I looked. I just wanted to be comfortable in the evenings as I propped myself up with pillows on my bed and attempted to relax. We never went to dinner; usually we were still full from our late Spanish lunch and too drained emotionally to face the world. Instead, we watched movies on Melanie's computer and grazed on our provisions from the gourmet grocery store near the hotel. I had cleared out the mini fridge in my room, replacing the tiny bottles of liquor and overpriced hotel snacks with gazpacho, jamón, olives, cheese, bread, and cava.

I loved that the Spanish people of Madrid had a love affair

with potato chips just like I did. There were salty chips cooked in olive oil in the Sanchez Romero grocery store, bowls of chips on counters in bars, an entire stall devoted to perfectly crisp chips in the Mercado, and even vendors on the street with chips spread out over tables. They used a big scoop to fill a paper cone so the Madrileños—and I—could eat them while walking around the city.

I was stiff from spending too much time in the bed, so we moved the sitting chair from my room into Melanie's room to watch movies. I left the mini bar in her adjoining room stocked, not knowing if any friends who might come to help me after her would want anything. I asked the cleaning staff for extra hangers.

In just days, I had figured out how to live in a hotel for an extended, unknown timeframe, and I was surprised to see how little in the way of clothes, food, or personal items I needed to live comfortably.

On the day Melanie arrived, we met Clodagh, the Madrid friend of my friend in Denver. They had met at a get-together for expat women in Madrid and had instantly become fast friends. This was coincidentally the same time Melanie and Rod's family had lived in southern Spain and other friends had lived in Barcelona. At the time, I couldn't believe so many Denver friends felt the need to live abroad; now I felt fortunate for the connections.

Clodagh picked up Melanie and me from the hospital. After a short tour around the northern end of the city, where her house and the hospital were located, she took us to a restaurant near our hotel for lunch. I wouldn't have noticed the nondescript building on my own. Inside was a warm restaurant with pretty, soft-white décor that I ended up coming back to every week. As we studied the menu, Clodagh asked if they had *lubina* that day. It was never on the menu, but I ordered it every time I ate at the restaurant. The delicate, flaky, white fish, drizzled in peppery Spanish olive oil, studded with roasted chips of garlic was a salve for my broken heart and weary soul. I was sure the maître d' wondered about me. I was American, couldn't speak Spanish, showed up each week with someone different, and always ordered a glass of cava. Sometimes I was calm, sometimes fighting back tears. I never found the courage to tell him why I was there, perhaps finding the language barrier too hard, perhaps still afraid stating the tragedy out loud would make it real. The restaurant was always packed with Madrileños conducting business over lunch, yet he always found me a perfect table. *"Muchas gracias,"* was all I said to him, but I hoped he understood I meant more than simply thank you. I hoped he understood I was more grateful for his kindness than I could possibly explain in Spanish.

After twelve days in Madrid, I realized if I just sat in my hotel for weeks while Greg recuperated, I would never have the strength I needed, emotionally or physically, to care for him. Melanie was asleep, still jet lagged, so I left her a note by the front door and found the hotel gym, relieved it was empty. I rode a stationary bike for a few minutes, then got onto the elliptical machine and stared at the Spanish news on the TV while I pedaled. It hadn't even been two weeks, but I could already feel the strain of caregiving, away from my routine and the comforts of home, the love of my life fighting to survive. I hoped some exercise would help, both physically and emotionally.

Melanie had traveled extensively with her husband's business and was adept at networking; they had friends and business colleagues throughout the world. I was more guarded and still tentative about letting anyone into my nightmare. Gently, she pushed me to meet people in Madrid and to accept their offers of help. We had coffee with a member of the Madrid YPO chapter who would rally any resources that could help. Melanie met Pedro, who assured her he would be available for anything I needed. Clodagh was warm and generous, intent on helping me. We were of similar age, her kids all launched like mine, and she and her husband lived in a pretty apartment in the neighborhood to the north of the hospital. Melanie urged me to accept her support.

I had run out of clean clothes and had grown tired of washing things in the hotel sink, so when Clodagh invited us to her home later that week for a home-cooked meal with her daughter, I heeded Melanie's advice and accepted her offer to bring my laundry. Looking out over the greenery from Clodagh's apartment, past the city perimeter to the mountains north of Madrid, my mind slowed, and my worries retreated for a few hours. Lunch with friends, a glass of wine, laundry, a movie in English—for just a few hours I found some respite, comforted by everyday activities and the embrace of friends both new and old.

Melanie came into the doctor consults with me as Cindy had. She didn't have formal medical training, but she wrote down our questions and translated them into Spanish for the constantly changing team. During the weekend after her arrival, the on-call doctors shared confusing reports about Greg's progress. One said the right side of his brain was completely dead, but the left was fine. Another said she had treated patients worse than Greg who had gone on to enjoy a good quality of life. But a third said his prognosis was very poor. The apparently conflicting reports made it impossible to understand Greg's true condition. Because many doctors struggled with English and required a younger nurse or resident to translate, I was never certain I understood correctly.

On Monday morning, seventeen days after Greg's collapse, Melanie and I sat in the waiting room, Melanie holding our list of questions. It was earlier than the scheduled family visitation, so the UCI waiting room was empty, except for one woman. Her hair was dyed dark, making her look younger, but I guessed by the lines on her face she was a little older than I was. She was dressed in simple clothes and wore her worry and sadness on her face. Her husband is very sick too, I thought. She, also, is terrified he might die. It seemed she preferred to sleep on the torn and dirty couches instead of traveling back and forth to her home between visits each day, and I felt guilty about my comfortable hotel room minutes away.

I noticed she was brave enough to eat from the vending machines—was that one of those shrimp salad sandwiches? *"Buenos dias,"* was all we said to each other, but our eyes locked for a brief moment.

I was tired of being in the dark, so I flipped on the lights for the waiting area, wondering when someone would turn them back off, and settled into the couch I now thought of as my assigned waiting spot.

As families began to gather in the waiting area, we were

the first called. *"Familia de Gregory?"* Being called first was a bad sign. Triage was the same everywhere—critical patients have priority. Melanie and I gathered up our coats and scarves and purses, having been told it wasn't safe to leave things unattended, and followed the resident down the stark, white hall, the fluorescent lighting harsh and relentless. We crowded into the small office for our consult with the young resident; thankfully, she spoke English. My questions were difficult enough in my native tongue and I didn't want the burden of translation.

"What have you been told?" she asked. She looked so serious. Her eyes were pinched together and boring into me through her glasses, scaring me immediately.

"The doctor on Saturday said the right side of Greg's brain is completely dead, but it's possible the left can compensate, and another doctor said he might recover to a decent quality of life," I said. Melanie was sitting on the edge of her chair with our notes, gripping them tightly. "But the resident yesterday said the prognosis is poor. I don't understand." I was rushing to get the words out, anxious to hear her response. When I finished, I leaned forward an inch in my chair, holding my breath, waiting for her to tell me Greg was stable and recovering.

"All of these things are true," she said, not answering my questions and in no way easing my concern. She saw my confusion and continued. "Yes, there have been patients with severe brain bleeds like Greg's who have recovered, but in his case, the prognosis for *any* recovery is very poor."

I stared at her, a cold wave of fear washing over me. The previous doctors who had talked about recovery were talking about Greg's long-term opportunity, through rehabilitation, to achieve a decent quality of life. But she wasn't talking about the outcome of rehab. She was saying Greg wasn't recovering medically, that Greg would likely not leave this hospital alive.

My eyes darted from her to Melanie to the window, barely able to focus. The blood rushing through my brain was trying to drown out her continued explanation. I was desperate for her to say they could save him. "But what about putting in a shunt to drain the fluid?" I asked.

"You don't understand. We already have a drain, and the pressure is still too high. The shunt is nothing more than a different drain." She sounded frustrated—whether because I didn't understand or because she couldn't save him, I wasn't sure.

I felt stupid that I didn't understand her and, at the same time, terrified I did.

"We can place him in a deeper coma," she said, "but he might never wake up." They had run out of treatment options, she explained, before dismissing us from the consult.

I had been sucker-punched. I couldn't catch my breath.

I threw my purse and coat and phone and tote bag into Melanie's lap so she could guard them in the waiting area while I went to see Greg, possibly for the last time. My legs were shaky, and as I pushed through the UCI door, I saw him right in front of me in bay ten. I stood beside his bed, trying not to faint, focusing on the display with his blood pressure reading and his pulse. The numbers didn't look bad, but the ventilator sent a soft whoosh of air to him at regular intervals, breathing for him and reminding me how very sick he was.

Barely able to speak, tears running down my cheeks, I touched him gently on the shoulder. I reached across the bed-rail to his face and stroked his cheek, clean shaven and smooth from freshly applied lotion. I spoke softly. "If this is too much for you, and you don't want to keep fighting, as much as it will break our hearts, the kids and I will survive." As I said the words, I was gulping down sobs and trying to breathe. How exactly would we survive? How would I carry on without the man who had been at my side since I was a teenager?

His lifeless body lay nearly naked in the bed. He was bloated, connected to fifteen different machines, and had a thick red scar running from the back of his skull up and over the top to the front.

"We don't want to lose you, but we will find a way to go on living without you. I don't want that, but this has to be your decision. If you want to keep going, you need to fight harder."

Was I being selfish by asking him to keep fighting? Was this what he wanted? Did he know how much I still loved him and still needed him after all these years together?

In January of 1978, I returned to Bucknell for the second semester of my freshman year in college, excited to see my friends and resume my newly independent life. The first night back, I went to a frat party with an upperclassman friend, and we were standing at the side of the room, listening to the music blasting and watching people dance under the mirrored disco ball.

"Hey, I think I'm going to get out of here," my friend said, nodding toward a pretty, petite brunette in the corner. "Will you be okay on your own?" He and I weren't romantically involved—he was like a big brother, looking out for me during those first wild months of college—and I assured him I'd be fine.

I watched him approach the girl with a smile on his face

and whisper something in her ear, and they were off. As I continued to watch people dance, I saw Greg across the room. He was thin but well-built—a wrestler's body, I knew, having dated wrestlers in high school—and he had a magnificent head of black-brown hair. When he smiled, his big toothy grin lit up the room. He was wearing a turtleneck, and I smelled his musk cologne as he approached me with a beer in his hand. I nervously sipped mine.

"How's it going?" he asked, and I smiled at him. God, he was good looking. With that full head of hair and million-dollar smile, he could have been mistaken for Donny Osmond. I didn't know him yet, just who he was. My roommate's cousin was in Greg's frat, so we had spent some time there during the first semester, and I had often seen Greg from across the room, leaning on crutches. I learned later he'd had knee surgery to repair a wrestling injury.

What I didn't know at the time was that Greg had seen my picture in the book that Bucknell put out each fall featuring the new freshman class. It was crudely called "The Pig Book," and lots of guys used it to seek out new girls. Years later Greg told me that when he saw my name was Michele Fugere, he had envisioned I'd have some exotic French accent. He had been eyeing me, it turned out, as much as I had been him.

"You want to get out of here?" he asked. Yes, I most certainly did. I was feeling a little buzz from the beer, but a bigger buzz from raw physical attraction.

The party was on the uphill portion of Bucknell's campus, the opposite side from Greg's fraternity, but not far from my dorm. It was freezing as we left the party, so we pulled our puffy down coats tighter, and ran arm in arm through the academic quad toward my dorm, laughing as it started snowing.

"Where's your room?" Greg asked when we were inside the dorm. I shared a room with two other girls, but they weren't back yet for the semester, so I had the place to myself. We sprinted up the stairs and rushed into my room, a double room with a small bathroom in between. One room housed three desks and wardrobes and was covered in posters of good looking movie stars and athletes; we slept in the other room. Two of the beds were bunked and since mine was on top, Greg and I tumbled into my roommate's single bed instead.

I had dated in high school, and wasn't a virgin, but I had never slept with someone the first night I met them. This felt different. I often reflected later that I must have known it wasn't going to be a one-night stand, that Greg was going to be the one for me.

"Are you on the pill?" he asked, as we began kissing.

"Yes," I said, as we started fumbling with buttons and zippers. The night was wild, passionate, and urgent, fueled by teenage hormones.

This was the beginning of our love story. Since that night, we'd been together for almost forty years. The only time we were apart was for a short time during my sophomore year in college when Greg didn't want to be tied down and had broken things off. He was dating a skinny, blond, large-breasted cheerleader. I knew I would never be any of those things and felt inadequate. I was dating one of his fraternity brothers, admitting only to myself that I was just using him to keep hanging around the frat and see Greg.

Through that spring and the following fall, Greg and I kept secretly seeing each other behind his girlfriend's and my boyfriend's backs. We weren't together, but we were most definitely not apart. By winter, I'd had enough of the ambiguity.

I was living with Cindy and two other girls in a house near campus, just a few blocks from Greg's fraternity. I grabbed my coat and put on boots to tramp through the snow to confront him. I had been around his frat enough that nobody questioned me as I went inside. I ignored the few guys I saw in the living rooms that flanked the front hallway and sprinted up the wide staircase to the second floor. Because Greg was an officer in the frat, he had a large corner room to himself.

I knocked lightly on his closed door. "Yeah? Who is it?" Greg answered, his voice raspy.

I pushed open the door to stick my head in. "It's me. Can I come in?" He was in bed in the middle of the afternoon, his blankets pulled up to his chin.

"Sure," he said, and I pulled his desk chair over beside the bed. I had spent a lot of time in that bed, but I needed to be strong, so the last thing I was going to do was crawl in with him.

"Are you sick?" I asked.

"Yeah. I don't know what it is, but I have a fever and I feel like shit," he said.

"Well, this might not be the best time," I said, "but what are we doing? We're both dating other people, but we keep meeting secretly, we keep having sex, you spend more nights at my apartment than you do here. I don't know what this is supposed to be, but I'm sick of it." I took a deep breath, waiting for his reaction. I had never before given him an ultimatum. I was in love with Greg, and though he might reject me, I needed to know if he loved me too.

"I don't know what we're doing either," he said, coughing.

"Look, I think we're great together," I said. "I love you and want to be with you. I can see a future together. But it's time to decide. Either we're dating and we're back together, or the secret meetings are going to end—your call." I was terrified waiting for his response.

"I love you too," Greg said, and I softened.

"Move over," I said, crawling into his bed. I put my arm across his broad chest so I could snuggle my neck into his shoulder. "Sorry you're sick. I love you."

During the first weeks we were in Spain, I had been adamant about not wanting the kids to come. It would be far too hard on them, I had argued, and I didn't want them to see their dad in this condition. Even if he died, I didn't want their final image of their dad to be his lifeless body lying naked in a hospital bed hooked up to machines. Greg's recovery was going to take a long time, I reasoned, and they were young adults with jobs and lives that shouldn't be put on hold. I had been defensive when people questioned my decision, but I felt I knew what was best for my kids, and I had defended my protective instincts.

Now, with the prospect that Greg might soon be dying, both Cindy and Melanie urged me to let the kids decide for themselves. As much as I hated the thought of them coming to Spain, I understood their point: "the kids" were adults now and had the right to choose.

If I had thought the initial calls telling them Greg was sick were hard, they were nothing compared to telling them I thought their dad was going to die. I needed them to know Greg and I had discussed this exact situation, not more than six weeks ago. He would not want to be kept alive artificially to endure the kind of life I suspected he would have. It was going to be nearly impossible not to fall apart on the phone, so Melanie helped me create a script for the calls:

The doctors are concerned that dad isn't getting better. They have tried many things with a small amount of success but there aren't many things left to try. At this point, most of the entire right side of his brain is dead. And while there is still a small hope he will survive and go on to rehab, there's a big concern now that he would not have any quality of life. Your dad and I have discussed our wishes and I know he would not want to live with the deficits they are describing to me.

I can't decide if it's important to you to see your dad's body before he passes away. It would not be my choice, and I think it would be very difficult for you to fly here and see him like this—probably more difficult than you can imagine.

If you're worried about coming to be with me and help me, please know I have support to get through this. You know I'm strong and I can do what your dad would want. Know that I will come home to you and we'll take care of each other. But you're an adult, and this is your dad, and if you feel you want to see him, then it's time to get on a plane.

Please don't feel like there's a right or wrong answer— whether you decide to come or not is a deeply personal decision. I don't want to tell you that you can't come, even though it's not my wish for you to see dad like this. There's always the chance for a miracle, but given dad's condition, I don't hold out hope.

Because it was still early in the morning in the U.S., I called Jon in New York first. I listened in agony as he collapsed with grief. "Am I a horrible person because I don't want to come there?" he said through his tears.

I was reminded of how Jon had reacted when our beloved nanny was dying—he'd been unable to face visiting her in hospice and had worried he was a bad person. Just as I had told him then, I told him now: "No, you're not a horrible person Jon. I don't want you to come either—I don't want you to see your dad in this condition. This is a highly personal decision and there is no right or wrong answer. You need to do what feels best for you." I held it together just long enough to tell him I'd be back in touch after calling Chris and Jenny.

As soon as I hung up the phone, I fell apart in my own pool of grief. I sat sobbing in the hotel room while Melanie handed me tissues, gently trying to comfort me. As a mother herself, she understood the enormity of the situation and felt my pain. She helped me settle myself to call the other two kids.

I was hoping neither of the boys would want to come to Spain and that they would convince Jenny to wait at home also, so I called Chris next even though it was very early in the morning in Colorado. Just a few years before, Chris had been struggling to find his path in life; he had put us through hell during those years. Now, as I talked to him, although I could hear him crying, I was struck at how mature he had become. Right before we had come to Spain, Greg and Chris and Katie had gone out for drinks to celebrate Chris's new job, and they had texted me a selfie of the three of them beaming—I was hosting a group of guests in Italy at the time. I knew this was what Chris wanted to remember. Chris trusted me, and now he trusted my instincts; he would not come to Spain. "I love you mom, and I'm here for you," he told me. As I hung up, I wailed—that we were losing Greg, but also that Greg would never see how mature Chris had become.

I called Jenny's store manager to find Jenny for me, explaining she needed privacy to take my call. Jenny walked out to her car and was crying as soon as she got on the phone, knowing I was about to deliver a blow. She had always been strong, but now she was collapsing into heartbreak. She was going to lose her dad and her special father-daughter bond was going to be forever broken. She couldn't speak, so I told her I was going to send a text with a call-in number so that we could all get on the phone together. She barely said goodbye before hanging up.

After another hard cry, I pulled myself together and sent the kids a text with a conference line number, so we could speak as a family. I could hear all three of them crying. "As hard as this is, it's important I honor your dad's wishes. This isn't what he would want," I said. "I've said this to each of you already—it's not my wish for you to see dad like this, but I can't decide for you. If you're going to come, you need to get on a plane immediately. Remember, it's a long trip—even if you leave soon, you might not get to Spain before he dies."

Jon and Chris quickly said they weren't coming, which I sensed gave Jenny the permission she needed to say she would also wait for me at home. I exhaled a small breath of relief and hoped I hadn't pushed them too hard to that decision.

After I hung up, I sent a text to Katie to tell her I loved her. I knew the prospect of losing Greg would be crushing for her. He was more than her father-in-law—for the past two years they had worked together and seen each other every day. He had been an important role model, helping her get started in business after graduating from college, and she loved him as if he were her own father.

I was worried that Jon, living in New York, was so far away from Chris and Jenny in Colorado. I reached out to his girlfriend, Keely, by text, hoping she would be able to stay home from work with Jon. I was glad they lived together, knowing they would be there to help each other through this.

Then, frantic about Jenny driving in her condition, I asked Ben's mom to find Ben and make sure he could leave work to help Jenny. Although she and I hadn't known each other well when the kids had dated in high school, she had known Jenny for a long time, and I knew she loved her. Having another mom step in for me in my absence eased my guilt at not being there to help Jenny through this.

Melanie had gone into her own room to begin calling people. I suspected she didn't want me to hear the sadness in her voice or see her tears as she shared Greg's condition. She called her husband Rod first, then Susan, who was scheduled to come to Spain in just two days. Melanie told her to cancel her flight. She called Rob and Lee, who were going to come after Susan, so they could also cancel. Later she would replay those conversations to me, sharing everyone's shock, disbelief, and crushing sadness.

I called my immediate family—my sister and Greg's brothers—and choked out what was happening. I remember few specifics of any of those conversations, just the overwhelming sense of pain and loss.

Next, we called Pedro, telling him we needed help, and with that call, my focus turned from saving Greg's life to preventing the hospital from keeping him alive artificially. I feared I'd be forced to watch him die slowly in Spain over the coming weeks; although I couldn't imagine my life without Greg after nearly forty years together, I certainly didn't want either of us, or our children, to suffer that kind of torture. I told Pedro Greg would not wish to be kept alive in this condition, and that we needed help either making sure his wishes were honored or getting him home to die peacefully there. I couldn't afford to be stumbling through translators, unsure of what was happening—I needed someone with Pedro's understanding of both the legal and medical systems in Spain to help navigate the next steps.

By the time we had made all of these calls, it was time for bed, but there was no way I could sleep. I spent the entire night awake, crying and texting the kids to be sure they were okay. It didn't seem possible this was happening. One word echoed in my head throughout the long night: widow.

By morning, an abnormal calm had washed over me. I heard myself discussing my finances with Melanie over breakfast, thinking how detached I sounded, like I was observing myself from afar, watching myself in my own drama. I was anticipating my husband dying very soon and was preparing to face the reality that I would be widowed, yet I was chatting mindlessly about 401K accounts and the equity in our house. I didn't know if this was a typical reaction to impending emotional devastation, only that I was unable to talk about Greg dying and needed to think about something other than losing him.

Pedro had offered to help in any way he could, and reached out to a friend of his, a cardiologist at Ramón y Cajal. It was highly unusual for one medical department to intervene in another's care of a patient, but Pedro had called in a favor and asked the cardiologist to verify Greg's condition. The cardiologist had made some calls and by ten that morning he confirmed to Pedro that we had understood correctly. Greg was not expected to recover.

Pedro called me when he heard, delivering an unfathomable blow, then graciously cancelled his own appointments to meet us at the hospital, knowing both the language barrier and the Spanish approach to end-of-life considerations would be challenging.

As soon as we arrived, we ran into the young resident from the day before and confronted her without sitting down, unwilling and unable to wait for our medical consult. I tried to explain that Greg wouldn't want to live like this and that I had to honor his end-of-life wishes. "He has a living will," I informed her, knowing as I said it that it would not be recognized in Spain.

She stared at me in confusion. "Our Spanish families ask us to save their loved ones," she replied, sounding shocked and angry.

Whether the language barrier was to blame, or my overly stressed mental state, the result was a massive misunderstanding. We fumbled through the conversation, Pedro helping, until we realized what she was telling us: they hadn't needed to put Greg into the deeper coma we had discussed. Miraculously, he had turned the corner overnight, and it seemed possible now he might recover.

The resident continued with her update. "The latest scan shows no new areas of brain damage. We think Greg is finally past the risk for vasospasm." She still looked so serious, her eyes boring deep into mine as she continued, "We need to see if we can close the drain without the pressure on his brain rising too high. If not, we need to place a permanent shunt to drain the fluid before he can go home." He also needed to have his intubation tube removed before he could fly home. They would replace that with a trach tube, she said, before removing the paralytics. Then they would slowly reduce his sedation, and start the slow process of trying to wake him up. That was the word she used: *trying*.

A day earlier I feared Greg was dying. Today, the medical team was discussing the steps necessary to transport him home. "Can we say we've already done the consult for today?" she asked. We had been standing in the UCI waiting area through the entire conversation, doctors, nurses, patients, and families of patients coming and going around us as we talked. There was nothing more to cover, so we thanked her before sitting down to collect ourselves.

I immediately called the kids. It was very early in the morning in the U.S., but I knew they had been awake all night, and I wanted to ease their pain as soon as possible. I hadn't posted to CaringBridge on Monday. It had been the only day I'd missed since starting the journal. Now I posted a quick update. Friends told me later they knew something bad must have happened on Monday when I'd gone silent, and they had been terrified to click on that post on Tuesday.

That's how I felt every day. That's how I felt every time I arrived at the hospital and every time the phone rang. Our friends had a choice whether they read along in my journal posts, whether they were on this journey with us. I didn't have that luxury.

Our doctors in Denver had requested Greg's medical records to prepare for his eventual transfer. I didn't know how to proceed, so Pedro escorted us to the medical records department. Spain is stricter about patient privacy than the U.S., and initially the clerk pushed back. She didn't care that I was Greg's wife, I understood her to say; unless Greg signed for his records, she wasn't going to release anything.

Pedro argued with her in Spanish, and I was grateful he had come along. He was tall and dressed in a dark blue suit, and as he leaned forward in his chair with his hands firmly planted on her desk, his body language portrayed both authority and urgency. While he pushed and argued, Melanie and I watched in silence. He finally wore her down, but only slightly. "I can work on it, but I cannot tell you when," she said, glancing at me as she spoke.

Pedro went back to his office—he had missed an entire morning of appointments to help us—leaving Melanie and me to work with the clerk. Melanie was from the south, although people rarely noticed it in her everyday speech. When she dropped into her drawl, when she started using "y'all," I knew she was intent on working her Southern charm on this woman, hoping to warm her up and get the help we needed.

"Have y'all ever been to the United States?" she asked.

Yes, the clerk said, she had a son in the Joffrey Ballet in Chicago.

"Wow, that's impressive!" Melanie said.

The campaign continued: Had she ever lived in Chicago? No. Had she always worked for Hospital Ramón y Cajal? No, she had spent many years working for the drug company Pfizer in Madrid. She pronounced it FEE-zer, but I understood.

I had been watching silently as both Pedro and Melanie had tried to secure the records from this clerk. I was so stressed, frustrated, and impatient that I would have snapped if I had tried to speak. Knowing that wouldn't help, I had done something I rarely ever did: I had kept my mouth shut. Now I said, "Pfizer? Did you know Guillermo Azuerro when he was in Madrid?"

"Guillermo, si!" she exclaimed, clearly excited. "I worked for him for many years when he ran Pfizer here. He and his wife are good friends with my husband and me."

Two weeks before we'd come to Spain, Greg had attended his fortieth high school reunion on Long Island. He had convinced a small group of his best friends to attend, including Billy—Guillermo—Azuerro, who had moved back to run Pfizer in his birth country of Columbia after his stint in Madrid. I knew this only because Greg had asked me to Google his friends before the reunion, so that he would be current when he saw them.

What were the odds I'd be cajoling medical records out of a clerk in Spain who happened to be great friends with one of Greg's closest high school friends? Was this just another inexplicable coincidence, or was it a sign? I explained what had happened to Greg and said, "My husband was with Guillermo in October for their high school reunion just a few weeks ago." I showed her the text from Greg with a picture of them together. "They're old friends."

And with that simple connection, the clerk softened. "Go to lunch," she said. "I'll let Pedro know what time to pick up the records. *Suerte.*"

Three hours later, we were seated in Pedro's paneled law offices near our hotel. One of his staff was scanning the printed medical records and transferring the CDs with images of Greg's brain into her computer to send electronically to the doctors in Denver, a task that would take time because of the sheer volume of records and the size of the digital images. Although I had never met her, she graciously worked into the evening and through the next day—her day off—to complete the work and return the records to Melanie to hand carry back to Denver.

We were chatting with Pedro while she worked when Melanie suddenly started to cry. In that moment, it struck me how stoic she had been for the past two days, helping me through the darkest part of this journey so far. She had sat beside me while I called my children to tell them Greg was going to die, and she had suffered my agony along with me. She had called both Rod and Rob, two of Greg's very best friends, to tell them Greg wasn't going to make it, and she had listened as these men had broken down on the phone. She had smiled her way through our meeting to coax medical records out of the clerk when she was exhausted. One of her good friends was critically ill, and her pain could no longer be contained. Watching her, I was keenly aware of the sacrifices my friends were making for Greg and for me, and I was humbled by their friendship and grateful for their support.

When we settled into the hotel for the evening, election day was just starting in the U.S. The world was watching, wondering whom the U.S. would elect as president. I had been ignoring the entire presidential battle, consumed by my own drama in Spain. Although the election coverage had now begun, the eight-hour time difference meant we wouldn't hear the results until very early in the morning. Melanie and I went to sleep, expecting to wake up and learn that Hillary Clinton had been the first woman elected president.

At five in the morning, deep into a fitful dream, I woke to Melanie pounding on my door. "I can't believe this! Donald Trump is going to be President!" she yelled. We huddled in bed watching the election results, in shock like much of the world. BBC Europe was the only channel in English, so we were hearing the news with a European slant, and it struck me that not everything is about the U.S. People around the world had their own concerns about our elections, and it gave me perspective as I listened.

Though I was disheartened to see such divisiveness and anger in our country, I couldn't allow myself to wallow in the frustration for fear of adding to my own despair. I needed to focus on something good, so I listed in a CaringBridge post the things people in Madrid had so generously done for me. People had joined me at the hospital to interpret. Pedro's sister had effortlessly handled legal paperwork. A secretary had spent hours copying records for me. I had been offered people's clothing to wear since I had no winter clothes with me. Clodagh had cooked lunch for me. A man from YPO in Madrid had invited me to join his wife for a workout with her personal trainer. I had been taken to the movies. I had been coddled by hotel staff. Concierge staff had called the hospital for me to check on Greg. Strangers had shown up at the hospital because a friend of a friend of a friend had told them I might need help. A clerk had bent over backwards to gather records for me. The kindness and generosity I had experienced during an incredibly scary time for my family had renewed my faith in humanity; expressing my gratitude publicly was uplifting.

Months later I was asked if I would ever return to Madrid: surely it held only tragic memories? That wasn't how I felt. Madrid would always hold a special place in my heart—these were the people who had saved Greg's life and done so much to help me during our crisis, and I never wanted to forget them or the perspective I had gained from the experience.

CHAPTER FOUR

#STARTBREATHING

SUSAN ARRIVED NEXT, her suitcase bulging with everything I had requested: clean jeans, another bra, my athletic shoes, a coat, yoga pants, and prescription refills. Susan and I had been friends for thirty years; we had worked together at IBM, had children at the same time, shared a nanny, learned to golf together, traveled together, and more. We had shared all the joys and sorrows thirty years bring—babies, deaths, weddings, career changes, illnesses, teenagers, successes, and failures. She knew me well and knew how to effectively counsel me, and I trusted her. If anyone would be able to talk me down from the ledge when I began obsessing or worrying about things over which I had no control, it would be Susan.

She arrived late in the afternoon, her head still spinning from the combination of exhaustion, jet lag, and waking up on her international flight to discover Trump had been elected president. As soon as she got to the hotel, the three of us huddled in the hotel room to debrief, Melanie and I manically relaying what had happened with Greg over the past forty-eight hours.

When doctors leave a patient's care, they leave call-out notes for the incoming medical team. In this spirit, Cindy had provided the first notes to Melanie.

> *The most important responsibilities for you: companionship and some needed diversion, logistics, therapist, political commentary, language assistance, acting as a second set of ears with the medical team, helping to keep track of Michele's questions. Additionally, you will occasionally need to talk Michele down from the ledge, offer encouraging words. Call me with any medical issue. Bring strength. Michele is so glad you will be here with her. Drink cava. It helps a little.*

Now Melanie was doing the same for Susan. The group was starting to bond, referring to themselves as my hand-holders. While Melanie handed Susan the baton, I sat mute.

My nickname in college—and for many years after—had been "The Little General." Everyone expected me to be in charge. But this was different. It was terrifying and humbling and sad and exhausting, and I both wanted and needed for others—good friends like Cindy and Peter and Melanie and Susan—to take the lead.

After Melanie departed the next morning, Susan and I went for breakfast at the hotel. The room was packed because of a cosmetics convention. Young Japanese girls kept pushing open the sliding door to the patio to smoke in between courses, the smoke annoyingly wafting in towards our table. I watched Susan moving around the noisy breakfast room, filling her plate with roasted tomatoes, Spanish tortilla, Manchego, and bread. I knew the sweet smell of cinnamon from the churros would eventually entice her. She didn't say anything about being nervous, but I suspected by the way she was eating—far too much food, far too fast—that she was steeling herself for her first hospital visit.

We had entered the "boring" stage of Greg's recovery, each doctor consult the same. "He's stable, no change. Greg's recovery will be very slow, *poco a poco*." Little by little. Two weeks before, Melanie had shared her experience with her son in a Spanish hospital with one of Greg's doctors. The approach had been less invasive than her experience in U.S. hospitals, and the inclination had been to allow things to slowly take their course, *poco a poco*. Greg's doctor had agreed with this approach—she didn't want to rush Greg's recovery, preferring to let him heal and get stronger before pushing him too quickly onto a plane for Denver. He could recover, she felt certain, just *poco a poco*. This had become our rallying cry. When my impatience bubbled up, my hand-holders would remind me: *poco a poco,* little by little, one day at a time.

But there was so very little progress every day. I was often disheartened and frustrated. Every night I lay in darkness in my hotel room, struggling to sleep or to shake a nightmare— Greg in a hospital bed, problems I couldn't solve, medical complications. All I was doing, I felt, was waiting. I stared at the tiny sliver of light from the moon shining through my hotel window, waiting for morning, waiting for Greg to wake up, waiting for his intubation tube to be replaced with a trach tube, waiting for the next surgery, waiting to go home, waiting for this nightmare to end.

One day, walking around Madrid, sad, scared, and uncertain, I saw an enormous sign, without any other context, that said #STARTBREATHING. I felt the universe was telling me to take a deep breath, that everything would be okay, so each day I tried to breathe deeply and to exhale before facing each day's new challenges.

Soon after that, amazingly, Greg started taking some breaths of his own. Each time he took a shallow breath, the ventilator stepped in to assist him, filling his lungs with a rush of air. I watched his chest move up and down, seeing the uneven pattern that signaled a departure from the steady machine-controlled breaths. I even heard a bit of his own breath in his throat, not just the swish of the ventilator. The strong drugs that had kept him purposefully paralyzed while he was recovering were slowly making their way out of his system, and his eyes now moved behind his still-closed eyelids, a small sign of hope to hold on to. I watched him, caressing his swollen arm, yearning for him to wake up.

That night, I couldn't seem to focus on the movie Susan and I were watching, when suddenly, a line in the movie caught my attention: "The plans I made didn't work out the way I planned." I had been endlessly ruminating on plans to bring Greg home, but too many things were out of my control. It was impossible to plan anything. I was driving myself crazy, and pitied Susan for having to listen to my impatient ranting. She calmly offered support, without any judgement, while I obsessed.

One thing that had been making me anxious was knowing that once the paralytics cleared from Greg's system and the trach was in place, the doctors would be slowly reducing the sedatives and trying to wake him up. This was the second time they used that word—*trying*. What if he never woke up? What if he woke up but had no idea who I was? What if he didn't remember our forty years together or the life we had built? What if he didn't recognize our children? What if he didn't love me anymore? I had made a life with Greg, and we were committed to each other, for better or for worse. We had weathered difficult times—in our relationship, with our children, in our professional lives—and had always emerged stronger as a couple. The thought that Greg might remember none of that scared me more than I could articulate.

Susan and I were sitting in the waiting area one morning as they wheeled Greg back from a CT scan, through the waiting room filled with families and strangers. Seeing my vulnerable husband in such a public space felt invasive, and I thought it strange they didn't use a private hallway. The gurney passed in front of us, nurses and doctors holding tubing and machines. Greg's eyes were open for the first time since his collapse, but in a fixed stare at the ceiling. I grabbed Susan's arm for support and was still gripping her wrist when the doctors called for me.

"Speak slowly," one of them said. "He can hear you, but he will be confused, possibly delirious."

Tentatively, I started talking. Greg blinked his eyes and moved his mouth, but his gaze was still a complete blank stare. I had been waiting for this day for weeks, for a noticeable step forward, but there was no way to tell if he could hear me or knew who I was. He didn't look like a vibrant fifty-nine-year-old man; he looked brain dead. I broke down, fled the UCI bay, and retreated to the overcrowded waiting area. I didn't care that I was surrounded by strangers, didn't care that I was sobbing loudly. I was so very afraid this would be the extent of his recovery—that blank stare.

One year before our trip, Greg had been diagnosed with rheumatoid arthritis. He'd had abnormal pain and stiffness for months, and while we were on vacation in Sicily in the fall of 2015, he had been unable to lift his arms or turn his head. Predictably, he tried to ignore the diagnosis while I launched into research mode.

"I feel good now," he'd said, as we stood in the kitchen a few weeks later. "I think I'm better."

"You're on massive steroids, that's why you feel better." I said. "They're masking the problem. Once you wean yourself, you are going to be a mess again. You need a plan."

"You sound like you want me to be sick."

Surely, I thought, he knows how ridiculous that sounds. I most certainly did not want him to be sick, I told him. I just knew he wouldn't take the time to understand his diagnosis. He'd be happy just taking a pill.

He let his guard down a bit, so I started to explain my research. "There are things that trigger your inflammation—you need to avoid or eliminate stress, sugar, gluten, and alcohol." As I recited the list of offending triggers, it seemed impossible even to me that Greg would be able to avoid, let alone eliminate them. He was managing a complicated merger with his company, he had a huge sweet tooth, his favorite meal was white pasta, and he drank far too much alcohol.

"I'll work on it," he said noncommittally.

"Really? You always say you'll cut back your drinking, but after a few weeks you fall right back into the same bad habits." I could feel my anger bubbling up and was trying not to let it boil over, knowing that wouldn't help. My father had struggled with alcoholism, and whenever I had been frustrated because Greg was drinking too much, I had made it clear I wouldn't put myself in the role my mother had. I wouldn't make demands or throw out idle threats like she had. But if he didn't manage the drinking, I had said, we'd keep repeating the same ugly arguments. "Our marriage will suffer," I'd said, wondering how much he cared.

He had aged noticeably in the last year. I didn't know if it was because he had stopped coloring his hair or because his face was more lined from the stress of the merger. After thirty years of marriage, and despite his flaws, I still loved him deeply. Uncharacteristically, I started to cry.

"Look, I plan to live a good long life," I said as he came forward to comfort me, "and I'd like to spend it with you, so you need to take care of yourself, okay?"

It was now four weeks since we'd landed in Madrid—I had never been apart from Greg for this long. We were physically in the same city, but we'd had no meaningful interaction, and I missed him terribly.

He needed a shunt to manage the excess fluid in his brain before we could fly home, but I was anxious about another brain surgery. Before the procedure, one of his nurses came to gather me. "Michele?"

I was surprised to hear the nurse call me by my first name, instead of calling for *familia de Gregory* as they usually did.

"You wish to kiss Gregory before the surgery?" he asked, speaking uncomfortably in English.

Because of the set times for UCI visitations, I hadn't been able to spend more than a few moments a day with Greg during the past month and hadn't kissed him on the lips at all. A kiss felt intimate and forbidden.

The nurse put his arm around my shoulder as we walked. He was being so kind that I worried about what he was trying to protect me from. As we walked past, the woman who had been sleeping on the couch of the waiting room locked eyes with me. "*Buenos dias. Cómo es su marido?*" she asked. Hello. How is your husband?

"*Así así,*" I said—so-so. I had been gradually learning key phrases in Spanish and could now communicate with her a bit. Her elderly husband had been fighting pneumonia, I'd learned. Later, when she was suddenly gone, I asked Greg's doctors what had happened. They glanced nervously at each other before telling me they didn't know, but I could see it in their eyes. Her husband had died. My heart broke for the stranger with whom I had shared the waiting room and the agony of watching a loved one suffer.

The nurse lowered the rail on the left side of the bed, where it was less tangled in tubes and lines. For the first time, I could wrap my arms across Greg's torso. I could reach his face with my lips to kiss him. It wasn't like we usually spent much time kissing—we had been together long enough that much of the fiery passion was gone from our marriage. But we had never gone this long without even a perfunctory kiss hello or goodbye.

I felt self-conscious and awkward as I leaned in, not knowing where to kiss him. I couldn't remember ever kissing him while he slept. His lips were soft and warm, but the kiss felt wrong; Greg was drugged and asleep and wasn't kissing back. I should have been happy for the intimate moment, but I felt sad and couldn't stop crying. The nurse, seeing my tears, thought I was worried about Greg's next surgery and pressed a small pink plastic rosary in my hand, struggling to find the few English words he could manage. "No worry, it be okay."

Weeks before, unaware of the tragedy that lay ahead, I would have tossed that rosary into the trash, even though I had been raised in the Catholic Church. At the age of fourteen I had dated a boy whose dad was an evangelical minister. When he wanted to baptize me in the small lake behind their house, I visited our priest to ask why Catholics didn't do immersion baptism. Instead of explaining that different religious groups had different traditions, he blustered, "You can't be baptized like that; it's against the rules of the Catholic Church."

From an early age, I rebelled against rules that made no sense to me, so I left his office—and the Catholic Church—that very day. Greg had been raised in the Protestant faith and early in our marriage asked me to try attending a Protestant church. It did nothing for me. When the kids were young, I attended a Unitarian Universalist church for a while before finally recognizing that I didn't feel a need for organized religion.

I hadn't followed Catholicism for over forty years, but the rosary from the nurse felt symbolic to me—not of the church, but of the absolute goodness and kindness of human beings. That rosary would forever remind me how these doctors and nurses cared not just for Greg, but for me too. I put the rosary in my purse, the first of what would grow to become a sizeable collection of items representing goodness, kindness, strength, and hope. A small stone inscribed with "breathe," a tiny pig, a penny, a dog, a silver circle with the word "hope," bracelets inscribed with "patience" and "always in my heart," a small silver square with a family tree in the middle labeled "Family Faith Friends," and many dragonflies, joined the pink plastic rosary.

Most of these things were given to me by friends throughout Greg's journey; some I had collected myself. Eventually a friend suggested that I had created my own totem bag of objects that held spiritual significance. Just as a medicine bundle is thought to possess powers of protection and healing, I believed these trinkets would do the same for Greg. The growing weight of my bag helped to ease the weight of my burden, reminding me of the strength of friendship while helping me hold tightly to hope for Greg's recovery.

It was draining to spend so many days in the UCI waiting room. I didn't care about the lack of amenities anymore—things I had taken for granted like toilet paper, clean tables, and lights. What sucked the energy out of me were the families of so many sick people. I had "friends" who had been here waiting for their loved ones to heal for as long as I had, and a few of us had been communicating using translation apps on our phones. One young Spanish woman with long dark hair and large green eyes tapped me on the shoulder to show me her phone after seeing Susan arrive to take Melanie's place. "You are lucky you have friends to come be with you," it said.

I nodded and smiled at her. *"Sí."* Yes, I knew I was incredibly lucky.

Inside the UCI ward, there were no doors or curtains for privacy on the bays, making it impossible to miss the many patients who rotated through the bay next to Greg. I knew it was a happy case when I saw the patient sitting in a chair, eating something bland, and watching TV, before being discharged the next day. I shared heartache with families when a priest arrived to say last rites. After that, the window between the two bays would be covered with a sheet until they moved the body and cleaned the room. It was unnerving to be so close to death.

Fortunately, I had distractions when I left the UCI each day. I had begun to know the city pretty well and enjoyed showing people around. Lunches provided a good two or three-hour diversion, and I ate with gusto. When friends sent me notes saying, "I hope you are eating," I was too guilty to respond. As a food writer, I had always blogged about restaurants on my trips, snapping photos of everything I ate. Greg had come to expect this and would even stop me from taking a bite if I forgot to photograph my plate. It felt foreign to dine out every single day and not write about it, but how could I? Wasn't I supposed to be too sad and stressed to eat?

Even being trapped in a small hotel room was less of a burden than friends at home envisioned. I could block out the tragedy because I had a friend with me, watching movies and sharing a glass of cava. We had room service and housekeeping every day.

In early November, Clodagh invited Susan and me for an early Thanksgiving dinner with her family, which reminded me I wouldn't be with my own family for the holiday. Greg and I always hosted Thanksgiving at our house, and long before I cooked professionally, I had been in charge of the meal, relishing the effort to create an elaborate feast. Who was going to cook for my kids this year?

"Before we eat, wouldn't it be nice to say what we're thankful for?" Clodagh asked, catching her husband with a fork full of stuffing close to his mouth. I'd had many private moments of thanks since we arrived in Spain, but to express my gratitude to people who didn't know Greg was difficult. How could I put into words to these relative strangers how grateful I was for their kindness?

I glanced around the table and said simply, "I'm thankful Greg is alive." I didn't say that I was grateful for the hotel staff who continually helped me, the incredible medical team, my friends who abruptly put their lives on hold to travel to Spain, the miracles of modern medicine, Clodagh, Pedro, my family, and, above all, Greg, for fighting so hard to get better. I couldn't say any of this aloud without breaking down.

By the end of Susan's time with me, Greg was healing from the shunt surgery. The place where the piece of skull had been removed was now a sizable sunken hole, the skin collapsing down to his unprotected brain. I tried to concentrate on the fact that he no longer had excess fluid causing dangerous pressure on his brain, and not that he looked like something out of a horror movie. I wanted to celebrate his small improvements—he was trying hard to yawn, swallow, move his mouth, take short breaths, and open his eyes—but he was still so very sick.

Every day as families entered the UCI to see their loved ones, they passed Greg, lying exposed with just a small sheet over his groin. I saw them try not to stare, but most were simply unable to not look at him. His eyes strained to see what was happening every time the door opened. Did he have any idea where he was? Did he know this was a hospital? Did he understand anything people said to him? Did he know who the nurses and doctors were? Was he scared? Did he know I was with him?

Even with encouraging reports from the doctors, I had trouble keeping my spirits up when Susan departed. It was unusually gloomy and rainy outside the day she left, the fog pressing down on my spirit, the wind and rain tearing into my soul. I had grown comfortable navigating Madrid; spending the days walking around with Susan had kept me distracted. But now that I was alone again, Madrid felt different. Rob and Lee wouldn't arrive for a couple of days, and the unbelievable sadness of the situation was unavoidable when I was alone.

Friends in Denver had thoughtfully arranged for some treatments at the hotel spa, and I had booked them specifically for this day, knowing I would be lonely after Susan left. In the dimly lit treatment room, an endless loop of soft-rock love songs played quietly, including everything from the theme from "Love Story" to "Thinking Out Loud," by Ed Sheeran, which had been Chris and Katie's first dance at their wedding the year before. I listened, thinking how little we know as newlyweds about how our lives will unfold, the joys and the sorrows we will face. I hoped the kids were thinking about the vows they had made—in sickness and health, in good times and bad. I also hoped they were proud of me, of how I was handling this, of how I was living up to my vows to Greg. We had spent thirty years telling our kids we were proud of them; to feel the need for their approval now felt strange.

Throughout my treatments, my throat tight, I hung on every word of every love song, the way I had listened to Jackson Browne songs over and over as a teen after a bad breakup. A favorite came on, "Stand by Me," stopping my breath. Every day for the past month I had been standing by Greg's bedside, repeating, "It's me. It's Michele. I'm here. I won't leave you. I love you." I ached to be rewarded for my bedside vigil. That day, Greg had moved his right eye slightly towards me as I spoke, trying to see me and listen to me, and my pulse had quickened. Yes! He knew it was me.

I had cried more in the past month than I could ever remember. I had expressed my sadness, anger, frustration, and fears repeatedly to myself, my hand-holders, and the world through my CaringBridge posts. Since I was an extrovert, it wasn't surprising that I was down when left alone for two days, but I hadn't noticed before how profoundly things like music or the weather could affect me. Still, it wasn't my nature to stay in a dark place for long, and when the cloud cover lifted the next day, so did my spirits.

CHAPTER FIVE

—✺—

GIVING THANKS

I SAT IN the hotel lobby watching a steady stream of flight attendants and pilots check in, waiting for Rob and Lee to arrive. Greg and I had met them twenty years before when we joined YPO, waiting to board a flight to attend a YPO couples' trip. We were all unsure about the purpose of the group, and more than a little worried we were joining some sort of cult. The four of us had bonded on that first trip, and in the twenty years since then, had traveled all over the world together.

I hesitated to ask friends to come to Madrid during Thanksgiving week, not wanting to interrupt anyone's family holiday. Why was this so hard for me? Why did I feel this need for a hand-holder by my side every day? I hated feeling so needy, but sent Lee a text. "Madrid has everything we look for in a destination—pretty city, great food, cheap wine. You'll love it here." It was a joke between the four of us that as long as I kept planning trips, the four of us would keep traveling together.

Rob and Lee arrived on schedule, and after a quick hug and a few tears, I led them to our rooms to drop their luggage. The connecting rooms had interior doors that provided privacy and a connecting sliding door in the entry area where our clothes hung beside the coffee makers and small hotel refrigerators. I had developed a routine with my hand-holders, closing the bedroom doors each night after we hugged goodnight, opening the doors when we were ready to face the day. Each week I used the translation app on my phone to write a short note to the housekeeping staff. *"Un nuevo amigo hoy. Por favor cambie las camas y las toallas. Muchas gracias."* A new friend today. Please change the beds and the towels. Thank you very much.

Not many people at the hotel knew my situation. Not the housekeeper who saw a steady stream of people come and go, not the host in the breakfast room, not the man who helped me find a table in that crowded room, not the waiters who brought my first cappuccino of the day, not the concierge who provided directions, and not the doormen who held the door open every time I came or went. If I told any of them, if I heard myself say out loud what had happened to Greg, instead of smiling at me every day, these people would look at me with pity and I would be constantly reminded how tenuous Greg's condition was. So I said nothing.

Rob and Lee arrived at Ramón y Cajal for the first time with me, dodging the cigarette smoke to enter the hospital, punchy from jet lag. I had been told Greg would fly home with the piece of skull still in his abdomen, but the surgeons had surprised me the evening before, saying they would be performing the cranioplasty today. Rob and Lee's first day would be torturous, waiting hours for the surgery. Rob, a big man, squirmed on the too-small plastic chairs in the surgical waiting area, trying to stay awake. Lee and I talked quietly. The room was filled with Spanish families huddled together, waiting for a post-op report, nervously tapping their feet and wiping away tears.

Hours later, after the surgery, I invited Rob and Lee to join me for the doctor consult and to visit Greg. After a month, I had grown comfortable with the process. Seeing Greg lying nearly naked, exposed to the UCI door, his head wrapped in gauze, and surrounded by machines dripping with drugs, fluids, and nutrition, didn't seem so scary anymore. I could quickly scan the machines, looking for key indicators like his blood pressure and oxygen saturation, and know he was stable. But each time a new hand-holder arrived, I was reminded how painful it was to see Greg broken. I was feeling upbeat about the visit, relieved that Greg's brain was once again protected by his skull, but I noticed Lee was struggling.

"Would you like to see him?" I asked her.

She shook her head no. "I can't stop crying."

I hugged her. "I know." I had been crying for a solid month, still in disbelief. It pained me to see Greg's friends also hurting. "It's okay. You watch the stuff while Rob and I go in." That this daily routine of visiting the UCI to see Greg in critical condition had become some sort of new normal was itself alarming.

The neurosurgeons who had saved Greg's life a month earlier had successfully replaced the piece of skull that had been tucked in his abdomen, which, along with his skull, was covered in scars from his many surgeries. He was bloated from lying in bed for so long, and he had lost weight. Rob looked so concerned. I was just relieved Greg had pulled through another surgery.

It was late in the afternoon by the time we left the hospital. Rob and Lee desperately needed a nap, so I took advantage of their down time to visit a hair salon near the hotel. It had been over a month since my hair had been cut or colored, my short hairstyle now overgrown and shaggy, my roots revealing the gray.

The locals in Madrid spoke little English, and I didn't speak Spanish. At the salon, I grasped for words and phrases, making a cutting motion with my fingers where I wanted my hair trimmed, gesturing where I wanted it left longer. *"Numero seis?"* I asked, knowing my stylist in Denver used color number six. I sat silently while she applied color to my roots and put my head under the heated hair dryer. I didn't speak as she washed my hair and massaged my scalp, my eyes burning slightly from the chemicals. I said nothing while she cut my hair, far shorter and edgier than I usually wore it, not caring that it made me look like a young boy.

When I met her at the desk to pay for the service, perhaps because having my hair washed felt almost intimate, I was compelled to share, *"Mi marido. Hemorragia cerebral. Hospital Ramón y Cajal. Muy enfermo."* My husband. Cerebral hemorrhage. Hospital Ramón y Cajal. Very sick.

As I shared those few words explaining our tragedy, a look of horror swept across her face, and she swiftly gathered me into her arms for a strong hug. *"Suerte, tu eres fuerte."* Good luck, you are strong. As I left the shop she was holding her hand over her heart, staring at me in disbelief, with that look of pity I had been working so hard to avoid.

For weeks I had hesitated to celebrate any good news about Greg, Cindy's early warning of the winding road to recovery always in the back of my mind. But on rare occasions, it felt right to cheer.

The day Rob and Lee had arrived, I had learned our insurance provider had approved my request for an air ambulance to transport Greg home. It wasn't just the staggering cost of such a flight—easily $100,000—that had weighed on me, but the uncertainty of knowing how I would get him home. I had recurring nightmares about wandering through airports with tubes and machines attached to Greg.

We arrived at the hospital the day after the cranioplasty optimistic, hoping they would tell us when Greg could depart. For weeks, the senior UCI doctor had been reminding me to take things one day at a time, *poco a poco*, telling me a few more weeks in Madrid would make Greg stronger for the long trip home. Until now, she had been very restrained in the consults. But on this day, she was so pleased about his progress after the surgery that she smiled at us and raised her fists into the air, signaling victory. It was the most upbeat report I had been given since Greg's arrival at Ramón y Cajal thirty-three days before.

Rob, Lee, and I headed into town after our hospital visit. I was looking forward to showing them around, slipping easily into my role of tour guide. I had become comfortable using the metro to travel from my hotel on the northern perimeter of the city into the historic center, and we emerged from underground near the imposing palace, a pretty way for first-time visitors to enter the historic center. We walked past the palace and the street performers in the square, stopping along the way for Lee to take some photos.

I had been in Madrid for over a month, yet still hadn't taken a single picture. Photography had felt wrong—I wasn't on vacation, I was trying to survive a tragedy, trying to get Greg home alive, so why would I photograph anything? But as Rob, Lee, and I wandered, I began to feel the need to capture the beauty of the city and the people who had saved Greg's life.

So I began snapping pictures. The opulent palace, the meticulous gardens, the pretty park with fall leaves gathering on the ground, the preserved buildings in the old part of the city, the Retiro Park with the green brain trees, the famous Metropolis building with the gilded golden winged statue on top, quaint Plaza Santa Ana adjacent to my first hotel, Plaza Mayor with its masses of tourists and vendors setting up Christmas booths, the imposing gothic Palacio de Comunicaciones on Plaza Cibeles with the enormous sign hanging from it that read "Refugees Welcome," the lake in the park, street performers, Madrileños crowded around the door of a bar silently watching a football match, the famous Bernabeu stadium near my hotel on the busy Paseo de la Castellana, the Melia hotel, Hospital Ramón y Cajal, and even the vending machines holding that scary food. The doctor's report had been so encouraging that I felt certain I'd be sharing these photos with Greg one day, explaining what I had done to stay sane while he was lying in a coma.

Beginning to believe Greg would heal, I had even discussed a return trip to Madrid with Pedro. We had talked about visiting the wine country with Rob and Lee, Cindy and Peter, and Greg; it would be the vacation in Spain that had never happened, only better, made sweeter because of overcoming this tragedy.

Rob and Lee and I wandered through the old city to Mercado San Miguel, which housed food stands, beer vendors, and wine bars. I had been here with Cindy and Peter, Melanie, and Susan, so I knew it was difficult to get a seat at the few sparse tables. The Madrileños preferred to stand at the counters, eating tapas while sipping drinks, but we were tired, Rob and Lee just one day into battling jet lag. We hovered until we found a small table with three stools.

I fetched glasses of cava while Rob found the stand serving thinly shaved pieces of the famous *Jamón Iberico*. We savored the jamón, sipped our drinks, and then moved on to the next course. We tried everything, including the mussels from the stall marked "MORRIS," thinking surely it was a sign. We shared a glass of the exquisite Spanish sweet vermouth, served with a twist of orange in a champagne glass. We ate slowly, Spanish style, returning with cones of potato chips when we craved something salty. We sipped our drinks, talking endlessly about Greg, sharing memories of better times together. When we teared up, we raised our glasses to toast Greg, then ordered more food and drinks.

We did this for six hours straight, eating and drinking far more than we should have. We needed to be together, needed a break from the hospital, and needed to ignore the tragedy for just a little while. We needed to embrace friendship, strengthen hope, and shed our worry, if only for one afternoon.

POCO A POCO

I woke the next day with the only hangover I had during my two months in Spain. I was relieved none of our friends or family in Denver knew, thankful for the privacy being so far away provided. It seemed irresponsible and selfish to be drinking with friends while Greg's life hung in the balance. I wasn't sure why I felt so guilty, not usually seeking approval from others, but I believed it was about expectations—our friends at home assumed my entire time in Madrid was awful, but it wasn't. I had learned early in Greg's journey that I needed to sometimes smile through my pain. Privately, though, I worried: was I a horrible person because I wasn't miserable all the time?

This was the first Thanksgiving I wouldn't be spending with my family, who was gathering at Chris and Katie's house for dinner. Katie had been working all week to decipher the recipes on my website for the traditional dishes I always made—garlic mashed potatoes, apple dressing with rosemary and sage, pancetta roasted Brussels sprouts, turkey with giblet gravy, and roasted cranberry-jalapeno relish. She sent me a text—"I don't know how you do this every year!"—but said she was determined.

Jon and Keely flew in from New York to be with the other kids. My sister, her boyfriend, and son would also join them, along with some friends and Katie's brothers. It would be good for all of them to be together, but it was agonizing for me not to have everyone gathering at my house, not to be with my kids on a holiday, and certainly not to have Greg healthy and with us. I missed cooking for everyone but missed more what cooking represented—a celebration of family.

Rob and Lee and I had our own Thanksgiving dinner of sorts at Asador de Aranda, famous for their roast suckling pig. We stuffed ourselves on the tender pork dripping in juicy fat, sipping wine, and toasting Greg and our friendship. Even though we were enduring the worst tragedy of our lives, I was overwhelmed with gratitude—for my family, our friends, the hospital staff, and the people of Madrid—and couldn't remember any Thanksgiving when I had felt more thankful.

I kept reminding myself that Greg's recovery was going to be a rollercoaster, *poco a poco*, two steps forward and one step back, baby steps, an up-and-down journey, one day at a time—every cliché described our experience—but I still struggled with the trajectory. On Thanksgiving, when Greg didn't respond to my voice, I told myself he was just tired from the cranioplasty surgery. But I was worried.

It wasn't until the next day, when the doctor told us the latest scans showed no swelling of the brain, no new areas of dead brain tissue, and no bleeding, that I realized the extent to which I had been holding my breath. I exhaled. When I saw Greg that afternoon he opened his eyes to my voice and was breathing on his own, and I was optimistic we would depart soon. They had turned on the Christmas lights in Madrid that day, and the hotel lobby was filled with lighted trees and decorations. The sparkling reminders of how long I had been away annoyed me, the Christmas carols in public buildings burning in my ears. Watching Spanish families gather to celebrate the season only made me yearn to have my family intact again. The early part of Greg's journey had certainly been made easier by being far away in Spain, but now I ached to go home.

After the consult, I stood at Greg's bedside discussing his condition with the on-call doctor. "It's going to take a lot of time and patience to get through this," he said. While the doctors and nurses had told me this every day, I still needed the reminder. When we finished chatting about Greg's potential transport home, he said, "You are a chef, no?" I wondered how he knew that, wondered if they had Googled me, and thought how my relationship with the medical team in Madrid had changed over the course of Greg's care. Six weeks ago, I had arrived at this hospital terrified and unable to communicate. Now I trusted these doctors and nurses completely.

The doctor interrupted my thoughts. "What do you like to cook?"

"I expect to cook a lot of Spanish food when I get home," I said. "It will remind me of all of you and how grateful I am you saved Greg's life. We have been married for thirty-one years and have three children. I need to take him home now."

He smiled. "All of us at Ramón y Cajal think you are a very strong woman."

Yes, I knew I was strong. I had raised three kids, guiding them through their difficult teenage years. I'd balanced a high-powered career—where often I was the only woman in a meeting full of men—with nurturing my marriage and our family. I had cared for aging parents and managed their estates when they died. Any of my friends would have attested: I was one of the strongest women they knew. But his words took me by surprise. I hadn't felt particularly strong during the past few weeks—I had felt weepy and weak, needy and unsure. As I prepared to embark on the next phase of this long journey, I thought, I was going to need every bit of strength I could summon.

Certain we'd be going home soon, Rob and Lee and I went for a celebratory lunch in the historic center. The Madrid weather had turned rainy and bone-chilling. Families lingered over their lunches, delaying the inevitable exit to find a taxi. We had just cut into our steaks when my cell phone buzzed. It was the insurance company arranging the air ambulance. We were going home the next day, they told me. Now that was worth celebrating! We clinked glasses, finished lunch, and headed to the hotel to pack.

I had developed anxiety about going home. In Spain, the tragedy had been mine to manage: it had been my job to strategize with the doctors, and my choice of hand-holders, what to tell the outside world, and what to keep private. Once we were in Colorado, would people show up unannounced at the hospital? I worried they would draw their own dire conclusions about Greg's condition and would gossip about him. I worried I'd no longer be able to have a glass of cava to relax without someone judging me. I didn't have the energy to see people, and I worried the tough armor I had developed to soldier through this journey would crack the minute people were kind to me. How could I control the situation once I left our bubble in Spain?

I knew people wanted to help, but I didn't know yet what I needed, so I posted a CaringBridge plea for privacy.

Greg will be admitted to the ICU upon arrival as he is still in very critical condition. I know many of you might be hoping to see him, but please understand that he will not be able to have ANY visitors other than immediate family for the foreseeable future.

The approval for Greg's transport on the air ambulance had come sooner than we had been expecting, so I was trying to arrange earlier flights home for Rob and Lee when a doctor from the hospital called. It was the only time in eight weeks they incurred charges by calling my U.S. cell phone, which I knew was ominous. "We haven't confirmed by CT scan that the small air bubble of air in his brain from his surgery is resolved," the doctor said. "Greg is not fit to fly."

"But the doctor in the consult today said the scan showed no pneumocephaly. And our doctors in Denver have said even if there is a tiny air bubble it's safe. I don't understand why he can't fly."

I had just been told we were going home and was already mentally prepared to be in Denver the next day, but despite my pleading and negotiations, the doctor wouldn't budge. I had been told the air ambulance company would not fly Greg without the hospital's approval. It was futile to keep arguing, so I relented.

I hung up the phone in a rage, frustration bubbling over beyond my control for the first time since we'd arrived in Spain. Rob and Lee had caught some of the phone conversation and were hovering in my doorway, waiting to hear what was happening. I screamed—at them, at the room, at nobody, at everybody. "I can't fucking believe this! They won't let Greg fly!"

I slammed my iPad shut and threw the closest thing I could find, one of my shoes, fortunately hitting nothing. It wasn't just that we weren't going home the next day; my frustration over the entire tragedy had finally erupted. I started sobbing. Rob and Lee, who had never seen me like this, tried to comfort me.

The next day, the morning I had hoped to go home, we arrived at the hospital an hour early, intent on understanding the disagreement over the small air bubble in Greg's brain.

"*Familia de Gregory?*"

Rob and I were ushered into the tiny consult room where all four of the UCI physicians treating Greg had gathered, including the head of UCI service. This was the first and only time I met with all of them together. My heart was pounding, and I was sweating—this must be serious, I thought. The head of service stood behind the young resident, who would translate for him. The air ambulance doctor and nurse joined us—they had arrived the night before, unaware that the UCI team had not deemed Greg fit to fly. Everyone was staring at me, which was unnerving. My mouth went dry waiting for them to speak.

"There is still a small bubble of air in the front of Greg's brain," the resident translated. The UCI head of service nodded in agreement. "We cannot declare him fit to fly until this is resolved."

Although air in the brain was normal after surgery, the air ambulance company simply wouldn't take the risk of flying Greg unless the hospital said it was safe. The UCI team was uncomfortable—they didn't like the responsibility of making the call, so agreed the air bubble had to resolve before flying.

"I think your decision is being driven more by legal exposure than medical necessity," I said boldly to the group. "His doctors in Denver say it's fine to fly." I was watching one of the senior physicians, the one with whom I had become close—she was as frustrated as I was, but when she didn't respond, I knew the team had agreed to unite behind their decision.

I had been fighting tenaciously for ten days to negotiate Greg's trip home—with multiple insurance companies in the

U.S. and Europe, U.S. doctors, the hospital in Madrid, the hospital in Denver, and the air transport company from Germany. Since it was clear we would not be going home today, I stopped fighting and listened to the new plan. If the CT scan in a few days showed the bubble had resolved, they would schedule a plane for transport. If not, we'd wait another week for the next scan. Though I knew we'd be going home eventually, the little bit of patience I had worked so hard to develop over the past five weeks had completely evaporated.

After the meeting, the doctors asked us to spend time talking to Greg. "He needs to hear you speak in English to stimulate his brain."

I wondered what it must be like for him, listening to Spanish nurses, Spanish music on his TV, and Spanish from the steady stream of visitors passing by his UCI bay every day. Was he massively confused? Would he emerge speaking Spanish? Months later, when I asked him if he remembered being in Madrid he shook his head no. But when I asked if he remembered people speaking Spanish, he nodded yes. I would never know for sure what he understood about his time in Madrid.

The young resident who was always tapped for translating approached me as I stood by Greg's bed. I felt bad about our difficulties communicating over the past few weeks. She had delivered the devastating news on day seventeen that they were running out of options to treat Greg, then taken the brunt of my frustration when we had misunderstood her report the next morning. Today, she had delivered the disappointing news about our delayed departure. Don't shoot the messenger, I thought.

"My boyfriend says good things come to those who wait," she said, friendlier than before, softly smiling at me. I sensed she also felt bad about our miscues. I assured her I understood. Greg had worked so hard to get this far—I didn't want to jeopardize his recovery in any way. Still, I couldn't shake the itchy feeling of anticipation. Going home would mean—at least to me—Greg was recovering. I had been told by doctors in Denver his rehab would start soon after his return, which would mean I'd be getting my husband back soon. I missed so much about home—my kids, cooking, family, my dogs, friends, my own bed—but more than anything, going home signaled success. It meant Greg was going to make it.

While we waited for the air bubble to clear, Greg slowly emerged. I held his soft, warm hand whenever I was with him, and sometimes it almost felt as if he was trying to hold mine back. Maybe that was wishful thinking on my part, but I needed to believe this was possible.

That night at Bucknell when Greg and I had first met, I had only been eighteen. I had been immediately attracted to him and had quickly fallen in love. It was much more than his outward appearance, muscled and good looking, that attracted me to him—he was strong and successful and committed. I saw it first when I watched him wrestle, his discipline so obvious, and I saw it in the leadership roles he took in his fraternity. I noticed it later as he landed his first job at P&G before launching a successful career in commercial real estate in Denver. And I had witnessed his commitment to our kids; he had always made family a priority.

Over forty years we had built a wonderful life together, but like most couples, we'd had our ups and downs. On our flight to Madrid, when I had looked across the aisle to Greg, he'd looked so tired. His job had been stressful recently, and it was taking a toll on him and our relationship. We had spent too much time lately either arguing or ignoring each other. I had smiled at him, reaching across the aisle to hold his hand briefly, a peace offering. He had smiled back and squeezed my hand; my heart had lifted.

In the months before we had left for Spain, I had harped at Greg about stupid little things, often annoyed by his imperfections. Now, as he slowly started to recover, as he started to respond to me, I began shedding any frustration and impatience I had felt. A little more of it faded each day, all of it seeming so petty now. I was reminded why I fell in love with him in the first place—because he was a good man who would always be there for me and our family, because he worked hard and was committed, and because he loved me unconditionally, despite my flaws. As he began to recover, I began to fall in love with him all over again. We had endured some difficult periods in our marriage, but we were devoted to each other. I hadn't given up on our marriage during any of those other tough times, and I certainly wasn't giving up now.

On some days I was hopeful, on some heartbroken, and on most days, both. I watched Greg struggle to make eye contact, trying to understand what was happening, and I ached. Would he ever recover? I was encouraged when the radiology team visited him to see his progress, the lead radiologist optimistic as he explained the case to his medical students. But when the doctor struggled to say in English, "I am sorry I cannot make him perfect," I knew he was telling me Greg would have deficits, likely major ones. It tore me apart.

Lee, worried about leaving me alone after seeing my rage and fury a couple of nights before, extended her stay when Rob left, and waited with me for the results of the next scan. It showed the tiny bubble was still there, so we'd be here for at least another week waiting for the next scan. I still didn't want to stay in Madrid alone, so arranged for my sister-in-law Lynn to come take over for Lee. Lynn was married to Greg's youngest brother Dave and was close to Greg. She was devastated by Greg's condition and wanted to help. It was fitting as we entered our seventh week in Spain that I would be joined by my seventh hand-holder.

I told family and friends I was at peace staying longer in Spain. In reality, I was anything but. I told people that I understood what the doctors had said: Greg was stable, he was getting better, and every day he stayed here meant he would be that much further along when we returned to Denver. That's what I said, but inwardly I was impatient to begin the next phase of this journey.

At night, alone in my dark hotel room, I obsessed about Greg's recovery and getting him home. In between googling pneumocephaly treatments on my iPad and scouring the Internet for solutions, I read comments from our friends on CaringBridge. I scanned messages of support on Facebook, and I emailed doctors in Denver to ask about oxygen treatments to eliminate the air bubble. I read emails from friends who had traveled this journey. One friend's cousin had had a similar bleed at the same time—he was already talking. The father of a friend had had a similar bleed—he had recovered fully and resumed his life. These reports were meant to encourage me, but I couldn't help comparing Greg's progress to theirs. Why wasn't he farther along? If the doctors said he could go home, that would mean he was getting well. My hope for his recovery was slipping away with every day we remained in Spain.

CHAPTER SIX

THE WAITING GAME

WHEN I'D FIRST told the kids we'd be in Spain for a month or two, I'd thought I was giving a worst-case scenario. Now, over six weeks later, we still had no definitive travel plans. Madrid wasn't the problem—I was comfortable living in a foreign city, and my new friends went to great lengths to care for me. The city was pretty, the hotel comfortable, the food delicious, and the wine cheap. No, Madrid wasn't the problem at all.

The problem was the endless loop of daily hospital visits and the enormous effort required to tease even the smallest response from Greg. Most days I woke up relieved to escape the nightmares I had been battling, only to remember I was living a nightmare. I felt so sad for Greg—about small things, like his not being there to see the completion of the new office space he had helped design, and big things, like how brutal his rehab was going to be. I constantly tried to guess the future, even when friends tried to stop me, fixating on how my life might change as a result of Greg's deficits. Would I become a full-time caregiver? Would we need to move? Would we be okay financially? And, most worrisome, what would become of our marriage?

Greg was relatively stable—at least I didn't need to worry every day about whether he would survive that day—and we'd been given more freedom to see him outside of visitation times. The team hoped extra time with him would stimulate his recovery, and it was refreshing to walk straight into his bay in the UCI instead of waiting for hours to be called.

Early one day, when we pushed open the UCI door, a team of nurses and doctors surrounded Greg's bed, all in sterile gowns and masks, talking rapidly in Spanish and working intently. I tried to ask if Greg was all right. Nobody spoke English, and I was pushed back into the hall. Lynn and I waited nervously for over an hour, as the waiting room filled with other families. He had been stable yesterday. What had happened overnight?

Finally, the nurse who had given me the plastic rosary weeks before called me. "*Familia de Gregory?*"

I jumped up quickly. As I followed him down the hall, he handed me a typed letter that was translated into English; I kept walking as I read it.

> *Good Morning! Greg it seems has a fever. Her nurse has channeled a central IV catheter. It has been channeled because he is given antibiotics and blood can be taken to analyze without having to puncture every day. We confirm radiologically insertion is correct.*

I suspected at least half of the time I had been waiting was because the nurse had been trying to translate the explanation for me. They wanted a central line in place because it was easier than trying to find a vein every time they needed to draw blood, and the nurses could administer antibiotics directly through that line. But it was the underlying cause that scared me: if he needed antibiotics, he had an infection. I had heard too many stories of patients who had survived their initial trauma only to succumb later to infection.

I spent my time with Greg that afternoon either choking back tears or crying with abandon. Greg tracked me with his eyes, looking right at me as I uneasily shifted my weight beside him. I was unable to take comfort from his eye contact, and I was frustrated I couldn't hold it together. Would crying so openly while Greg stared at me frighten or confuse him? I ripped off the sterile gown and gloves I now needed to wear to control the spread of his infection. Could he tell I was sad? Did he recognize I was crying? Did he know what crying meant, or know these tears were for him, for me, for us?

My moods swung every day, along with Greg's level of responsiveness. When he was groggy or wouldn't open his eyes—most of the time—I worried about his ability to recover. If he showed any small sign that he understood, I felt hopeful, but remained guarded, afraid he would relapse again. He had begun turning his head a few degrees in each direction, making solid eye contact, and when I told him, "I love you," he seemed to be trying to form a word with his lips. I imagined he was mouthing the word "love," because I desperately needed to believe he remembered me and still loved me. These tiny improvements were a glimpse into what rehabilitation would be like, showing me how long and difficult it would be.

I had a feeling my friends didn't get it. "When I say Greg will need a lot of rehab to recover," I complained to Cindy one day, "I think people picture him on an exercise bike at the gym watching the golf channel." I knew why they couldn't grasp how challenging Greg's journey would be: because I was still protecting him and his privacy, still sanitizing the information I shared on CaringBridge. I was unable to say out loud to anyone other than my hand-holders that Greg's road to recovery would start with relearning how to breathe, swallow, speak, eat, lift his arms, control his bowels, and sit upright. It was hard enough for me to accept what the future held for him, so how could I expect people who hadn't seen him yet to understand?

Although a second family visitation was allowed in the evenings, I had never until this point returned to see Greg at night. I battled my guilt—how could I not want to spend as much time with him as possible? Publicly I blamed the hospital, saying long visits weren't allowed in Spain, but in reality, I wasn't emotionally strong enough to return at night. By late afternoon every day, I needed to escape the hospital, my sadness and fear, and Greg's tragedy. I rationalized my decision by telling myself he would be sleeping and wouldn't know if I was there or not. Still, I felt guilty unwinding with a glass of cava in my hotel room when I could have been with Greg.

Lynn was fighting the same cold every hand-holder before her had contracted. The worry and stress and long international flight combined to create a storm of sickness that so far nobody had been able to avoid. I decided to let her rest while I returned by myself for the evening visitation for the first time. The nurses had told me earlier that day Greg was becoming more responsive, and I was hopeful this might be a turning point. I hopped in a cab alone as the sun was setting over the city, willing Greg to be alert when I arrived.

When I pushed open the UCI door to his bay, Greg was wide awake, his eyes darting wildly around the room. He was watching everything, moving his arms, his mouth, and his tongue in a state of constant motion. He was unable to speak with the trach tube still in place but was forming words silently. "Many movements are just electrical impulses firing," the nurse said, "but I can tell he hears me. I asked him to blink his eyes to answer my questions, and he did it!"

The nurse was beaming, and I wanted to share her excitement, but I still worried about Greg's slow progress. I was still scared he might not ever recover enough to know his family, to communicate, or to understand. Needing more, I stood close to him, holding his hand, and looked into his hazel eyes. "You can see me, right?"

He nodded his head ever so slightly. I wanted to believe he was seeing me, wanted to believe he heard and understood me, but it was hard to tell.

"You know it's me, Michele, right?"

Another small nod. My pulse was picking up. Could he finally be coming out of the darkness?

"Do you want to go home to Colorado?"

A stronger nod. Yeah, you and me both, I thought.

"Do you see the pictures of the kids?" I pointed to the wall where I had taped up family photos.

Yes, he nodded.

"Do you see Chris?"

His eyes moved up and right, to the top photo of Chris and Katie. He remembered the kids! I had been so terrified he wouldn't remember his family.

Everything that was happening around him must have been so confusing and scary. He jerked his head toward the UCI door every time it opened. The constant flow of traffic seemed to startle and scare him. I knew he had no idea what had happened or where he was, but he was in there, and this man I had fallen in love with was a fighter. When he faced difficult challenges, Greg never gave up; he only fought harder—for our kids, his career, and our marriage.

For as long as I had known him, Greg had needed to be told I was proud of him, of what he had accomplished at work, in the community, and as a father. I regretted not telling him enough over the past forty years how proud I had always been; now watching him fight to come back to me, I had never been prouder. "I'm so proud of you," I said. "I'm going to help you get through this. I love you."

I returned to the hotel buzzing with excitement. Maybe he was going to be okay after all. Maybe he needed more time, but he could rehab like everyone else I had heard about.

The next morning, for the first time in nearly seven weeks, I didn't have a sinking feeling of worry and dread when the taxi dropped us off in front of the hospital. Lynn and I raced up the stairs to the UCI and into Greg's bay. He was wide-awake and alert. The medical staff said they couldn't gauge his comprehension since they were speaking mostly in Spanish. We started asking him questions in English.

"Do you see the picture of you and me?" I asked, pointing to the family photos mounted on the wall. Yes-nod. "Do you want to see the kids?" Yes-nod. "Did you feel me kiss your hand just now?" Yes-nod.

"Do you want me to kiss you too?" Lynn asked. No-nod, making us laugh. "Do you know you're handsome?" Yes-nod. More laughter. "Do you like to drink beer?" Yes-nod, making the nurse laugh.

More than just nodding his head, his responses signaled nuanced understanding. I let out a massive sigh of relief. I hadn't lost my husband.

I still didn't know if it would take days or weeks to clear the air bubble. If someone was going to arrive to replace Lynn when she left on Friday, they would need to depart on Thursday. Despite my independence and self-sufficiency, despite traveling solo frequently, despite the friends I had made in Madrid, despite how easy living in a hotel had become, and despite Greg having reached a level of stability and responsiveness, I dreaded being by myself, even for a single day. What made it worse was that Christmas was quickly approaching. I called Gail, one of my best friends.

"I hate to ask you to come. We could be coming home soon if the scan Friday shows the air bubble is gone. You'd have to turn right back around and fly home." I hoped she heard the fear in my voice and would in some way intuit my need for a friend, would insist on coming.

"I don't care if I have to turn back around," she said. "But do you want some time alone with Greg? Would you rather I didn't come?"

I blurted "No!" so fast that it surprised both of us. She booked a flight to arrive Friday morning.

We had been friends for a long time—since she and Susan and I had worked together at IBM in the 1980s—and we had always been close. Gail would have been at the top of my list of friends to ask to come; she knew me well and had navigated many hospitals with her own family. I had held off asking her only because her father was elderly and quite sick.

When she arrived, I was eating breakfast alone at the hotel, not expecting her to get there so quickly in morning rush hour traffic. From across the room, I saw the host greet her. He showed her to my table, telling her, "Your colleague is over here," and pulled out a chair for her. I still hadn't told any of the staff in the breakfast room about Greg. They catered to business travelers, and surely assumed I was in Madrid on an extended business trip. Each day they had seated me for breakfast, brought me a cappuccino, cleared my dishes, and told me to have a nice day as I left the room, never knowing about my burden, my worries, or my sadness. Now, as Gail and I embraced, both of us breaking down in tears, I finally told them why I was there. *"Mi marido—Hospital Ramón y Cajal—muy enfermo, hemorragia cerebral."* It finally felt safe to share our story; Greg was recovering, and we'd be going home soon.

It didn't surprise me that Greg lit up when he saw Gail that morning; she had been a close friend of his for thirty years. His reaction to her helped to ease my worries about whether he would know his family, friends, and colleagues.

Gail smiled at him. "Isn't Michele pretty?"

He nodded yes.

Not only does he know me, I thought, but he thinks I'm pretty? My heartbeat quickened, and I got that fluttery feeling in my stomach, something I couldn't remember feeling with Greg in many years. We still loved each other, but after forty years together, much of the passion of our early years had faded, I had assumed inevitably. This was what it had felt like in those early days, when we were young and falling for each other.

I watched his crooked half-smile, the way he looked at Gail with a smirk when she joked with him. I observed him nodding yes and no to her questions, and I was overcome with gratitude she had come.

While we were visiting with Greg, the head of UCI service came to tell me the news himself: the air bubble was gone. We were finally going home.

Unfortunately, the air ambulance company wouldn't schedule the plane until their doctor also read the scan. They had incurred significant expense by sending a plane and crew two weeks earlier based on misinformation, so now they insisted on confirmation before approving the flight plan. It was already late in the afternoon on Friday, which meant there was no time to arrange anything before another dreaded weekend. On Monday, Chris would be turning thirty. Months ago Greg and I had made plans to be in the Colorado mountains for a big surprise party this weekend. I was sad Chris's celebration would be overshadowed by his dad's crisis, frustrated I hadn't been able to negotiate an earlier departure, and heartbroken that Greg and I would miss this parenting milestone.

Since it would be Monday before we heard about flight plans, Gail and I went to lunch to distract ourselves. I glanced at my watch—it was 4:15, the same time Greg had collapsed exactly seven weeks earlier.

CHAPTER SEVEN

MADRID TO DENVER

WE WERE ENTERING our eighth week in Spain. Those weeks had been made bearable, in large part, because of the eight hand-holders who had come to help me—Cindy, Peter, Melanie, Susan, Rob, Lee, Lynn, and now Gail. They had selflessly put their own lives on hold, never once balking at the time or the cost.

It had been the same for all of them: they had arrived in a foreign city, jet-lagged from the flight, fighting a cold, intent on helping Greg and me, but unsure what they would encounter once they arrived. For me, near the end, it was different. Madrid, the hotel, and the hospital no longer felt foreign. I had been in Spain a long time and had settled into a routine—workout in the morning, shower, breakfast at the hotel, gather my things for the day, taxi to the hospital, consult with the doctor, spend time with Greg, text or call the kids, taxi or metro to

124

lunch, enjoy a leisurely meal, walk through the city, stop by the market for snacks, return to the hotel, change into my lounging clothes, post on CaringBridge, relax with my hand-holder, watch a show or movie while nibbling on snacks and sipping on cava, then call it a night. Every day was virtually the same.

Although my life had stalled, each week a new conference group rolled into the hotel—everything from make-up to medicine. Each morning, flight crews checked in from their international arrivals. Each weekend families met at the hotel for a grand Sunday brunch. In the beginning, I had been shocked to see the man in the apartment across the street watering the plants on his patio naked. After weeks, I had grown bored with the show.

One of the quirkier things about living in a hotel for so long was that I had memorized the soundtracks. In the breakfast room each morning, a female vocalist sang covers of various soft love songs. "All I Need," was followed by "Loving You," its high-pitched, whiny chorus of *"la la la la la...la la la la la...la la la la la la la la la"* repeating over and over, making me want to stab my leg with my fork. Then came "Stand by Me," and I struggled to maintain my composure in the crowded noisy room.

In the gym, the soundtrack pounded out current American pop songs intended to push people during their workouts. A few songs, like Pharrell's "Happy," did help me pedal faster. But Pink's "Just Give Me a Reason" followed that song, and my heart felt like it was being ripped apart each time I heard it:

It's in the stars
It's been written in the scars on our hearts
You're not broken just bent
And we can learn to love again

Every time it came on, I self-consciously choked back tears, thinking about the long wait for Greg to recover and respond. I desperately hoped he was only "bent," not completely broken, and wondered how long it would take for him to learn to love me again.

The elevator loudly blurted "eighth floor!" every time the door opened on my floor. Each hand-holder had quickly become annoyed by it; after so many weeks, I was ready to rip out the speaker. Even worse, the walls of the elevator were covered with mirrors and illuminated with harsh, overhead fluorescent lighting. Every time I entered the elevator, I came face to face with my grief. I stared at the floor to avoid seeing the new frown lines and dark circles under my eyes.

From my hotel room, I had a view of the sky above the apartment building across the way. I watched the jet streams of passing planes, knowing they were destined for the same airport where Greg had collapsed. I also watched the moon each night as I closed my curtains. It had grown to a full moon in the middle of November—on the day Greg had started breathing on his own—then then faded to a sliver, only to begin getting larger again, and I fixated on it during our final days in Spain. Gail was hopeful we might hear first thing Monday that we were going home that day, which would get us to Denver by the night of Chris's birthday.

"I wish that were the case," I said, "but it's going to be a full moon on Wednesday and I have this weird feeling that's the day we're going home." It was only an intuition, but on Monday they told us we were approved to fly on Wednesday when there would be not only a full moon, but a rare super moon. I had known people who claimed they could intuit things, and I hadn't thought it really possible. Now I stared at the moon that would soon be full, trying to comprehend how or when I had become so intuitive.

When friends heard we'd be back soon, they began bombarding me with offers of help. Instead of being grateful, I was overwhelmed. I had no idea what I might need. My sister, Janine, who had been frustrated she hadn't been able to be with me in Spain, kindly offered to manage a support system for me. As the older sister, I had often helped her. Now I was relieved to tell people, "Call Janine." The role reversal was likely good for both of us.

I still wasn't ready for people to see how sick Greg was and knew he would hate being the center of attention or fodder for gossip. I didn't want to experience pity from friends, either. When had I become so sensitive about what other people thought or said, I wondered? I hadn't been with the kids in two months—the longest I had ever been away from home—so I told our wide network of friends in Denver we needed time to be together as a family without the intrusion of others. I told people to call Janine and I let her manage the chaos.

The night before our departure, Gail came into my room, both of us anxious about the next day and unable to fall asleep. "How do you feel about going home?" she asked. I didn't know what she was asking: if I was relieved they were allowing me to fly with Greg on the air ambulance, or nervous about the small plane, or dreading the many stops on the long flight plan.

"Scared," I said.

She had known me a long time and knew I wasn't afraid of flying. "What do you mean? What are you scared of?"

"I'm so scared to see the kids," I said, breaking down in sobs. For two months, I had been spared seeing their pain. In Denver, there would be no way to avoid it. I would be staring straight into their eyes and would feel their agony as only a mother can.

People had suggested I use FaceTime to chat with the kids when I was in Madrid, but I had purposely chosen to talk on a traditional phone call instead, not wanting to see their worry and fear and sadness, not wanting them to see mine. I had been so strong with them, my voice rarely cracking on a call. Instead, I had cried by myself at night or in private with my hand-holders. I worried I would break apart as soon as I saw them, and, once broken, not be able to recover. I needed to help Greg in his long recovery, so I couldn't let that happen.

Gail left early the next morning, so when the time came to check out of the hotel, I was alone. The housekeeper had kept the rooms clean, made sure we had coffee, replaced my tiny shampoo bottles, and prepared the adjoining room every week for a new hand-holder without ever knowing about Greg. It was unusual to tip in Spain, but I put some euros into an envelope for her and used my phone translation app to write a note. *"Yo estaba aquí porque mi marido estaba en el Hospital Ramón y Cajal—muy enfermo, hemorragia cerebral. Amigos vinieron a ayudarme. Gracias por todo. Nos vamos a casa hoy."* I was here because my husband was at Hospital Ramón y Cajal—very sick, cerebral hemorrhage. Friends came to help me. Thank you for everything. We are going home today.

I handed her the envelope and watched her read the note with the same shock and disbelief as the hair stylist a few weeks earlier. *"Gracias,"* she said. She looked worried for me, and I ached when I saw her pity. *"Viaje seguro. Buena suerte."* Safe trip. Good luck. She smiled, holding her hand over her heart, as so many other Madrileños had done. I smiled back, then turned with my luggage toward the elevator and for the last time headed down to the lobby and out through the busy re-volving doors.

When I arrived at the hospital, I went directly to Greg's bay. Wearing a sterile gown and a mask, I tried to explain that we were going home. As I waited for the doctors to turn over his care to the air ambulance team, the many nurses and doc-tors at Ramón y Cajal began coming by to wish me well, to hug me, to smile at Greg. They were proud of their patient and hopeful for our future. I found it impossible to say any-thing, my throat frozen, tears rolling down my cheeks. These people had saved Greg's life and had cared for him for two en-tire months. They had also cared for me, in ways I could never have imagined. They had given me letters of encouragement, smiles to acknowledge his progress, pats on the shoulder when I was suffering, advice about our future together, and more. I would never forget these people or the incredible kindness they had shown me.

I stepped out of the UCI to let the doctors transfer Greg to a gurney. In the waiting room I saw the young woman with the big green eyes. She had been here the entire time I had, caring for her father. I hadn't understood what his initial illness had been, but he was now battling a secondary pneumonia which was proving difficult to treat. I showed her a translated message on my phone. *"Vamos a casa a Colorado hoy en una ambulan-cia aérea. Buena suerte con tu familia."* We are going home to Colorado today on an air ambulance. Good luck with your family.

"Suerte," she said, smiling to wish me luck while holding her hand to her heart.

"Suerte," I replied, holding my own hand to my heart while blinking back tears. I wasn't just sad for her or sad about what

we had been through. I was sad to leave my fellow families from the waiting room. We had bonded over our shared tragedies and worries, knowing our experience made us comrades, though we could barely communicate with each other. These people had been part of my support system in Spain, the ones rushing me into the UCI when there was a crisis, smiling when I shared that Greg was stable, and now wishing me well on my journey. Leaving them would leave a gap I didn't yet know how to fill at home.

And then we were off. The ambulance driver pushed Greg's gurney, the flight doctor and nurse followed behind, and I struggled to keep up as I wheeled my luggage through the massive hospital—through the UCI waiting room where the *"familia de"* friends watched, through the long, dank corridors of Hospital Ramón y Cajal, through the Urgencias door where the nightmare had begun, and outside into the mild December air and the awaiting ambulance. I was terrified and thrilled and overwhelmed.

As we drove the short distance to the airport, I sat in the front seat, thinking back to when I had been prohibited from riding in the ambulance after Greg collapsed. I glanced out the window as we passed *Calle Gregorio,* where an office building had a Cushman & Wakefield sign posted on the side. Just a few years earlier Greg had been running a small, local, commercial real estate firm in Denver. Greg had led the company through three mergers since then, and now ran the Denver office for Cushman & Wakefield, a massive, worldwide, commercial real estate firm. The past three years had been difficult for Greg, but also invigorating and exciting, and selling our stock in the original company had given us some hard-earned financial freedom. I wondered: were his name on a street and his company's name on a building signs that he would one day return to work?

At the airport, I was whisked into a large, well-decorated, private waiting room where I sat alone while they prepared Greg for the flight. It was impossible not to notice that the airport lounge was cleaner and nicer than the hospital. It was well stocked with safe-looking snacks and drinks—no scary vending machines here—but I was too nervous to eat. I wanted to fast-forward twelve hours, to have the trip over, to be back in Colorado where the hospital waiting rooms would surely be cleaner than the airport lounges.

An hour later, the concierge led me to a waiting van and drove me far out onto the airfield to the plane. He stowed my suitcase below, and I climbed aboard. Greg had been transferred to the plane and was being cared for by the nurse and doctor. Many people asked later about the flight, envisioning some sort of tin can prop plane that bounced through the air all the way home, but it was a LearJet 60. I had flown on the same kind of plane when taking clients on business trips for IBM years ago, so I knew the flight would be smooth and comfortable.

But the space, which had been outfitted as a flying ambulance, was much tinier than I expected, and I was happy I had sent Greg's suitcase home with Rob, barely finding room near my seat for my travel tote. The cockpit in front had just enough space for the two pilots. Directly behind the cockpit was the door hatch on the left and a small storage place for snacks to the right. My seat was behind the door; although the steps that folded in were great for propping up my legs, it was freezing because of the cold climate of our flight path. I had to wrap my legs in my coat for most of the flight.

His doctors suspected Greg was blind in his left eye, so I had asked them to position him with his right eye facing the aisle, not wanting him to be staring at a wall the entire flight. The doctor was seated directly behind me, and the nurse behind Greg. The proximity of my seat to his gurney meant we faced each other, and the aisle was so narrow I could comfortably reach Greg without even moving from my seat. Having had such limited time with him during the past two months, it felt forbidden to be so close. Without a mask, he could see my face. Without gloves, he could feel my hand. I could touch him as much as I wanted. My fingers tingled as I stroked his smooth skin and I held tightly to his arm, unwilling to let go through the entire trip.

He looked frightened as the engines revved and we began to taxi. "It's okay," I told him, "we're on a plane and we're going home." He blinked at me and nodded his understanding. The plane bounced down the runway and lifted into the air. Our flight plan from Madrid required refueling stops in Iceland and Canada. Because of the late afternoon start, we wouldn't land in Denver until eight in the evening. Greg stared out the window, seemingly mesmerized by the long setting sun painting the sky orange. When he dozed during the flight, I stared out the same window, mesmerized by the super moon.

Beyond knowing that the thirteen-hour flight required multiple stops, I didn't know what to expect. I had worried for days about whether the plane would have anything to eat, so I'd stuffed my tote bag with snacks. Now I had zero appetite. I had been drinking a bottle of water, but after learning the toilet on the plane was broken, I abandoned it, fearing I'd be forced to pee into a portable urinal bag in that tiny space, in view of strangers.

At each refueling stop, passport control opened the plane's side door to greet us. In Iceland, nobody looked at our documents, and we ran through the icy rain across the tarmac to use the bathroom inside. Greg and I were supposed to be coming to Iceland with his brothers and their wives in June for his sixtieth birthday; that seemed unlikely now.

The weather in Madrid had been fall-like. When we landed in Canada, the thermometer on the building registered twenty below zero. I cursed my ankle pants and summer sneakers as I ran thirty yards in the snow to the small outpost for the bathroom. Back on the plane, I immediately pulled on some thick socks and gently wrapped Greg's head in my pashmina to keep him warm.

The doctor was on board in case of an emergency, but the flight nurse did the real work. She cleaned Greg's diarrhea, suctioned his secretions through his trach, and turned him to prevent sores. For the first time, I was up close with his actual care. It was a stark contrast to visiting at the appointed hour to find him cleaned and smelling of fresh lotion; on the small plane it was impossible to escape the sights, smells, and sounds of his care. The cabin was so tight it was difficult to reposition him, and the doctor and nurse needed me to protect his head when they turned him, the shunt tubing pushing through the skin on one side and the cranioplasty scar still healing on the other side. It was like passing a crash on the highway—I couldn't turn away. I stared in shock and disbelief at his thin, frail, scarred, naked body.

When we landed in Denver, the agent took our passports, glanced only briefly at Greg and me, and handed me the documents. It took him just minutes to review the passports of the pilots and medical team. Then we were off the plane and in an ambulance.

As I sat in the front seat on that cold December night in Denver, I couldn't quite believe what had happened. It was like waking from a long, complicated nightmare. The entire time in Spain had been surreal, but being home in Colorado felt equally strange. The EMTs already had Greg's assigned room number on the Neuro ICU ward. I texted it to the kids as the ambulance took off so they could meet us at the hospital.

I had been prepared for the transfer to take a couple of hours, but less than thirty minutes after touching down, we were wheeling Greg down the long hallway of University of Colorado Health on the sprawling Anschutz medical campus in Denver. It was smoke-free, clean, modern, tastefully decorated, and softly lit, and it felt foreign to be surrounded by such luxury after two months at Ramón y Cajal. As the automatic doors opened to the hall leading to the neuro ICU, the EMT almost pushed Greg's gurney right into Chris, Katie, and Jenny, who were heading to his room.

Jenny ran straight towards me as Chris yelled, "Jenny, stop! You're going to get hit!" She kept running straight into my arms, and I grabbed her, both of us sobbing uncontrollably. She was, in that moment, my baby girl all over again, and I knew my instincts to protect the kids had been right. Katie had also started to cry. I had dreaded seeing the pain on their faces for two months, and now I was staring straight into it. How was I going to take care of them? The EMTs kept moving down the long hall with Greg, forcing us to let go of each other to keep up.

The ICU secretary kindly escorted us to a private family waiting room while they got Greg settled. She pointed out the vending machines; I stared at the familiar products and brands. The hallways of the hospital and the waiting room were empty at this hour of night, and I missed the empathetic smiles from the Spanish families at Ramón y Cajal. I felt that uncomfortable mix of adrenaline and exhaustion.

When the medical team was finished with Greg, we suited up in sterile gowns and gloves. This hospital had been forewarned of the rare Spanish bacteria Greg carried and knew it was resistant to antibiotics—they would take no chance of that spreading to other patients.

I had been visiting Greg in the hospital for almost eight weeks, rapidly gowning up and snapping on my gloves, talking to his sleeping form, holding his hand, hoping for a glimmer of recognition and understanding. But this was the first time for the kids, and it was as brutal—for both them and me—as I had anticipated. I had known they would be shocked and saddened to see Greg in this shape. I had known they would be unable to understand the tragedy fully until they came face to face with their dad. Mostly I had known that seeing their pain and anguish would cut me to the quick.

We had left Madrid over seventeen hours earlier, and Greg was worn out and sleepy. Although his scars had healed, and his hair had grown over the tubing from the shunt, he looked frail and sick. The kids had no point of comparison to understand how far he had come. They were in shock.

"Talk to him," I encouraged.

"Hi Dad," Chris choked out, before turning away to find tissues.

I hugged him hard. "He's okay. We're home."

Though the kids were in their late twenties, they were still my children and I their mother. They were looking to me to determine how worried or hopeful they should feel, and I needed to show them I had hope. I didn't know if Greg was okay and didn't know with any certainty where this journey was heading, but we were home. It meant Greg was moving into the rehab phase of recovery. This was the progress I had been waiting for, but it was too complicated to explain all of this to the kids in this moment.

"Dad, it's Jenny." Her face was contorted in grief. She stroked his arm while he slept. Seeing her anguish and despair felt like being stabbed.

Katie watched with such sadness that I scooped her into my arms. Greg was important to Katie, and she loved him deeply. "He loves you so much, Katie. He's going to get better. Try talking to him."

Chris was still wiping his eyes, still unable to find the strength to speak, and he was hugging Jenny as she cried on his shoulder. It was more than I could bear. I turned away, pretending to search for tissues, to let myself cry for a few short seconds.

It was ten o'clock at night in Denver, but that meant it was already six in the morning in Madrid, and I was exhausted. After a few minutes with Greg, I asked the kids if we could leave for the night. After the two-month nightmare abroad, I was finally home.

CHAPTER EIGHT

HOMECOMING

I HAD NEVER been away from home for so long, certainly never under such grueling circumstances. I entered my house, put down my luggage, and prepared to be assaulted by our two golden retrievers. I had missed them horribly and had been anticipating their wet kisses welcoming me home. They barely wagged their tails; did they remember me? When I tried to turn on lights, I had trouble remembering which switches worked which lights.

I had been up for over twenty-four hours, my head was throbbing, and although I was dizzy from exhaustion, I was still buzzing from too much adrenaline. "Here, Mom," Jenny said, handing me a glass of cava. I wanted to go straight to bed, but I sensed that after our emotional reunion, everyone needed to numb themselves in order to fall asleep. I took the glass from her and sipped, hoping to silence the noise in my head. We spoke about random things, not the big thing on everyone's mind.

"I thought since Susan comes here so often that she'd know where everything goes," I said, looking around.

Susan had handled moving everything back into the house in early November after the floors were refinished. Several things were in the wrong place, and much of the art Greg and I had collected from our travels was sitting on the floor unhung. She had remembered correctly where our newest piece went— an oil painting of a classic car we had purchased in Cuba a few months before—and had hung it back above the living room mantle. The trip to Madrid was the first time we hadn't brought home a souvenir piece of art from a trip. I had found a poster on the street one day that was the kind of thing Greg would love—colorful, showing the dates we were in Madrid— and it was tucked in my suitcase. Months later I threw the poster away; it didn't feel right to hang it.

I tried to dim the lights, my eyes dry and fatigued from the long flight, but still couldn't figure out which switch to use.

"We said the same thing while you were away," Chris said. "You have too many lights." As he tried various switches, we noticed several bulbs had burned out while I was gone. "I'll come over tomorrow with the big ladder to change those," he said, stepping into a role that would continue long past Greg's battle. He was going to help me through this, in some way repaying me for helping him through his tumultuous years.

Katie and Jenny were wiping away tears between sips of cava. I hated to leave them, but we all needed rest. "I can't stay up another minute," I said. "I have to get some sleep so I can get back to the hospital in the morning." Chris let the dogs out as I got them a treat, hoping to entice them to follow me to my bedroom.

Even with the help of a sleeping pill, I tossed and turned all night. People rave about coming home to their own bed, but after two months, the hotel bed was familiar and mine felt uncomfortable. I adjusted the pillows repeatedly, yet I couldn't get my bearings. At the hotel, the bathroom had been to the left of the bed. Here, looking through the darkness, I reminded myself that the door to the bathroom was at the foot of my bed. In Madrid, I'd heard taxis through the night; the quiet here sounded wrong. All night, I stared at my clock. One o'clock. Two-thirty. Four o'clock. At five o'clock, unable to shake the feeling that I was in a foreign place, I gave up all hope of sleeping.

I wandered into the kitchen, in need of caffeine. Susan's daughter and her husband, who had stayed here with our dogs, had left only that morning. They had little notice of my return, but had kindly stocked the refrigerator with some food and cleaned up the house. Still, as I looked around my kitchen, I couldn't shake my disorientation. On the dining room table, they had left a pile of legitimate mail to open, neatly separated from catalogs and junk mail. I didn't have the energy to start digging through things, but I worried about unpaid bills lurking in the piles. I dragged myself back into the kitchen to make breakfast. When I peered into the refrigerator, it looked foreign. I hadn't made my own breakfast in two months. Even my beloved Nespresso coffee didn't taste right after the cappuccino in the hotel.

Coming home felt like what I imagined it would be like coming home from war. I had been pressing the team in Spain for weeks to clear Greg to fly, playing out the reunion with my dogs, my kids, and my house in my mind over and over. Yet now I found myself struggling to re-enter, experiencing my own version of PTSD.

Later that morning, Jenny and I met with the neurologist at UC Health who had advised me by email while I was in Spain. He had explained weeks before that once Greg was in Denver, he would be examined, admitted to ICU for a few days, then transferred to a regular ward for a week or two to get stronger before moving to a rehab facility. I had grown to trust this doctor, and I was anxious to meet with him, anxious to hear about the next steps, and anxious for Greg to begin rehab.

Greg was asleep as we sat down with the doctor in his room—a spacious room, with a sliding glass door, a privacy curtain, a full-sized sofa for visitors, and a private bathroom. It was like being admitted to first class after flying coach my entire life. The hospital channel on the TV rotated through stunning nature scenes while playing tranquil music. The Spanish songs that had blared from the old TV in Greg's bay in Madrid certainly hadn't done much for his recovery. Maybe this more familiar setting would.

The doctor looked at me, his face pinched and serious looking. My throat tightened.

"Greg had a respiratory failure last night that led to cardiac arrest," he said, "but we were able to revive him with CPR."

I was jetlagged and punchy from insomnia. What was he saying? He was explaining in English, not in Spanish, roughly translated into English, so why was I struggling to understand him? I glanced at Jenny, wondering if I had heard him correctly.

She was gripping her chair so tightly her fingers where white. Greg had been fine on the plane. What had gone so wrong?

"We think the air ambulance didn't use humidified oxygen on the flight," the doctor said. "We believe this caused his membranes to dry out, which caused respiratory failure, which led to cardiac arrest."

"Why didn't they know to use humidified air?" I asked angrily, wanting someone to take responsibility for Greg's setback. My mind was racing to determine whom to blame.

They hadn't called me during the night when it had happened, I learned, because they had forgotten to get my phone number when they had admitted Greg. I wouldn't let that happen again.

For so many weeks, I had anticipated this homecoming. We would have an uneventful flight home on the air ambulance. The kids would arrive at the hospital and would see Greg was improving. Greg would be alert, his eyes traveling to them when they spoke. He would squeeze their hands as he had mine in Spain, and they would be reassured that he was getting better. The doctors would tell me he was going to be fine, that the rehab would take time, but he could recover.

Everything in this room seemed wrong. The familiar faces who had cared for him in Spain were missing, and I had yet to befriend his new nurses. In Spain, they had been weaning him from machines and he had been breathing on his own, but now he was hooked up to tubes and lines again and was back on the ventilator. The doctor looked serious and cautious—later I would learn that was his natural facial expression—yet he was freakishly calm in light of what had happened. In contrast, I was livid. My fury and terror, along with my confusion and jet lag, left me feeling as if I would combust.

I desperately wanted to rewind twenty-four hours and have this not have happened.

Why was Greg so weak and sick? He had a blood clot in his leg. He needed blood thinners, which put him at risk for another brain bleed. He still carried the exotic antibiotic-resistant Spanish bacteria and now had a lung infection. And he had a low white blood cell count they couldn't explain. "We are worried he might have bone marrow disease," the doctor said.

I had gotten a medical briefing every day in Spain. Despite their efforts to communicate with me in English or to translate things on my phone, had I missed something about Greg's condition? Or were these new problems? How much had been caused by the unavoidable stress of the long trip? I struggled to comprehend the situation and immediately started second-guessing my decision to bring Greg home, uselessly arguing to myself that had we stayed in Spain he might right now be moving to rehab instead of recovering from cardiac arrest.

Jenny was sitting bolt upright beside me. She was still gripping the arms of her chair. This wasn't even close to what the doctor had told me to expect as next steps. "Look, we believe the hospital in Spain did all the right things—exactly what we would have done—to treat Greg's ruptured aneurysm and resulting complications," he said, trying to help me digest the news. "But he's just still really sick."

I chewed on my cuticles as the doctor explained their treatment plan, not daring to look at Jenny.

He shifted his weight to face me, his face softening a bit. "You've been away for a long time. Go home, be with your family, and get your life under control. We've got this—he's in good hands here."

That night, I lay in my bed, tears slowly trickling onto my pillow. I had been sanitizing the news for the kids, and now that they saw how sick Greg was, I worried about their ability to cope. In Spain, I had vented my emotions with my hand-holders, then distracted myself and pushed my sadness and worry aside. Being home with my family meant facing their raw emotions all day long, which naturally intensified my own despair. I had guessed things would feel more real when I was home, and unfortunately, I had been right. I could no longer hide.

As the long night passed, I stared at Greg's side of the bed. This was our home; he should be here with me, like he had been for the more than ten thousand other nights of our marriage. Instead the dogs had taken over his side of the bed, twitching as they slept, blissfully unaware.

The kids could do little to help Greg, so they focused their energy on helping me. We were finally navigating the journey together as a family; I was no longer isolated. They hesitated to leave me alone and helped with everything from changing light bulbs and putting out the trash to hanging pictures, moving furniture, and decorating for Christmas. I wasn't in the habit of filling the dogs' water bowl—Greg had always done that—so Chris bought a larger bowl with a built-in reservoir that would last for days. Jenny fed me, making rice bowls filled with whole grains, low fat proteins, and lots of vegetables so I'd stay strong and healthy. They all tried to stay upbeat, but their demeanor was guarded, their eyes downcast to hide their pain and worry.

One day, we hovered by the bullpen where the staff worked as the doctor explained Greg's status: "We still don't know the cause of his low white blood cell count. We're having trouble getting rid of his infection. We can't control his diarrhea, and we're concerned his kidneys aren't functioning well."

I was only half listening. My mind raced forward past the report to assess how it would affect the kids. In Spain, I could digest the news on my own to decide how much to share and how to spin it. I no longer had that luxury. I had known once I came home I'd need to help my kids battle their own fears, worry, and sadness. I had felt confident staying so long in Spain would ensure that by the time the kids saw Greg, he would seem more like their dad than a sick patient, but he remained unresponsive and lethargic, sleeping most of the time. The ventilator softly pressed air into his lungs while he fought infection and exhaustion.

I glanced at the kids, knowing I needed to ask the doctor some tough questions. Alone in Spain, I had been able to ask the doctors anything, then brace myself as I listened to the answers, without worrying how others would hear it. Now I had to consider that the answers to tough questions might scare the shit out of the kids. I asked anyway. "The kidneys are worrisome to me," I said. "What's the treatment plan for that?"

The kids listened to the doctor's response along with me. He said they would eliminate drugs that might be hurting Greg's kidneys. Then he explained the plan to treat his long list of other problems. The minute the doctor was out of earshot, the kids bombarded me with questions.

"He's going to be okay, right?"

"They can fix these things, right?"

"Do they know what they are doing?"

Surely they were old enough to understand that the medical problems Greg faced were life-threatening. I wanted to hug them and tell them their dad was going to be fine, but I didn't want to make promises I couldn't keep. Despite heroic efforts to save his life after the initial crisis, he was still very sick. I was barely able to admit to myself that Greg could still die. There was no way I could say that to the kids, so I buried my thoughts.

Jon and his girlfriend, Keely, arrived from New York a few days later. During their first hospital visit, although the ventilator was still helping him breathe, Greg was awake and alert. As we put on gowns and gloves and gathered at his bedside, I watched the kids' faces relax into soft smiles. Keely was nervous, speaking rapidly and in a high-pitched voice. "Hey Greg! Hey Greg!"

"Woah, slow down! You're scaring him!" Chris said, trying to calm her by teasing her. He was smiling, not wiping away the onslaught of tears the way he had the night we arrived.

Katie, who I feared was more fragile than the others, had been taking longer to gown up. Just the day before, she had cried all the way home. She was heartbroken to see Greg so sick and felt guilty that we were leaving him alone in the hospital.

"Come in to see him, Katie," I said gently.

"Hi Greg," she said from the doorway, "it's Katie." She entered the room.

Greg not only looked in her direction, he gave her a thumbs

up. My heart soared, and Katie smiled as she approached Greg's bed. She held his hand for a few minutes before the other kids took turns.

"You know," I said to Katie, "he sees you and hears your voice more than he does the rest of us, since you work together." This was the first time I understood that close friends with whom Greg spent a lot of time might be helpful in his recovery.

After one of the kids set his hand down, Greg moved his whole right arm to his belly, in and of itself something to celebrate. Jenny asked, "Dad can you move your arm back to hold my hand?" He moved it back and held her hand; my pulse quickened. "Can I have a kiss?" she asked, and Greg puckered up while the rest of us laughed.

"We knew she was your favorite!" Chris and Jon said at the same time.

Greg smiled at them with a half smirk.

The kids were relieved to see their dad smiling at them, but didn't know Greg's smirk was a telltale sign of the stroke damage to his brain. They only saw that he understood their joke. They didn't know how concerned I was that he was still so very sick. They only understood that he had opened his eyes, recognized them, and interacted with them after two long months. I could tell their hope was blossoming, and I didn't have the heart to dampen their celebration.

Later, at lunch with the kids, I kept tearing up. I couldn't shake my fear that Greg might still die.

"What's wrong, mom?" Jenny asked, putting her arm around me while Jon and Keely looked for my reaction.

POCO A POCO

"I just miss dad," I told them, not wanting them to know what was racing through my mind.

"We need to stay positive," Jon said. His optimism about Greg's ability to fully recover would continue throughout Greg's journey, highlighting for me how differently each of my kids would cope with the tragedy. Jon needed to believe, even against all odds, while Chris had trouble with that unbridled optimism and kept probing in order to prepare himself for the worst-case scenario. Jenny needed to stay busy with work to keep from breaking, her tears flowing far more easily than her brothers'. She was so much like me.

"We're here for you," Keely said. I forced myself to stop crying and relax into their love and comfort.

Many friends were anxious to help in any way they could, but I was terrified to interact with anyone. I dreaded confronting them and was scared I'd cry uncontrollably if anyone hugged me. Seeing people would require updating them on Greg's condition, and speaking those words, I feared, would confirm the horrible reality. If I said it out loud, Greg's critical condition would be fact. So I hid from people—not answering the door, returning phone calls, or accepting offers of help. In the process, I continued to hide how grave Greg's condition was, putting forth optimistic CaringBridge posts instead of speaking the truth.

Just a few days after we returned, there was a blustery snowstorm in Denver. The climate in Madrid had been mostly mild, and I wasn't prepared to be assaulted by winter, the snow piling up like my worry. I got up early, still jetlagged, and peered into my refrigerator. Nothing appealed to me, so I grabbed my keys and drove to the store, hoping a refrigerator stocked with familiar foods would make my house feel more like my home. It felt strange to walk through my regular grocery store after shopping only for cava and snacks at the small gourmet store in Madrid.

Back home, as I pulled into the driveway, I saw one of Greg's brokers and his son shoveling. I waved tentatively as I drove past them into the garage, feeling my frustration rising. Why were they shoveling when I had a service to do it? I hadn't asked for this help, I thought. I don't need help.

I wanted to shut the garage door and run inside to hide, but I knew my reaction was irrational. This was a close colleague of Greg's and a well-meaning friend who merely wanted to help. He was teaching his son a life lesson about caring for others; in any other circumstance I would have commended his parenting. I couldn't ignore them. Taking a deep breath, I turned off the car, and, instead of running inside, walked through the crunchy snow tracks toward my friend and his son. They were putting down their shovels. I was moving in slow motion. They were turning to hug me. This was my first hug, outside of my immediate family, since I had returned from Spain. While I had been certain I would break, I didn't. We stood in the driveway for a few minutes, tearing up from both the icy wind and our sadness.

"I've been waiting for two months to give you that hug," our friend said, his son watching me shyly.

"It sucks, doesn't it?" was all I could respond. If I said more, I was going to fall apart. If I confided how scared I was that Greg might never recover, that we still might lose him, I feared I would crumble. I couldn't afford that. "I have groceries to put away," I finally said, and thanked them for shoveling.

I had made it through my first face-to-face meeting with a friend. I would need friends to survive this tragedy, I knew, but as I put my groceries away, I struggled to identify any specific ways they could help me. I had managed this crisis virtually alone for so long, it would take time for me to relax my intense need to control.

I couldn't stop thinking back to the early days of our journey—not the first few dark days of crisis when I really thought we'd lose Greg, but the days he began to show signs of recovery. Although I'd felt the uncertainty of what the future would hold in terms of his neurological deficits, I hadn't anticipated the medical complications he would endure. I had expected he'd be much further along in his recovery by now.

I knew he faced extra health challenges because he had been forced to stay in Spain longer and had endured a brutally long flight home that had resulted in cardiac arrest. I was angry—at nobody in particular, at everyone, at myself—not just that he had suffered this tragedy, but that it had happened this way.

The kids worked hard to make the holiday season seem normal. One afternoon, I sat at the counter in the kitchen watching Jenny make whiskey caramel sticky buns while Katie and Keely decorated Christmas cookies. The kitchen smelled of holiday spices, and the fireplace glowed, the dogs sleeping soundly near the warm glass. We were listening to Christmas music as everyone busied about. Greg would love this, I thought. He adored when the kids came home for the holidays. It felt strange to be watching instead of cooking, so I made dinner that night for the first time since my return. Cooking was familiar, and it was comforting.

After dinner, the kids watched a favorite childhood Christmas movie while I lay on the couch in my favorite spot and tuned out. It was hard to stay awake because I was still battling jet lag and insomnia, but I fought to keep my eyes open, not wanting to bail on the kids. Everyone was trying to get through this holiday, even if it felt like we were just going through the motions. Greg's absence pierced our Christmas spirit; I ached for him to be with us.

"I can't stay awake," I finally said, and dragged myself upstairs. I flopped into my bed, desperately hoping for a restful sleep, but couldn't turn off my mind, couldn't stop thinking how much I missed Greg. Oddly, although I had slept alone every night in my hotel room in Spain, I hadn't felt as lonely and hadn't missed Greg as much as I now did in our home. I had felt a lot of other things—anger, sadness, terror, homesickness, frustration, confusion, and shock—but not loneliness. It had never felt strange that Greg wasn't at the hotel in Spain—I often traveled solo—but it seemed completely wrong that he wasn't here. I had shared a home with him for nearly thirty-two years, and his absence was painfully obvious everywhere I looked, every minute of every day.

The next day, after going to see Greg, I pulled into the garage, and when I saw his car, my heart leapt for a minute. Oh good, Greg's home from work early! But within a split second, I was pulled back to reality. In the months to come, I would have this reaction nearly every time I pulled in next to his car.

When I sat down to watch TV that evening, the kids out with some friends, I reclined on the couch in the living room, and glanced back to the counter stool where Greg always sat.

I was willing him to magically appear. The silence was eerie—and a bit unnerving—because even in a best-case scenario, I would be living here without Greg for months.

In an unconscious attempt to keep running from the loneliness I made a conscious effort to stay busy. I soaked in the winter sun shining through my office windows as I wrote out a list of tasks, the sort of things I could control: groceries, laundry, thank-you notes, dog pills, bills. Then I started tackling the list, pausing mid-day to drive to the hospital, returning to the list when I got home, until I wore myself out.

The next day I checked a few things off, added a few new things to the list, and started all over again. But no matter how much time I spent cleaning out my email, reconciling VISA statements, paying bills, contacting insurance, reviewing medical information, handling home repairs, or organizing my office, no level of staying busy was going to take away my pain. After a few days of this self-induced frenzy, as I lay in bed one night, I thought: I need to find a therapist.

Every day, just as I had in Spain, I went to the hospital. But that's where the similarity ended. I'd had only a few outfits to choose from in Spain and almost no jewelry to speak of. In Denver, I had my entire closet and a large jewelry box from which to choose; the selection overwhelmed me.

I drove myself now instead of taking a taxi, fighting the growing traffic in Denver. Smoking was not allowed anywhere on the massive medical campus where UC Health was located. The hospital had every convenience for patients' families: a concierge desk, a gift shop, and a massive, modern cafeteria. I didn't have to wait for a doctor consult because the doctors sat in an open bullpen, right next to Greg's private room. I could call them, or his on-duty nurse, any time day or night. They responded quickly to my emails.

The biggest difference was that, other than at night in my hotel room, I had almost never been alone in Spain. I'd had a hand-holder with me at all times, and we had waited with the other *"familia de"* Spanish families to be ushered in for visitation. Now I drove back and forth to the hospital each day alone. I was completely alone with Greg for hours, without the moral support of my hand-holders. While I had yearned for privacy in Spain, the private room with the closed door and curtain where I now sat with him for hours felt isolated. I had never experienced that in Spain.

They couldn't shave Greg now that he was on blood thinners, and his gray beard made him look old and unkempt. His hair hadn't been cut in months and lay shaggily over his scars. His recovery was moving in slow motion and was fraught with one setback after another. Every day, they explained, in crystal-clear English, how very sick he was. Every single day, I saw the sadness on my kids' faces. Every minute of every day, the tragedy was right in front of me, and I felt as if my heart were breaking over and over again.

We had left the surreal, fantasy-like setting of Madrid, and I missed it.

"Mom, it's the hospital," Jon said, jolting me out of my sleep two nights before Christmas.

I glanced at the clock—eleven, which meant I had barely

fallen asleep—and took the call.

"Greg's blood count is dropping," the nurse on the phone said. "We need your consent for a blood transfusion." She explained the risks, and I listened numbly, reminded of the doctors in Spain explaining the risks to me before Greg's many procedures there. As an afterthought, she added, "Greg isn't in crisis." When the kids were getting into trouble as teens, Greg and I had an agreement to start any *non*-emergency phone call with, "Everything's fine." If only nurse had understood how differently this call would have gone if she had begun that way.

How many times had I listened to a scary list of possible outcomes—infection, rejection of the transfusion, more bleeding, or death—and still consented to treatment? How many times had I struggled with pervasive guilt that I was keeping Greg alive against his will? How many times had I doubted that I was doing the right thing?

I hung up, my mind racing. Why was his blood count dropping? How low was it? Shit, I was fully awake now.

I was annoyed by the call and frustrated, afraid that I might not be able to fall asleep again. But the next thing I knew, it was six in the morning and the dogs were breathing down my neck for breakfast. Greg had never loved having the dogs in the bed, but I had started letting them sleep with me, comforted by their warmth and unfailing love. Alone in our king-sized bed, I was grateful that they were helping to fill both the space in the bed and the hole in my heart.

On the morning of Christmas Eve, I felt numb. Although my heart wasn't into the holiday, I feared the minute I stopped doing things I'd collapse into my grief, so I worked on my menu for Christmas dinner before setting the dining room table. I pulled out the red place mats with holly leaves from Greg's mom and my mom's Christmas china. I opened up the silver boxes and removed forks and knives and serving utensils, thinking of the Christmas Greg had surprised me by completing our set. I picked which glasses I would use—our wedding crystal—and gathered the red napkin rings. I was carefully putting the twelfth plate in place when I caught myself and put Greg's place setting back into the cabinet. I left his place next to me at the end of the table empty, a bitter reminder.

Jenny wouldn't be back in Denver until Christmas morning, Keely had flown to California to be with her parents for Christmas, and Chris and Katie were working, which left Jon and me with too much empty time after visiting with Greg. We went to see a movie, which filled a couple of hours but also made me sad, reminding me of Christmases when the kids were little.

That evening, Jon and I went to Rob and Lee's house for an early Christmas Eve family celebration. They were some of our best friends—and the hand-holders who had given up Thanksgiving to be with me in Spain. For the past few years, if Greg and I had found ourselves alone on Christmas Eve, we had joined their extended family—three married kids and eight grandchildren—for dinner. Jon and I pushed open the front door to the chaos—babies on the floor, toddlers running with toys, adults serving drinks, and several big dogs trying to stay out of the way. One by one, everyone hugged me, as I blinked away my tears. One of the preschool-aged grandkids wrapped his arms around my legs and asked, "Is Greg going to be okay?"

"Yes," I told him. I have no idea, I thought.

We stayed only long enough to have a quick drink before heading to Chris and Katie's for dinner. While I appreciated the effort they were making, nothing was right about the evening. I was supposed to host the holidays at my house. I was supposed to cook the meal, not my friend who had kindly made a lasagna for our family, knowing it had been our traditional Christmas Eve meal when the kids were small. We should have been listening to the Christmas play list on our music server, not Chris's mix of oldies and rap.

Glasses rang as they touched the glass table after each sip, and forks clinked against plates as everyone ate the lasagna and garlic bread and salad. It was excruciating, and I had to escape, so I told the kids I was worn out. "I think I'm going to call it a night. Jon, why don't you hang out with Chris and Katie for a while, so you're not bored at my house?" I was in the car for only seconds when the tears began to flow. As I drove out of Chris and Katie's neighborhood, I thought about heading back to the hospital to spend Christmas Eve with Greg. Instead, I turned left at the light and drove home. As much as I didn't want to be alone on Christmas Eve, I feared it would be more painful to return to the hospital only to watch Greg sleep, so sick and broken.

I burst into tears the second I opened my eyes on Christmas morning, trying to shake the nightmares—Greg in a wheelchair on a bus, Greg unable to speak, blood everywhere, and the sound of suctioning. I have to get busy, I thought, pulling myself out of bed, or I won't make it through this day.

Preparing a grand holiday meal would be therapeutic, and I was thankful I knew how to cook. I still hadn't adjusted to Denver time, so it was early when I got going in the kitchen. I was intent on making a feast—far more food than we needed—because I needed to stay busy. I pulled out a cutting board and a chef's knife while some greens steamed in a pot on the stove. When the greens had wilted, I wrung out the moisture and chopped them. I minced some shallots and mixed them into the greens along with a wheel of Boursin cheese before spooning everything into a buttered casserole dish and topping it with breadcrumbs and a drizzle of olive oil to bake later in the day.

I pulled out my favorite homemade dry rub—salt, pepper, dried porcini mushrooms, and garlic powder—and smeared it over a pork loin roast from a Colorado farmer. It went back into the refrigerator to roast later. I diced a good amount of my homemade pancetta and cooked it until crispy in a wide sauté pan. I halved Brussels sprouts and spread them on a baking pan, tossing them with the crispy pancetta, the rendered fat, and grated Parmesan. I sliced apples and onions and sautéed them in butter with some fresh thyme to make a compote for the pork.

I thawed a glazed ham that had been lurking in the freezer, thinking an extra roast couldn't hurt. I had braised some bison short ribs the day before in a cherry chipotle sauce and began separating the tender meat from the fat and bones. I thinly sliced potatoes, tossed them with heavy cream and thyme, and spread them into a greased baking pan, topping the whole thing with grated Manchego cheese, pausing briefly to think about the Manchego in every restaurant in Spain. I kept slicing, dicing, chopping, browning, baking, sautéing, and cleaning for as long as I could, desperately working to keep my hands busy and my tears at bay.

At some point during my frenzy, Jenny came into the kitchen. "Do you need help?" she asked.

"I don't think so," I said. "This is good for me—it's so cathartic. What the hell do people who can't cook do when they are in crisis?"

"Pretty sure they drink!" she said laughing. We both knew our family would try to drown our sorrows later.

Throughout the day, emails and texts were arriving in a steady stream—from Cindy, my hand-holder group, my sorority sisters, friends, family, Greg's brokers, and neighbors. Each message was meant to comfort me on what people guessed was going to be a very hard day for my family, yet each communication only reminded me of the tragedy and triggered more tears. I waffled all day between wanting to cry with abandon and being annoyed that I couldn't stop crying for five minutes. Being so sad all the time was sucking the life out of me.

Later, as we sat down to dinner, I looked around the table at the faces of my family—Jenny and Ben on one side of me, and Chris and Katie on the other, my sister and her son at the end of the table, Jon slipping in next to me where Greg should have been. Everyone looked on the verge of tears. "To Greg," I said, just as I had been toasting him at every single meal since his collapse, desperate for anything that might help him recover.

Throughout the meal the kids kept the conversation light. They poked at each other good-naturedly, trying to make each other look worse at managing money. Jon and Jenny teased Chris and Katie: "Don't you think it's time to get working on a grandbaby for our family?"

I didn't think Chris was considering having a family yet, but my mood lifted slightly at the thought. He tried to divert the attention. "What about you, Jon? Isn't it about time you got engaged?"

In the end, we raised our glasses to everything we hoped for in the coming year. "To health, wealth, engagements, and babies!"

Everyone over-ate before retiring to the living room to share our Secret Santa gifts. Jenny's boyfriend Ben had been assigned to Greg and me, and I opened his gift: two copies of a book called *My Life Story So Far* for us to fill in and leave for our kids and grandkids. I stood to hug him, my throat closing with the threat of more tears, wanting to believe Greg would be able to complete his own book someday. I was relieved Jenny had found such a sensitive soul mate, no matter which way this went.

I fell into bed that night with the dogs cuddling up to me and pulled out my iPad to check for messages. A good friend who had lost her husband years before had been sending me an email every single day since Greg's collapse, ending each one with an inspirational quote. During the first dark days, I had desperately clung to her messages, looking for much needed hope, strength, and perspective. On Christmas, a day I knew must still be difficult for her own family, she shared this quote:

What is Christmas? It is tenderness for the past, courage for the present, hope for the future. It is a fervent wish that every cup may overflow with blessings rich and eternal, and that every path may lead to peace.

I had survived Christmas without Greg, but the painful day had left me drained, and I cried myself to sleep.

CHAPTER NINE

ARE WE LOSING HIM?

IN THE QUIET, early morning hours of the day after Christmas, the kids still asleep, I sat at the kitchen counter with my coffee, trying to grasp Greg's declining condition. His doctors were struggling to find effective treatments. I leaned heavily on the counter, warming my hands on my mug. We're losing him, I thought. My cell phone buzzed on the counter. It was a text from Melanie, asking, "What's happening?"

"Can you come over?" I texted back. I needed someone who had been on this journey with me to help me unravel the data and analyze the situation. Melanie had been the first handholder to come to Spain after Cindy and Peter had left—she was there when we thought we were losing Greg on day seventeen. She lived just three blocks away and was at my house in minutes.

"I think he might be dying," I said. I said it quietly, not

wanting the kids to overhear. We both started to cry. Although I had been thinking it for ten days, I had not been able to say it aloud. I had worked so hard to make sure he had the best care, to make sure the right decisions were being made, and to negotiate his transport home. "How do I prepare the kids? They thought I was bringing their dad home to recover." Melanie hugged me, and I sobbed in her arms. "I've failed them."

A few hours later, I entered the ICU with the kids. They were now keenly aware of Greg's critical condition. "You go see Dad while I talk to the doctor," I said, choking up. I quickly put on sunglasses so they couldn't see my tears.

Jenny looked at me suspiciously. Gently, she tugged on my arm to make me face her. Her eyes were shaped like Greg's, one eye slightly more closed. Now both eyes were pinched as she frowned at me. She was so tiny—barely over five feet tall and barely over a hundred pounds—and I sometimes struggled to see her as the adult she was. She was fighting back her fear and trying not to cry. "I want you to tell us what the doctor says. Okay Mom?"

"I will," I said, trying to sound calm and in control.

"Really, Mom—everything, promise?"

"I will, but please let me do this alone, Jen. I need to ask some hard questions before I can talk about it with you kids. Okay?"

She nodded slightly.

The kids went to see Greg as the head neurologist walked me through the floor trying to find a private room to talk. Pulse racing, adrenaline shooting through my body, I prepared to hear bad news. The head neurologist was older than I was, his years of experience showing on his face. He closed the door of an empty conference room and looked at me with soft eyes.

"Greg has the team stumped," he began, sitting down across from me. "We've never had a patient with a suppressed immune system who didn't respond to drug treatment. That has us worried. His kidneys are also in bad shape—we hope we don't have to put him on dialysis."

Dialysis? Was it possible Greg had survived a massive brain hemorrhage only to spend his final weeks or months on dialysis? I forced myself to ask, "Are we losing him?"

"We're not losing him. He isn't in crisis right now."

I sat on the edge of my chair, hugging myself tightly, while the neurologist talked through the complexities of Greg's case. "We've ruled out HIV," he said. HIV? I hadn't even considered it. Greg had been given blood transfusions in Spain, the doctor explained, so they had needed to test for HIV. "We'll do a bone marrow biopsy soon to make sure there aren't any other diseases suppressing his immune system."

I had spent the past ten weeks worrying about Greg's brain recovery, focused on getting him into rehab. I hadn't given a thought to the myriad of complications that might arise. Any of them might kill him.

The doctor didn't take his eyes off me. When he finished speaking, he asked gently, "How are you holding up?"

For months, I had remained strong in the face of tragedy and uncertainty, and throughout this journey I hadn't cracked once when asking the doctors hard questions and bracing for what might be scary answers. But whenever people were kind to me, as this doctor was now, I lost my composure and was unable to contain the grief. Tears welled, my throat tightened, and I could feel my face contorting. "I don't know what else to do but wait," I said.

When I got home, I went straight to my office and turned on my computer. Although I had been trying to heed Cindy's advice to stay off the Internet, the mystery of Greg's failing immune system catapulted me back into research mode. He had seemed healthy before Spain. Right before we'd left, he had seen his arthritis doctor, and I knew they had done blood work. I called the clinic and explained what had happened in Spain, then tapped my foot waiting for the doctor to pick up, hoping he wouldn't stonewall me about sharing Greg's medical information.

"Oh my God," he said when he picked up the phone. "I'm so sorry to hear about Greg."

"Thank you. I need to know about his blood work from October. Was there anything to indicate something wrong with his bone marrow?"

No, he confirmed, Greg's lab tests had all been normal.

I hung up and hunched over the keyboard of my computer. If Greg's blood work had been normal except for an RA diagnosis in October, why would his bone marrow be unable to produce the proper cells three months later? Although it was theoretically possible that Greg had suddenly developed something like leukemia, that didn't seem logical to me. It was also possible he didn't have a disease at all, that his immune system had simply been crushed by the massive amounts of drugs he had been given since his collapse—sedatives, paralytics, antibiotics, blood thinners, anti-seizure meds, blood pressure meds, and more. I wasn't certain which was scarier: knowing there was something wrong and moving forward to treat it or finding no cause for his suppressed immune system and worrying whether he could recover from the damage caused by the treatments meant to save him.

Jon and Keely would soon head back to New York. I needed to make peace with being alone instead of continually wrapped in the warm blanket of my family's love, continually distracted by their conversation. So that night, I stayed home while they went to dinner. I was immediately overwhelmed by the quiet, the faint hum from the refrigerator the only sound in the house. I turned on mindless television, hoping to fill the void with a sitcom laugh track. My legs twitched as I continually changed positions on the couch, willing myself to stay awake until a reasonable bedtime. I drifted in and out of sleep for two hours until I gave up, staggered upstairs, and promptly fell into a deep sleep. A week before, I had been unable to fall asleep. Now I found it impossible to stay awake, and I worried about this sudden excessive need for sleep. The cumulative exhaustion from the past ten weeks of trauma could easily be the reason, but still. Was I sick? Was I slipping into depression?

The next night, I had just sat down to unwind when Greg's doctor called. Dr. Cava—a name that made me trust him even before he started to speak—was Spanish and spoke with a slight accent, reminding me instantly of Madrid. "Greg's white count is improving slightly, and his kidney function seems to have leveled off. We're withholding antibiotics now so we won't further stress his kidneys or immune system. Also, I thought you'd want to know, Greg was responsive to my commands this morning."

It had been a week since a doctor had been able to tease even the smallest response out of Greg. I wanted to leap for joy, but first needed to be certain I'd understood correctly. "I hear you saying his kidneys are stable, his white count is rising, and he might be slowly turning the corner—is that right?"

"Yes," he agreed, "but remember, it's going to be a long road to recovery." The message was spoken in a different language, delivered by a different doctor, but it was the same: *poco a poco*.

I could barely drag myself out of bed the next day. I had repeatedly told the kids, our families, friends, and even myself that as long as Greg continued to get well, I could handle a long journey and would attempt to take things one day at a time. With his recovery dragging on, though, I had begun to question whether I had the strength and stamina the journey would demand.

It was harder and harder to get my act together each morning. I was having trouble getting showered, organized, and out the door with any speed, often wandering in circles and not remembering what I was supposed to be doing. Being scared all the time had depleted me. Despite making a concerted effort to avoid worry—trying (miserably) to meditate, experimenting with marijuana edibles to sleep, hashing things out with a therapist, and using a deep breathing app on my phone—I couldn't shed the worry.

Greg had been sleeping through most every visit now, so after putting on my wedding ring—I had only started wearing it regularly again after returning from Spain—I filled my tote bag with things to occupy my time should I find him unresponsive:

a needlepoint Christmas stocking I was working on for Keely, a Sudoku book from a friend, my iPad for research, my cell phone, tissues, and some snacks. As I packed my bag, I thought back to the conversation with Dr. Cava the night before, and I left the house hopeful, anticipating that Greg might be awake today.

I had just started the half-hour drive to the hospital and was barely out of my own neighborhood when one of the doctors called my cell phone. I answered as I drove, not wanting to delay my arrival. He sounded so serious, though, that I eventually pulled off the road and put on my hazard lights to take the call.

"We're concerned Greg might have sepsis," he said.

His words terrified me—sepsis meant an infection spreading throughout his blood, which could infect multiple organs and eventually kill him. Cindy had explained that some doctors used the term sepsis loosely to mean there might be a broad-based infection, not necessarily that the patient was spiraling towards death. But I had heard horror stories about people with sepsis—a friend of a friend had died from sepsis the same weekend Greg had collapsed in Spain, and an employee of Greg's had required multiple amputations after her recent bout with sepsis. The doctor on the phone certainly had my full attention.

"What about his white count?" I asked, knowing if he did have another infection he'd need a stronger immune system to fight it.

"It's 6,500," he said.

"6,500? Wasn't it just 1,900 yesterday?" I asked, struggling to understand why he wasn't excited that Greg's immune system was rebounding.

"Yes, his white count is up. But Greg's neurological response has declined again; he wasn't following any commands today."

My mind was reeling; in just twelve hours Greg had once again become unresponsive; his life was again hanging by a thread. I gripped the steering wheel tightly, trying not to hyperventilate.

The doctor continued: "The white count rising might mean his immune system is responding, but it could also signal a serious infection. We want your consent to do a lumbar puncture to culture his spinal fluid to see if he has a broader infection."

I was trying so hard to piece together the complexities. Cindy had explained that in medicine, a treatment meant to produce an outcome could also cause other problems, which required new treatments, which could cause even more problems. Everything done to a patient could have both the intended outcome as well as unintended—and often dangerous—side effects.

Greg had been given so many treatments that those unintended side effects had been mounting. He was colonized with an antibiotic-resistant superbug, so when they found some spots on his lungs, they had no choice but to treat him with heavy-hitting antibiotics. The antibiotics were hard on both Greg's kidneys and his bone marrow, causing kidney function and immune system challenges. Even more dangerous, the longer he stayed on antibiotics, the greater the risk that every type of bacteria in his system would start morphing to become resistant to antibiotics. If that happened, the doctors would eventually run out of options for treating infections.

When I arrived at the hospital, I went straight to the neuro

ICU bullpen. "Given the long time he's already been on antibiotics, the infectious disease team wants all antibiotics stopped," the head doctor said. "They think Greg is too weak to handle more drugs."

"Do you agree?" I asked. In Spain, a single doctor had briefed me each day. There must have been other medical professionals involved in Greg's care, but I never interacted with them. Here a vast network of doctors worked as a team, with specialties ranging from neurology to hematology to nephrology to infectious disease, and I was fed information daily from all of them. They each had their spin on what was best for Greg, leaving the ICU doctor to negotiate all of that input and determine a treatment plan.

"We're still concerned there might be an infection somewhere, so we're not keen to stop antibiotics yet," the ICU doctor said. "I still suspect the seizure drug used in Spain is what hammered his immune system, but we can't be sure unless we rule out infection."

The doctors in Denver had replaced the suspect medication two weeks before and were now tweaking the dosage of the new drug because Greg was having small seizures. His movements had become so spastic that they were also giving him an additional drug to settle him. It was potent and would make even a healthy person sleepy—in Greg's case it might explain why he was unresponsive, the doctor explained.

Or you could be wrong, I thought, staring at the floor. He could have sepsis. If you're wrong and you stop antibiotics, he's going to die.

The doctor said, "There's a possibility the hardware of the shunt they inserted in Spain could be infected—that's not uncommon. That would cause a broad-based infection throughout his cerebral spinal fluid." An infection in the spinal fluid would theoretically be treatable, but very dangerous, especially if the antibiotic-resistant bacteria he was carrying had caused it. Alternatively, if he had no infection and was getting progressively weaker and unresponsive for unknown reasons, the next steps in his treatment were entirely unclear.

They couldn't do anything for a few days the doctor explained—the blood thinners in his system would need to clear before they could tap the shunt or do a lumbar puncture. As I put on my gown and gloves to visit him, I thought: this is why they say, "practicing medicine." They just keep trying things, because none of these doctors know what's wrong with Greg.

The bone marrow biopsy results came back normal a couple of days later and, combined with his rising white count, made a strong case that Greg's suppressed immune system had been a drug reaction. But his white count continued to rise, worrying his doctors. "We don't know if the white count is high because of all the drugs we pumped into him to stimulate white blood cell production, or if it's the result of an infection," they said. The only way to know was to culture the spinal fluid, so I authorized the procedure.

Greg was asleep when the team showed up for the culture. As the attending doctor laid out the supplies, I chatted with the second-year neurology resident who would assist, realizing I understood more than he did about Greg's illness and prognosis. How did people without a friend like Cindy, a doctor who had been personally on call to me since Greg's collapse, navigate the complexities of care? How did people without

POCO A POCO

my aptitude for technical, medical information advocate for a loved one?

When the spinal fluid culture showed no infection, the doctors ruled out every frightening diagnosis. Unfortunately, that meant they had no explanation for Greg's lack of responsiveness. With few remaining options, they eliminated antibiotics and reduced some of the harsher drugs. And we waited, hoping Greg would soon wake up.

For over thirty years, Greg and I had hosted a New Year's Eve party with friends. In the early years, we sent the kids to stay overnight at their nanny's house, relishing the night without kids and welcoming the first morning of the New Year alone together. When the millennium rolled around in 2000, the kids started joining us for the celebration until they eventually moved on to parties of their own. For the past ten years I had been cooking a massive gourmet dinner paired with wines for a group of friends. As we aged, it was getting harder and harder to stay awake until midnight, but a long spate of eating, drinking, and laughing at the table helped pass the time until the magic hour. It was my favorite holiday—the New Year symbolized new beginnings, and it always filled me with hope.

There would be no party this year. Instead, I made a simple steak dinner for Jon and Keely, and we ate at the kitchen counter. I asked Jon to open a bottle of champagne.

"Doesn't Dad have that sword thing to open it?" He was referring to the sabre Greg had been given by his YPO friends.

"Really? You want to do that?" I asked. The sabre was meant for celebrating momentous events in life, and I didn't have any enthusiasm for a celebration. But when Jon seemed eager, I relented, unboxing the sabre. Walking to the back porch, I peeled off the foil and removed the cage from the cork. "You line the sabre up along the seam of the bottle—see here?—and swipe it away from you in a firm stroke," I explained. "Let me show you." I swiped the blade up the neck of the bottle, using the technique I'd been taught, but failed. "Fuck!" I screamed into the dark back yard. We all knew I was angry at far more than my inability to sabre a bottle of champagne.

I was ready to give up and call it a night—and a year—but Jon begged to try. I turned the bottle and sabre over to him, and on the first try, he expertly sabered the cork off. We all screamed, hugging each other and jumping up and down on the cold back deck. We just needed a victory of any sort.

I lay in bed that night with the dogs by my side and wondered how many times I had wished people a happy and healthy new year, using those words so freely, giving little thought to the meaning behind the wish. This year, the words had weight; they felt substantial (as Greg liked to say). I desperately wished for Greg to recover, and hoped that the kids and I would also remain healthy. I hoped our friends would never have to endure the pain we had this year. My wishes were delivered with a depth of understanding that came from surviving difficulty. That perspective was a gift; I hoped I'd never lose sight of it.

I would never forget 2016, despite the advice of friends who suggested I wipe the entire year from my mind. To erase the memories of the difficulties, I told them, would be to also erase the memories of everything wonderful that happened before Greg's collapse that year. Moreover, I never wanted to forget the generosity and kindness I had experienced, initially in Spain and now in Colorado, as a result of Greg's illness. I had seen goodness, found hope, and been showered with an abundance of love in the face of tragedy and uncertainty. Instead of forgetting that experience, I needed to draw strength from it.

CHAPTER TEN

ACCEPTANCE

I HAD BEEN telling the kids since Greg's collapse they shouldn't put their lives on hold while he recovered, yet as I got dressed one morning a few days into the new year, I realized that was exactly what I had been doing for seventy-four days. I needed to reclaim some small piece of my former life or the stress of caregiving would kill me.

I sat down at my desk and shot off a couple of emails to accept a few work assignments. I checked the volunteer schedule for one of the nonprofits I supported and signed up to teach an upcoming class. I sent notes to a few close friends and made plans for lunch. I had always been very independent, but this felt different. I was testing how to live alone, possibly for a long time, maybe even forever. I needed to figure out how to have a meaningful life, one that didn't revolve exclusively around hospital visits, doctor calls, and medical bills.

I still worried endlessly, and my current obsession was our finances. We were fortunate money hadn't been a problem so far during Greg's crisis; we had great medical insurance and solid financial resources. When friends had offered to set up a donation site to cover Greg's care, I had politely declined. But the realization that he might never again have an income caused me to panic. Neither of us was sixty yet, and he had planned to work for several more years.

I had always been in charge of paying bills and managing our investments, and every month Greg had pressured me to provide him a snapshot of our finances. I'd always thought he was being obsessive—we were making good money and were saving—even though I acknowledged much of the pressure to earn had fallen to him in the past ten years.

Years earlier, in late 2008, after what was generally considered the worst financial crisis since the Great Depression, I was still in bed early one morning while Greg was getting dressed. I watched through the bathroom door as he put on his tie and grabbed his suit coat. He said, "This is bad, Michele. The commercial real estate market depends on banks lending money, and nobody wants to lend anything right now. I'm scared."

It was stressful for him, and I could see it wearing on him. The frown line between his eyes was permanent now, his gray hair thinning. Not only was he concerned about his ability to make enough money to support our lifestyle, he was also worried for every broker in his company. Many of them had worked for him for twenty or more years, and he considered them family. He didn't say it, but he was worried about the company's ability to stay afloat.

"When do you think things will start turning around?" I asked.

"Who knows, but I'm really worried about our personal financial situation."

We had two kids in college and had just taken on a hefty mortgage for our new home in Denver. In the absence of commissions or bonuses from his work, we were borrowing from our equity line of credit and our insurance policies. I was confident we'd bounce back and pay off the loans eventually, but debt always made Greg nervous.

"You might need to get a job again," he said. "Maybe you should go back to work at IBM."

Just two years before, after a successful 25-year career with IBM, I had taken early retirement and launched my cooking business. I'd known I wouldn't make anywhere near what I had made as an IBM executive, but at the time, Greg's business had been strong, and the risk had seemed small. Greg had supported my decision. "I don't care how much money you make," he'd said, "as long as you don't lose money." Now he was questioning the soundness of that decision.

I sat up in bed to see him better. "I can't just go back to IBM. The tech world changes fast and I've been out of it for two years already. I don't think they would hire me back. Besides, I already have a job, my cooking business."

"You mean that hobby?" As soon as Greg spoke, his face showed his regret, but unfortunately, the words were out, and they stung. Up until I'd left IBM I had always worked full time in high-powered positions. I had earned good money, I provided the benefits for our family, and Greg and I were partners. I knew he was proud of me, relieved I hadn't chosen to stay home with the kids like many of his friends' wives had. My income had taken much of the pressure off him.

I understood where he was coming from now: I too had a hard time defining success in my new career. Initially, when I'd been offered twenty-five dollars to write a recipe column for a local magazine, I'd balked. At IBM, my commissions had been in the thousands. I forged ahead anyway, over time putting passion ahead of my paycheck and feeling intangible rewards like my growing reputation in a new industry. But that wouldn't pay the bills during the current financial crisis.

"Look, I'm sorry," Greg said. "I didn't mean that." But I knew, sadly, that he did. He missed being able to show off his successful IBM executive wife to colleagues, and he especially missed being able to share the financial burden with his partner.

"I think you did mean it," I said, "but I'm not giving up the business I just started. If we need to cut back in other areas, we will." His comments hurt, and I felt unsupported, but I was most definitely not going back to work at IBM.

Over time, the crisis passed, and we managed to dig ourselves out of debt. More importantly for our relationship, Greg began to identify with my new success. When my first cookbook won the prestigious Colorado Book Award, when the governor came to our home to support a fundraising event I was in charge of to help end childhood hunger in Colorado, when Greg heard me interviewed on public radio while he was driving to work, and when a regional magazine ran a multipage story to feature my business and philanthropic work, I knew he was proud. I was lucky to have a partner who enabled me to pursue my passion.

I thought about my "hobby" as I sat alone in my office, and I began pulling up spreadsheets on my computer to review our assets and expenses. The small amount I earned each year from my business could never fill the gap in Greg's earnings, and I finally empathized with Greg's worry over money. It felt strange to be doing the analysis for myself, knowing I wouldn't show it to Greg for his review, but I dug in anyway. I was having trouble reading the numbers, so I put on my reading glasses. How could my vision have declined so much in the past few months? Could stress do that? And if so, what else was it doing to me?

Pushing aside my worries over my health, I reviewed our expenses from the past year, trying to make realistic projections for the future. I could live without the cleaning ladies so frequently. I reduced our budget for travel, tearing up as I did it. I reduced the line item for groceries and alcohol. I'm a household of one, I thought, though it seems only yesterday we were a family of five.

Later that day, standing at Greg's bedside while he slept, I told him I had the financial statement ready for him to review, aching for him to open his eyes and give me his input.

Winter had settled into Colorado, the long, dark, cold days weighing me down like a heavy blanket. As I stared out the window at the falling snow one day in early January, Susan called, interrupting my inertia. I fell apart on the phone. I had been afraid I was becoming numb to grief and sadness. Suddenly I was unable to contain it.

"I'm so frustrated," I said. "We've been back in Colorado

for three full weeks, and yet Greg is completely unresponsive. I'm terrified they won't find a way to bring him back. How could it be that three weeks ago in Spain he was smirking at Gail as she showed him a picture of you with a big glass of wine?"

I didn't know what I had expected would happen over the course of the eleven weeks after Greg's collapse in the Madrid airport. During those first scary days, I hadn't known whether he was going to survive, but as he healed, I had become hopeful. While I knew his recovery might be slow, I was in no way prepared for the journey we had been on since returning to Colorado.

Later that day, Greg's colleague Don Kortz called. He had been texting for updates regularly, so I knew a phone call instead of a text meant he had something important to discuss. "The company would like to announce a replacement for Greg. He's a good guy, someone Greg has worked with for years and respects," Don began. "He'll be announced as interim, of course, and I wanted to be sure it's okay with you."

"Of course, do what you need to do. You have a company to run," I said, wondering why he was asking for my permission and why anyone would pretend this was an interim move. We both knew Greg wasn't going back to work there any time soon, and probably never in his full capacity. I tried to process my mixed feelings. I was scared that Greg would be depressed about ending his career at the company he had nurtured for thirty years, but I didn't want him to work in that pressure-cooker environment again. The kids didn't want him to return to work at all, ever. They believed the stress of his job had somehow caused his collapse.

But if he never worked again, what would our life be like?

Would we be happy as a couple with if he was forced into retirement early? Would we be financially secure? How would he cope with the reality that his deficits might make it impossible for him to work? Would he be angry? Would he blame me?

I wanted to talk to someone who had been through this sort of life-changing event, so accepted the invitation when my friend—who had lost her husband twelve years prior—asked me to dinner one evening. I had been hesitant to discuss my journey with her because I hadn't yet suffered the loss she had—Greg was still fighting to live. I believed her loss was in some way greater, but she was quick to disagree. "That's not how I see it," she told me. "Just because Greg is still alive doesn't mean you haven't lost something huge—your life plan. It's been replaced with complete uncertainty, and that's significant. I don't think you should dismiss it."

We were tucked in a booth at the back of a small French restaurant, scarves wrapped around our necks to ward off the chill. The duck confit, coq au vin, and wine were comforting as we chatted through dinner about how loss affects a family. She shared what it was like for her as a mother of two young teens when her husband died and their life was upended. "I hated living in our house," she confessed. "Every time the back door opened I thought he was home from work. I was miserable."

"I can totally relate. I hate seeing Greg's car in the garage every time I pull in because it reminds me he's not coming home from work. I keep wondering if our marriage is strong enough to get through this. My self-doubt terrifies me."

My friend, of course, was right. Greg and I did have a plan for this phase of our lives. The company was hoping to go public, and Greg was planning to lead his team through this final transaction before retiring, proud of what he had accomplished through his career, financially secure. Our kids were all launched, working, and doing well. They were in strong, long-term relationships and we were getting ready for more weddings and eventually grandbabies. We both wanted to travel more and were planning several big trips in the next year.

I hoped Greg would recover. I hoped he would make it to those weddings. I hoped he would one day hold his grandbabies. I hoped we could make a life together, despite any residual deficits he had to live with. I hoped we could someday travel together again. I wanted to show him Madrid, to introduce him to Pedro and Clodagh, and show off his recovery to everyone who had helped us. I hoped our marriage would survive. I hoped we'd still be happy together.

Exactly four weeks after Gail and I had been at the hotel in Madrid discussing our return to Denver, Jenny and I met with the head of neuro ICU. "No change—he's stable," was all he had to report.

When we entered his room, Greg's eyes were open, and he glanced at Jenny and me a couple of times. I held my breath, hoping for more. "Dad, can you pick up your arm to hold my hand?" Jenny coaxed, and he did. "Can you give me a thumbs-up?" she continued, and he did. I exhaled slowly and unclenched my fists.

"Jen, I'm so grateful you're willing to drive back and forth from the mountains through the snow each week to see your dad," I said. "I think after so many weeks he's sick of me telling him what to do. Clearly you're his favorite and he responds to you." The way she was looking at her dad—she wouldn't be anywhere else right now, I knew, despite the emotional and physical drain I saw on her face. I worried she was going to push herself too hard—possibly to the breaking point. "Maybe next week you should stay up in the mountains and spend some time with Ben," I suggested gently, knowing she and her boyfriend had hardly seen each other since we returned from Spain.

"I don't know—let's wait and see how dad is" was all she would commit.

I had been fixating on Greg's numbers—blood pressure, white count, seizure activity, creatinine level, INR, PT, oxygen saturation, and more—for weeks. After we left him that afternoon, I tried to quantify what had happened by compiling a list:

81 days since Greg's collapse
81 days in UCI/ICU
WBC as low as 500 and then as high as 47,000
Creatinine as high as a scary 2.98, now at a respectable 1.1
Blood pressure ranges all over the map
8 brain surgeries/procedures
At least 25 CT scans
Several angiograms
75+ chest X-rays
1 bone marrow biopsy
1 lumbar puncture to rule out infection in the cerebral spinal fluid
1 shunt tap to definitively rule out infection in the cerebral spinal fluid

1 MRI to rule out more brain damage from seizures or bleeding
1 MRA to definitively rule out more brain damage
Hundreds of labs tests
2 blood clots
20 or more physicians
40 or more nurses
2 hospitals
3 drugs for controlling seizures
1 antibiotic-resistant Spanish bacteria
5 courses of antibiotics for 4 different infections
2 sedatives, 1 paralytic, 1 eugeroic, 1 dopamine promoter
2 PICC lines, 2 catheters, 1 drain, and 2 tracheostomies
1 EMG to rule out neuropathy and myopathy
Mortality rate for this type of brain injury: 80–90%

I was paralyzed as I stared at my notes, unable to get the last number out of my head. Greg was a fighter, but could he beat those odds?

While Greg was fighting to survive, my attempts to live some semblance of a normal life plagued me with guilt. How can I enjoy dinner with friends while Greg lies in that bed day after day? How can I get my nails done, schedule a massage, or go to a movie when he is suffering? I knew all about caregiving, having been the primary caregiver for all four of our parents before they passed away, and I knew it was critical to take care of myself first. My guilt stemmed from a much deeper and more complicated thought. "If I make a life alone, it's as if I've already said goodbye to Greg and moved on without him," I told my therapist one day. "I'm terrified if he survives we'll find it hard to be a couple again. I've lived alone now for three months. What if it's hard to have him come home?"

"Are you afraid if you try to fill the giant hole his absence has left that you won't be able to let him back into your life?" she probed.

"Yes," I said softly, reaching for the tissue box in her office and petting her small therapy dog.

"Why do you think that?" she asked.

"What if I learn I like being alone, that I prefer living alone? What if over time I don't miss him so much? What if he doesn't know me or love me anymore? What if it's too hard? What if we can't live in the house we were so happy to build for our empty nest years?" My head was spinning, guilt pressing down on me. I didn't say it out loud, but what if we could no longer have an intimate relationship? What if he was childlike? Would I want out?

"Your feelings are completely normal, but I feel certain that's not going to happen. I can see how much you love him," she tried to assure me.

I still felt guilty and conflicted.

"Look, I've had clients in your shoes who had a strained marriage filled with conflict before the tragedy. They're the ones who aren't strong enough to make it through a crisis like this. That's not you two—your marriage is strong, your love is deep, and your commitment is solid. You've survived difficulty before and you'll get through this together."

That night I was still chewing on my guilt, replaying her words in my mind, when I was startled out of my preoccupation by my cell phone buzzing. It was Chris texting: "Can we come over? We need help understanding how to get a home equity loan to pay off my car."

I let out a groan before responding yes. If only Greg were here, I thought, he could share some of the parenting burden with me.

Ten minutes later, Chris and Katie walked through the door and sat down at the kitchen counter where I was sipping on a glass of cava.

"Do you want one?" I asked Katie, but she declined. Wearily, I asked them, "Do you need me to explain the HELOC process one more time?"

"No," Chris said, "but we might need to discuss this." He thrust a small plastic bag into my hands. I was tired and didn't have my glasses on. What was I looking at? Then I read through the plastic bag: YES + was displayed on a stick inside the bag, and my heart skipped a beat. Could it be?!

"We're having a baby!" both Chris and Katie screamed in unison, unable to contain their excitement. I jumped up and hugged them both, screaming along with them. Only two weeks before, at Christmas, the family had been teasing them about having a baby, and I had thought it would take months. For once I was happy that Chris shared my propensity for impulsivity. "We couldn't wait to tell you!" he said. "We knew you'd be excited!"

I had been anxious for a grandbaby for some time, but Greg had repeatedly told me not to pressure them, believing it would happen when the time was right. They had only been married a little over a year. During the previous summer, right before we left for Spain, Greg had finally started warming to the idea of becoming a grandfather. Learning the exciting news alone, without him to join in the celebration, only added to the feeling that my life was moving on without him.

For the first three months after Greg's collapse, I didn't make any major financial decisions. Even though I had always managed our finances, it felt strange to make decisions in a vacuum without Greg. I needed to be smart, but some of the decisions felt disloyal to Greg.

I asked Melanie's husband Rod if he thought I should sell Greg's car. It wasn't just a matter of the painful reminder every time I entered the garage. The car was sitting unused, depreciating, and of course Rod would advise me to sell it—he had spent his entire career in the car business, and it was an obvious financial decision. Greg loved his sporty convertible. I had joked that it was better he got a luxury car than a mistress in mid-life, and it felt cruel to sell it. Rod reminded me I could always buy Greg a new one when he recovered, but he didn't say what we both were thinking: Greg might not ever drive again.

Greg and I had been members of our country club for twenty-five years, and although I rarely attended the club, Greg golfed there regularly with friends and colleagues. It was a chunk of money in dues each month. Unsure if Greg would ever be able to golf again, I reached out to one of his golfing buddies to tell him I was thinking of resigning. I knew it saddened him—he would be losing his favorite tournament partner—but he convinced the club to let me resign with a provision for Greg to rejoin if he recovered.

I drove to the club to pick up our things. I walked out of the club with the contents of my golf locker and our two golf bags and threw them into the car. As I drove away I looked at the pool where the kids had swum when they were young and where Jon had been part of the dive team. I saw the courts where Jenny had played tennis, somehow winning ten trophies one summer. Beyond the pool and tennis courts was the eighteenth fairway along the lake, and I remembered the first time Greg had taken me golfing. Our entire extended family had gathered here just a few years ago for a celebration of Greg's mom's life and I could still hear their laughter. I was closing a chapter on our lives without even asking Greg's opinion.

Driving home I thought of a passage by David Crosby that I had read. Discussing his long-term marriage, he had referred to his commitment to his wife as "a second pair of hands." He shared an example: one of you is doing the dishes and knocks over a glass, but the other person catches it before it hits the floor. A second pair of hands. That's what Greg and I had always been for each other. Now I didn't know if he would be happy about the decisions I'd made or angry and resentful. I didn't want to do this alone; I wanted my second pair of hands, and I ached to hear his reassurance that I was thinking clearly.

What frightened me most was that these decisions seemed to signal an acceptance on my part that Greg wasn't going to recover.

CHAPTER ELEVEN

DRAGONFLIES

IN AN ATTEMPT to gain some control over my life, I returned to my volunteer work as a chef educator for a local nonprofit organization. I had been teaching families in need how to shop and cook nutritious meals on a budget for ten years, and I missed the work. As I set up for the class in the kitchen of a mental health facility, my assistant helped me lay out the cutting boards, knives, and vegetables. Although I had been away from teaching for months, everything was falling into place, and I was looking forward to the class. The classes would take only a couple of hours once a week, so I could easily work around my routine of hospital visits and doctor consults.

I was shaking off some pre-class jitters when my cell phone rang. The hospital social worker said bluntly, "It's time for Greg to leave the neuro ICU and move to another hospital."

Just forty-eight hours earlier they had been performing

tests to rule out additional neurological issues, and they had yet to determine the cause of Greg's lack of responsiveness. He had barely recovered from the many complications—a low white count, kidney problems, seizures—yet now they wanted to move him. I had grown comfortable communicating with the head of the neuro ICU and trusted him—was he giving up?

"Hasn't anyone talked to you about this?" she asked after my prolonged silence.

"Nobody said anything. I don't understand. Why does he have to move?"

"It's what the doctor thinks is best—he wants Greg to move to Kindred, a long-term, acute care hospital. I'm sorry, but I thought he had talked to you already."

I had never heard of Kindred. The move from Spain to Denver had nearly killed Greg, and it was terrifying to think he would be leaving the world-class facilities where he was currently being treated.

"Let me start working on it—the referral process and insurance approval takes time anyway. You can talk to the doctor when you get here later this morning," she said.

If I had thought I could sneak in a simple two-hour class to bring back some sense of my prior life, the call proved I had been wrong. I was frazzled as I tried to get organized. The students were arriving and washing their hands, but I was busy texting people. "They want to move him—to an LTAC—a long-term, acute care hospital," I sent to Cindy. I had never heard of an LTAC and hoped she could help me make sense of the plan. Then to Don Kortz, who was well connected in the Denver medical community: "They want to move Greg to Kindred—what do you know about them?"

I was sweating and unable to concentrate, completely

caught off guard. It wasn't clear if the move was good news or bad news. I was frustrated and more than a little angry—all I had wanted that morning was a pleasant, two-hour cooking class.

I shut off my phone and turned to greet my class. "Good morning, I'm Michele and I'll be your Chef Educator today."

After class, I drove to the hospital, still in my chef coat, and confronted the head of the neuro ICU. "I don't understand why you want to move Greg. I always thought the plan was to stabilize him, then move him to a regular ward *here* before moving him to a rehab hospital." Others might have been hesitant to confront a senior physician like this, but I wasn't. Over the months of Greg's care, I had developed the confidence and strength to push for what I believed he needed. One of the things I appreciated most about this doctor was his complete honesty, so I locked on his eyes waiting for his answer.

"Listen, between you and me, UC Health does a lot of things very well, like this neuro ICU and cancer treatment," he explained, "but I'd give our rehab a B-minus. At this stage of Greg's recovery, I'd rather have him in a place that will provide intensive rehab alongside his medical care. This just isn't what we do well."

I knew he was likely overstepping by speaking poorly about any aspect of his employer, but I appreciated his frankness. Okay, I thought, here we go again—another new hospital.

I had just gotten out of my car at home when the social worker called again, and I stood in the garage with my cell phone pressed to my ear. That morning she had said the insurance referral process would take at least a few days, but the approval had taken only two hours. It had taken weeks of negotiating with the insurance company to approve Greg's air transport home from Madrid, but they certainly had moved quickly when the decision would reduce their cost. I hated feeling cynical but couldn't shake it.

I ran inside to research Kindred and to call their liaison to discuss the process for moving Greg. Both Cindy and Don returned my calls—Cindy agreed the move was a reasonable next step in Greg's care, and Don shared that Kindred had a solid reputation as an LTAC with a specialty in intensive neuro rehab.

At four o'clock that afternoon an ambulance picked up Greg to move him to his third hospital in less than twelve weeks. My stomach churned as I drove through rush-hour traffic into downtown Denver to meet them. I had plugged the address into my GPS, and when I arrived at the point indicated, it looked more like an office building than a hospital. There was a sign posted in front that read "No Emergency Care." What did that mean? Across the street loomed the massive medical complex of a different hospital system. What if Greg had some sort of emergency? Would they take him there?

I drove behind the building to the parking lot, but in the dark, I couldn't figure out where to enter the building, so I walked around to the front door, pulling my scarf tighter around my neck in the cold wind.

Inside at the guard desk, I entered my name on the sign-in sheet, and the guard gave me a stick-on Visitor badge. "He's on the 3rd floor—the elevators are over there," he said, before adding, "I'm the X-ray tech, but since it's night time, I'm covering for admissions. I'm going to bring some paperwork to the room for you to fill out, okay?" I nodded, wondering how thin the staffing was that an X-ray tech was also acting as security guard and admissions clerk. I walked down the hall toward the elevators, through the dark, old building, and thought back to Ramón y Cajal. Décor had nothing to do with medical care, I tried to remind myself.

The elevator doors opened on the third floor, right in front of the nursing station, and the desk was eerily empty. It was six-thirty in the evening—where were the nurses and doctors? Where were the people who were going to care for Greg? I turned left toward Greg's room, hung up my coat, and put on a gown and gloves. He was alone in the room and groggy from the move. I hadn't had enough time to digest the change and was disoriented from the speed of the transfer. I sat down and waited for someone to tell me what was happening, staring mindlessly at the TV with the sound off while I held Greg's hand.

Eventually the on-call doctor came to examine Greg. He gave a cursory glance at his chart from UC Health, checked a few vitals, and then said they would do more evaluation in the morning. That's it? I tried to make myself believe the brief consult meant Greg was getting better, that nothing critical was threatening his recovery at this point, but I couldn't shake the worry that this change in hospitals would mean he'd be getting less attention and potentially substandard care.

The night nurse came in, cheerily introducing herself and enthusiastically assuring me Greg was in a wonderful facility. "You'll be impressed with what we'll help him do, I promise. I know he was off the ventilator in Spain, and I don't know why the neuro ICU team didn't work on weaning him again. Doesn't matter—this is our specialty and we're good at getting patients weaned quickly." She was talking too rapidly for me to keep up, full of energy at the start of her shift, a sharp contrast to my exhaustion at the end of my day. As I tried to keep up with her chatter, all I could think was how much I hated starting over again, hated figuring out how to work with a new care team. I understood they needed time to assess Greg, but I had been here over two hours at this point and had learned nothing.

No matter how much I willed it, Greg wasn't waking up, and it was now nine at night. I hadn't eaten dinner, and nothing else would happen until the next day, so I went back down the elevators to leave for the night. The X-ray tech was still at the guard desk. "I didn't have a chance to get you the paperwork, but we'll do it tomorrow," he said. I didn't care. After the omission at UC Health when they had admitted Greg, I knew they needed my phone number and had already written it on the white board in Greg's room. The paperwork could wait, so I turned toward the door to leave.

"Call me if you need anything," the X-ray tech/guard/admissions clerk said. "Even if you just need someone to clean the snow off your car, I'm happy to help."

"Thank you," I said. The kindness of yet another stranger, I thought, pushing open the door to the cold night air. As I walked through the parking lot to find my car I glanced up and saw that the moon was full again. The last full moon had escorted us from Spain to Denver, now this one from the ICU to the long-term acute care hospital. I slipped into my car, slamming the door against the winter chill, and thought: will the next full moon, in February, finally take Greg to the rehab hospital?

I had wanted a small tattoo for a few years, for reasons I couldn't quite articulate, even though Greg didn't approve. When Jenny had shown up with a large tattoo covering her ribcage several years before, all he could say was, "Oh, Jenny." She had given considerable thought to a design that would be inspirational: a clock with a Latin inscription that translated to "time waits for no one." It was meant to remind her to live her life fully every day. All Greg saw was that she was covered in ink, and that years later, if she hated it, there would be no removing it.

Still, I had been considering everything from a small whisk or pig to document my love of cooking to the words "fuck you" in a bold font that I could throw into someone's face when they spewed the racist, misogynist hatred that had permeated our country recently. I hadn't followed through on any of my ideas—if I was going to get a tattoo, which would last forever, then the message it conveyed every day should be powerful. None of these carried enough weight or significance.

On the day of Greg's cranioplasty surgery in Spain, Rob and Lee and I had been trying to fill the time with anything that would provide a diversion from our worry over another surgery when I had mentioned wanting to get a tattoo. "What about a dragonfly?" Rob had asked, pulling out his phone. He had been considering a dragonfly tattoo himself and had been compiling notes about the symbolism of dragonflies.

"Greg loves dragonflies, you know," I said. "When we sit on the patio in the summer with a glass of wine, he gets so excited when they start showing up." I smiled, picturing the scene, remembering happier times, as I started reading Rob's notes on his phone:

The dragonfly symbolizes change, the kind of change that has its source in mental and emotional maturity and the understanding of the deeper meaning of life.

The way they fly low and scurry across water symbolizes going beyond what's on the surface and looking for deeper implications and more profound aspects of life.

The dragonfly's agile flight and its ability to move in all six directions exude a sense of power and poise, things that come only with age and maturity and experience. They symbolize the depth of character we develop by enduring significant life events.

The dragonfly exhibits iridescence. Some cultures say this symbolizes the end of one's self-created illusions, a clear vision into the realities of life, and the discovery of one's own abilities by unmasking the real self.

Because the adult dragonfly flies only for a fraction of its life and usually not more than a few months, they are meant to remind us of the virtue of living in the moment, living life to the fullest, and living life without regrets.

Almost 80 percent of the dragonfly's brain power is dedicated to its sight, and it can see in all 360 degrees, a symbol for the ability to see beyond the limitations of the human self, to see beyond the mundane into the vastness of our universe and our own minds.

Everything I read resonated with me. This would be a powerful symbol for the journey Greg and I were on, one that would be significant for the rest of my life.

After nearly three months of Greg's hospitalization, I wasn't the same person I had been when Greg and I had boarded the plane for a vacation in Spain.

I wasn't as angry anymore—I didn't feel the need to scream "fuck you" at the world so much, which was ironic because the journey could have left me angry and bitter.

I was more understanding and more empathetic. It was impossible to know what other people were going through, and I reminded myself to consider that before lashing out with impatience or frustration.

Despite so much tragedy and pain and uncertainty, I was more grateful, perhaps having taken too much of our charmed life for granted before. I felt driven to write thank-you notes for any kindness shown me; expressing gratitude was uplifting.

I had been forced to erase any plans or expectations for what the future would hold, which caused me to live more for what was happening each day.

I wanted to be around friends more and separated my true best friends from my many other casual acquaintances in the community. I told those true friends how much they meant to me.

While I spent more time alone, I was at the same time less independent and accepted help more.

I appreciated Greg's friends more and learned more about what he meant to them. My respect for Greg's reputation as a business leader grew.

I developed a new admiration for health care workers and understood more about medicine than I ever thought possible.

I cared little about the things Greg and I had fought about before his collapse. I loved him more—or perhaps was simply reminded how much I loved him.

I was more in tune with the universe, noticing signs, symbols, and synchronicities in ways I never had before.

I understood, finally, how very little I controlled.

No, I wasn't the same person I had been three months prior, and a dragonfly tattoo would be the perfect symbol for my personal journey.

Jenny drove down from the mountains one snowy Monday in January to see her dad. She still hadn't agreed to skip a week of visiting Greg, despite my gentle prodding. The staff at Kindred had been working to try to wean Greg off the ventilator, but he was sleepy and unresponsive while we sat with him. Frustrated, we left the hospital after a short visit. As we got in the car I asked, "Want to go get dragonfly tattoos?"

I had reached the point in Greg's recovery—or lack of recovery—that I needed a visual reminder; I needed to see that dragonfly on my wrist every day for strength and encouragement. Jenny was excited to get one too, and we drove south to the tattoo shop Rob had recommended.

My heart was racing as we pushed through the door of the shop. The tattoo artists were covered from head to toe in tattoos, some of them running up their necks and onto their faces. Almost all had their ears gauged, leaving them with those freakish-looking loopy, long earlobes. They had piercings in their ears, noses, eyebrows, lips, tongues, and God knew where else. What was I doing here?

As we stood at the desk, Jenny and I pulled up the images on our phones we had found for our tattoos. Mine was a simple, loose dragonfly design, while Jenny's was more intricate, with lacy wings that would require lots of tattoo dot work. We waited while the artist prepared the images.

"Who's first?" he asked, calling us to the desk to sign waivers.

"Me," I said, anxious to get it over with, not knowing if it would hurt, and fearing I'd lose my resolve if I thought too much about it.

"Where are we putting this tattoo?" he asked. He was only twenty-four, he was covered in ink, and his tongue had been split like a serpent's tongue—which I tried to avoid noticing.

"On the inside of my right wrist," I said. I didn't understand the point of getting a tattoo in a hidden place—I wanted to see mine every single day and draw much-needed inspiration and strength from it.

As I sat in the chair and the artist did his work, Jenny took pictures to send to Chris and Jon, who were disappointed not to be with us getting a tattoo of their own. I visualized myself trying to explain to Greg one day why I had done this as the artist followed the stencil outline with ink.

The tattoo only took five minutes because it was so small, but I had done it. I now had a tattoo. I stared at the small, feminine dragonfly, a little over an inch long, on the inside of my right arm just above my wrist. I was mesmerized, the symbolism Rob had shared with me running through my mind, and I couldn't stop smiling.

Because Jenny's tattoo had more detail, it took longer. I snapped a couple of pics, and then scrolled through the artist's Instagram feed while he worked, looking at other tattoos he had done, wondering if this would become addictive as my kids had suggested, wondering if I would get another one. I didn't need to wonder for long: within six months I added three more tattoos. Eventually Rob got the dragonfly tattoo he had been wanting. In time, Chris, Katie, Jon, Keely and many of our friends also chose tattoos to honor Greg.

Jenny and I drove home and opened a bottle of cava to celebrate our new body art. "To dad," we toasted. I knew my tattoo had no bearing on Greg's journey—it had no power to dictate his recovery—but it was deeply significant to me, and I hoped when I eventually showed it to him and told him why I had gotten it, he would understand my intent and appreciate the symbolism.

CHAPTER TWELVE

RECOVERING

THE NURSE WHO had admitted Greg to Kindred had been right to be optimistic. Within ten days of his transfer, he had successfully weaned from the ventilator and was given a special valve that allowed him to speak with his trach still in place. He had been silent for three months, and his first words were whispers and out of context, so it was hard to understand what thoughts might be going through his mind. When a nurse asked if he would rather be called Gregory or Greg, he said, "Greg," which reassured me that he knew who he was. But then, right afterwards, he said, "1986," without any explanation.

One of my earliest concerns was that too many people would want to see Greg, something I feared he would hate. He was very private, and he wouldn't want the community to see his deficits and vulnerability. He had little control of his arms and legs, was still tube fed, was incontinent, and couldn't put a sentence together. But despite my worry over how he'd feel about it, I sensed it was time for selected friends and family to visit. I had seen how he reacted to the kids—hearing the voices of people he loved, I hoped, would provide more stimulation than I could on my own.

The nurses requested I limit the number of visitors, so I asked only a few of his very best friends to start visiting. Some were happy to go alone, while others wanted me to show them the process. Some wanted privacy to say what they needed to say to Greg, while others needed their wife along for support. They all reported back to me after their visits—not because I asked them to, but because they now felt they were part of Team Greg.

"He was sleepy, but I held his hand for a while."

"His eyes were open, but I couldn't tell if he could hear me."

"I reminded him of a funny story, and he smiled a little."

They also told me how hard it was, many of them sharing how they had cried in their car after visiting him. Seeing one of their best friends in such bad shape was difficult, a too vivid reminder of their own mortality, but they were intent on helping Greg find his voice, hoping one day to have him become part of their lives again.

One day, Susan's husband Scott called to report after seeing Greg. He had been vigilant about visiting Greg, trying to sneak in time with him early in the morning before his work day started. I was on my way to Kindred when he called, and as I listened on my cell phone while driving, I could feel the smile in Scott's voice. While he was there, the doctor had come by and was surprised to see Greg interacting with a friend. "We haven't had much luck getting him to respond," he said, before asking, "How are you, Greg?"

"Fucking wonderful," Greg replied. Scott and the doctor burst out laughing. Classic Greg, I thought. Greg was always a man of few words and used to joke that everyone in my family talked just to hear themselves speak. He wasn't social with strangers, and probably didn't have anything to say to the doctors, so he had been remaining largely silent. But his buddies mattered, and he was trying hard for them.

His short answers continued for some time. His voice was soft and raspy, he didn't always enunciate well, and sometimes his words came out jumbled. But he was clearly answering with "hi," "yes," "no thanks," "pretty good," or "a little bit." His responses seemed to convey understanding. He also smirked at jokes or funny stories his friends told, prompting one of his best friends—a broker he had worked with for twenty years— to call and say, "It's happening!!!"

Yes, it's finally happening, I thought. I had been waiting months for this day, hoping beyond all hope he would begin to recover eventually and I'd have my man back, complete and healthy. But my excitement was always tempered by the reality. Despite all of the encouraging signs his friends noticed, Greg still slept most of the time, which made me uneasy and anxious. He had made such little progress in the three months since his collapse compared to other patients. Friends were surprised by how good he looked; his face looked like Greg, the scars from his brain surgeries now long healed, his cheeks a rosy pink. But our friends didn't see what I saw. They didn't know his grimace meant he was having an uncontrolled bowel movement. They didn't see his emaciated body when the nurses bathed him. They didn't see the fear in his eyes when the orderlies turned him on his side to clean him from the soiled bed pads.

They didn't witness his confusion when he opened his eyes to the doctors. They didn't watch him frantically grabbing for his tubing, his arms flailing in spastic motions because of his brain injury, forcing the nurse to strap his arm down or place a ball in his hand to keep it occupied.

They saw only their buddy Greg.

I saw my husband developmentally at the stage of an infant, and it broke my heart—for him, for me, and for our family.

I had become frustrated that I couldn't get anyone to take care of Greg's freakishly long fingernails and toenails, so one morning I arrived at the hospital with everything I needed to take care of them myself. I started trimming his fingernails with the clippers before gently filing off the sharp edges. I dug in the drawers in his room to find some bacterial wipes and used them to wipe away the crusting that comes from unkempt nails. Next, I unwrapped the boots that kept his feet in their proper position and began clipping his toenails. The nails were hard, and I worried I would cut too close, but I persevered. When I finished clipping, filing, and cleaning, I massaged the heavy duty unscented lotion the nurses used into his toes and fingers to relieve the dryness and cracking.

Greg slept the entire time.

Until his collapse, we had only been called on in the tiniest ways to care for each other: pick up cough syrup, schedule a doctor's appointment, administer meds on schedule after surgery. Even then, I had never doted much on Greg when he was sick, expecting him to be an adult and deal with it. If he whined when he was sick, I was annoyed. If he had asked me for help before this, I would have done it begrudgingly. When I was sick, I took care of myself, so why couldn't he? Now he wasn't asking me for anything, yet I felt compelled to do everything I could to care for him.

When Greg and I were married in 1985, I didn't give much thought to the words "in sickness and in health" that were woven into our wedding vows. We were young and healthy, and it was impossible to envision what might happen over the course of the coming years. The only illnesses and deaths we had experienced at that time were those of our grandparents, which we accepted as the inevitability of aging.

Greg used to joke: "If I ever have to wear a diaper, just shoot me." I had heartily agreed. But now that I'd encountered a true medical crisis for which I didn't know the ending, my perspective had changed. A diaper at this stage of his recovery was a small inconvenience, and although I could never have imagined it when we said our vows, I had grown comfortable assisting the nurses in changing and cleaning him.

After I had trimmed Greg's nails, the therapist came into his room. "We need to stimulate his muscles, so he can remember how they work," she said, as she showed me how to smooth his eyebrows and mouth to stimulate muscle movements that would eventually, hopefully, help Greg open his eyes and talk. It was tedious work, but I followed her instructions, slowly pressing his eyebrows up, out to the side, and back down, over, and over, and over. I wished our friends understood: this is how rehab starts for Greg, and it's going to take a very long time.

As I worked, Greg eventually opened his eyes, and when I finished, he puckered up for a kiss. For the past couple of weeks, he had been working his mouth into some sort of pucker when I requested, but this time he did it on his own, without my prompting, and made the sound of a kiss when he did it. I leaned in, and we shared a brief kiss, his lips warm and dry. After forty years together, kissing had become perfunctory, a small peck on the cheek before heading out the door to work; our kisses hadn't felt fiery or romantic for a long time.

Since our nightmare had begun, I had rarely kissed Greg on the lips. When the nurse in Spain had put the side of the bed down so I could hug and kiss him before his shunt surgery, he had been asleep, and the kiss had felt desperate. But this single kiss, this single pucker, was completely different. It wasn't filled with the lusty passion of our youth, but it was filled with more love than I had experienced in years kissing Greg. This kiss filled me with hope for our future.

Early one morning a few days into February, I arrived at the hospital as Greg's nurse was starting his assessment. His room always felt too hot to me, but I reminded myself that he had no body fat to keep him warm. I pulled off my scarf and pushed up my sleeves. I stood close, expectantly gripping the bedrail while the nurse began the exam.

"What's your name?" the nurse asked.

"Greg...." His voice trailed off, so I asked him to say his last name. "Morris," he answered.

"What's your birthdate?" the nurse continued.

"6-20-57." Yes, he knows his birthdate! It didn't seem to me that saying words like "hi" or "yes" show much brain recovery, but remembering dates seemed significant. It meant he remembered the past, which I desperately hoped meant he would remember us and our life together.

"Do you know where you are?"

Greg nodded his head slightly.

"Where?" the nurse asked.

"University Hospital," he answered.

"You're at Kindred Hospital in Denver," the nurse corrected him, and Greg nodded his head ever so slightly before the nurse placed the stethoscope on his chest. "Take a deep breath for me."

Greg took a deep breath.

"Does it hurt when I press here?" the nurse asked, pressing on his abdomen.

"No."

"Do you have any pain?" the nurse asked him.

"No."

"Does your back still hurt?" the nurse asked.

"Not now." Greg often had back pain, and it was astonishing to hear him answer the question with such clarity—not just "no," but "not now."

"Do you want some water?" I asked.

"Sure," he answered.

"Do you need something on your lips?" I asked.

"No."

My heart was beating wildly. The entire conversation sounded like a completely normal exchange with a patient. Greg didn't seem like someone recovering from a massive brain injury, he seemed like someone who knew exactly what was going on, and my heart soared as I smiled at him. I hadn't remembered feeling happy in a long time, the stress and worry over Greg's journey overshadowing everything, but I actually felt happy. Happy Greg was still in there and making progress, and hoping there might be a happy ending after all.

I liked to be at the hospital for the first rounds in the morning, because I hoped Greg would be awake and rested and the morning routine might stimulate him to communicate with me. One morning a few days later, the same nurse made a comment about the disco music I had selected on the small portable radio I had placed on the windowsill in his room. The nurse was smiling, amused by my choice, not knowing I had purposely picked it to remind Greg of our past, of our years at Bucknell, when disco was so popular. I had been hoping the music might stimulate his neuro recovery. As I looked out the window towards the office buildings downtown where Greg worked, I said to him, "You like to dance, don't you?" and he nodded yes. "We were the disco couple in college, weren't we?" I asked, and he smiled. Yes, we were, I thought, as I pictured those frenzied dance parties in the basement of Greg's frat house when he was social chairman. I wondered if we would ever dance together again.

The nurse interrupted my thoughts by asking how long we had been married. I looked at Greg. "It'll be thirty-two years soon," I said to him as I looked him in the eyes. He nodded. "What's our anniversary?" I asked, still looking at him.

"April 20th," he answered. Yes.

The nurse teased him—"Good thing you remember that date!"—and all three of us laughed.

Although I only witnessed Greg awake and alert a very few times, he often responded well to his male friends. I tried not to feel hurt that Greg was more communicative with them than he was with me. I made light of it by joking with everyone that he surely must be sick of me after months of my bedside vigil. Intellectually, I knew he was comfortable with me and probably felt safe to rest while I was there, but emotionally, I ached for more interaction with him.

I suspected part of the reason he was communicating well with friends was because he was trying hard to show them he was going to be okay. When they came into his room and said hi, he perked up and reached out his right arm—his left was still paralyzed from the brain injury—to shake their hand. He smiled and tried to mouth some words from a song when a buddy came to sing for him. He accurately told the nurses the names of his friends. When one friend joked that maybe he could finally beat Greg in a wrestling match, Greg told him, "I'll put a figure four on you," referring to a classic wrestling move, making it clear he knew exactly what he was saying.

Unfortunately, as soon as my hopes were boosted by an exchange like that, there was inevitably another communication from Greg that was garbled and confused and caused me to question whether he was making progress or not. He would cite names as if his brain were going through a rolodex of people from his past, but not provide any details about what he was thinking or trying to say, which made it impossible for me to respond.

I would endure days of watching him sleep, or struggle with these incomprehensible conversations, and then, just when I was about to give up hope, he would say something lucid. One day, Chris and Katie reminded him they were having a baby, and Greg asked, "How far along?"

Although I discovered early that Greg was better equipped to handle simple yes or no questions, I couldn't stop trying to press him for more, because I needed to know how much of his brain and memory were intact. Greg and I had always agreed it was great that we shared long-term memories of growing up together at college. After the hemorrhage, I worried he would lose these memories and without a shared past, our marriage would suffer. So, I persisted in testing him.

"Do you know our kids' names?" When he didn't answer, I concluded it was too much to digest. I tried another tact. "What's our oldest son's name?"

"Chris."

Yes!

"And what's his wife's name?"

"Katie."

"What's our other son's name?"

"Jon."

"Who is his girlfriend?"

"Keely."

"What's our daughter's name?"

"Jenny."

"And what's her boyfriend's name?"

When Greg didn't respond, I told him his name was Ben.

"Yeah, Ben," he said softly. He sounded disappointed in himself. I wanted to tell him: It's okay. You're doing fine, it's going to take time for you to remember everything. You'll get there. But he had yet to initiate any conversation himself. I didn't know if I believed he would get there or not.

One day as I sat at his bedside, Greg's arm was thrashing about wildly, his brain still unable to control his spastic movements. When the thrashing jolted him from sleep, I said, "Hold my hand."

He squeezed my hand as he looked at me.

"It's nice to have a hand to hold, isn't it?" I said. He smiled and nodded yes. Those were the moments I felt like my husband was still there, and that Greg truly would recover. Those were the interactions I lived for, even if they happened only sporadically.

I had been repeating the *poco a poco* mantra ever since Melanie first shared it with me in Spain, but I still needed a visual reminder to take things one day at a time when I spun out of control with worry. So, I added *poco a poco* to my tattoo, in a loose script that trailed up the inside of my right forearm, from the tail of my dragonfly tattoo all the way to the inside of my elbow. In five short minutes my small tattoo had become quite large, and although I wondered how Greg would eventually react to seeing it, I didn't care. For now, it would help me stay grounded and focused.

CHAPTER THIRTEEN

FILLING THE VOID

WHILE GREG SLOWLY and painstakingly started emerging, I tried desperately to fill the long gaps between meaningful interactions with him. I was looking for anything to keep my mind off my worry, intent on regaining control of any aspect of my life I could.

The quiet in our house, interrupted only by the dogs barking or the furnace, left me alone with my thoughts for far too long, which led to my imagining worst-case scenarios. My therapist had suggested I try meditating, which sounded like torture. I had never learned how to meditate properly—my mind had always been too busy making lists and checking things off to settle into the required mental stillness. But when Chris mentioned he used a short, guided meditation app on his phone to calm his overactive brain so that he could fall asleep, I decided to give it a try.

I sat down in the suede chair in the corner of my office on the first floor of the house. The dogs, who liked to lie in the sun while I worked, were sprawled out on the rug. I opened the app and placed my feet flat on the floor as instructed. When I pressed start, a man's pleasant British accent filled my office, explaining the guided meditation. Within seconds, my confused dogs started licking my knees. Frustrated, I shut down the app.

Over the coming months I used the meditation app daily— I never actually meditated, but for at least ten short minutes each day I thought about something other than the tragedy that had struck our family. My thoughts weren't deep or spiritual, more like distractions: Why is a British accent more soothing than a southern accent? Is this helping to lower my blood pressure? When did Chris start using this app? How do people sit and meditate for hours? I don't know that I experienced any emotional growth, but I did calm myself for those few minutes each day.

Without my work or Greg at home, I had so much time to fill. Every day, I took on the challenge of trying to find anything to chew up some of that time. I'd always enjoyed reading, but I was completely unable to focus on a book, my mind wandering too much to stay connected to the story. I exercised because I wanted to protect my own health, but my workouts were short. My primary motivation for exercising had always been to stay trim. What was the point now if Greg couldn't acknowledge my efforts and tell me I looked good?

I did the laundry and the ironing, chores I ordinarily ignored for as long as possible. I tried working on needlepoint Christmas stockings for the family, having committed to picking up the tradition my mother-in-law had started, but I tired of the work quickly. I stepped back into volunteering for two nonprofits, having experienced many times how doing for others made me feel better, but that filled only a couple of hours each week. Since I missed cooking for Greg and was looking for something to do in the kitchen, I baked more than usual. My family had made chocolate peanut butter fudge every Christmas when I was a child, so I pulled out my mom's recipe book and mixed up a double batch. I knew that was a colossal mistake when I glanced in the pan a few days later and realized I had eaten a pound of fudge by myself.

I took the rest of it to Greg's nurses, as I did with other baked goods whenever I felt susceptible to another binge. I had always hated Greg's criticism about my weight or my diet and had recoiled when he said things like "Are you really going to eat that?" Now I missed his help in controlling my stress eating.

I sorely missed writing my food blog. Occasionally I worked on a post, but I had trouble finding any creativity. I made my bed every day—it gave me some small sense of completion.

With the financial worries created by Greg's medical condition and his likely forced early retirement, I had scaled back the cleaning professionals after returning from Spain. It was embarrassing to admit I hadn't cleaned my own house in thirty years. When Chris had been an infant, our nanny, with time on her hands while he napped, had begun cleaning the house while Greg and I worked. Over the years, we officially "hired" her to clean, which provided her some extra cash and cleared the responsibility of cleaning the house from our busy schedules. Once the kids were grown, I was so accustomed to having my house cleaned by someone else that I couldn't face doing it myself. But the problem of dog hair—the reason Greg had wanted the housed cleaned weekly—was overwhelming. So I did something I hadn't done in thirty years: I started cleaning my house. I bought a new vacuum and Swiffer pads for my dry mop and started doing the carpets and floors. As I wandered back and forth across the family room, watching the ever-growing mass of blonde dog hair accumulate on the mop, a small, hard-to-explain sense of peacefulness washed over me. I didn't move on to what I considered "real" cleaning—toilets—but I finally saw why many people felt cleaning was every bit as therapeutic as cooking.

If nothing else, it filled a small part of my long, lonely days.

In Spain, I had lived out of a small hotel room with just six changes of clothing. When I returned home, I was overwhelmed by the sheer amount of stuff Greg and I had. Neither of us was a hoarder, we had cleaned out extensively every time we moved, and I gave things away regularly. But now, nearly every day I pulled something out of a closet, off a shelf, or up from the basement and put it in a pile for Goodwill. When friends came over I gave them things, whether they wanted them or not. I just felt I needed to get rid of stuff. Subconsciously, I was preparing to move, believing it was less and less likely Greg would recover well enough to return to this house. There was no first-floor bedroom and no first-floor shower, and the open modern staircase would be impossible to navigate if he had trouble walking. I had looked at putting an elevator on the outside of the house, changing my office to a first-floor bedroom, and adding a shower to the first-floor powder room, but couldn't see any of these options working.

Possibly more overwhelming than the things we had

accumulated was the volume of food we had on hand. Years before, I had started buying meat directly from Colorado ranchers and farmers, no longer willing to settle for the quality of industrially produced meat. Storing all that meat required an additional freezer in the garage and it was completely full of Colorado beef, bison, pork, chicken, and lamb. I had a massive professional-sized refrigerator-freezer in the house and a second refrigerator-freezer in the garage for overflow. When we'd built the house, knowing I'd be teaching cooking classes along with cooking for our family and catering jobs, I had requested a large walk-in pantry. It had thirty sections of shelving, and most of them were crammed full of food: three bags of oatmeal; seven kinds of rice; ten pounds of pasta; canned and dried beans; ten varieties of sea salt; Asian, Mexican, and Italian food products; six boxes of cereal; dried fruits and mushrooms; baking supplies; and more.

I had lived out of a dorm fridge in a hotel for two months, subsisting on lunch at a restaurant and snacks of meats, nuts, and cheese in the evening. Now, faced with this massive volume of food, I was ashamed. I had spent considerable time as a volunteer fighting issues of food insecurity and hunger, and hated wasting food, so couldn't allow myself to throw any of it out. Instead, when I returned from Spain I declared I wouldn't buy any meat or pantry items until I had eaten what I already had. I purchased only fresh produce, eggs, and almond milk for months. This need to clear the house of all this food was the same as the cleaning and giving stuff away: I felt strongly, albeit silently, that I would be leaving this house, either with or without Greg.

What I didn't recognize at the time was that, unable to control Greg's recovery, I was directing my energy at things I *could* control. The meditation, the exercising, the baking, the cleaning, the discarding, and even the eating down of the food in the house, were attempts to take control of my life. They had nothing to do with Greg's recovery—none of them helped him to respond to me. But at least I filled a few hours each day obsessing about something other than his care.

CHAPTER FOURTEEN

Respite from Caregiving

On Valentine's Day, Greg's nurse—the chatty one who had admitted him in mid-January—called me. "Greg has a Valentine's Day present for you," she said.

I could hear the excitement in her voice.

"He got his trach out finally, and he's grinning from ear to ear!" She put the phone to Greg's ear so I could talk to him. It was awkward, like talking to a baby who couldn't respond. After silence on his end, she finally took the phone back and we said good night. I should have been celebrating Greg's progress, but I ached for more from him.

By late February, trach or no trach, Greg was still largely unresponsive and slept most of the time. I was scheduled to leave for a week-long vacation with friends, an annual trip Susan and Gail and I had started taking thirty years earlier, and I had vacillated about whether I should go. I desperately needed a break, but I was uncomfortable leaving Greg.

During the previous weeks, I had been told what Greg's rehabilitation might involve: it was going to take more time and effort as he progressed. Would I have the stamina for his long recovery? The nurses suggested this would be a good time to take a break. Friends gently insisted I take the vacation. My kids pushed me hard to go. I was terrified—I had been at his side every single day since this started—but I decided I would go.

On the Friday afternoon before I was due to leave, I went to see Greg. He was about to be transported to UC Health for some additional tests—they were still managing his ongoing neurological care, and his neurologist wanted to check for underlying seizure activity that might be contributing to his lack of responsiveness.

When I arrived, he was sitting in a special chair, his arms propped up on several pillows to prevent bedsores. I still didn't know what he understood, and I struggled with whether to tell him I was leaving or just not show up for a week. He was awake and seemed focused, which was rare, so I said, "I'm going away with Gail and Susan for a few days." I watched to see if he understood me.

"Where?" I thought I heard him whisper.

Thinking it would be too complex to explain the details of our cruise, I said simply, "Florida." Greg nodded and blinked, actions I had come to accept as signifying understanding.

He had been in the chair for a few hours already, which always tired him, so the aides put him back into his bed just as one of his brokers came to visit. The two of us stood on either side of Greg, visiting across the bed while he slept, softly snoring. His trach had finally been removed, the scar on his throat had healed, and he was breathing completely on his own, complete with snoring. While his snoring had annoyed me for forty years, listening to him snore now was oddly comforting. He seemed like himself.

Suddenly he opened his eyes. He stared to the right where the friend was standing. He seemed to be in some sort of trance; he was struggling to breathe.

"Is he okay?" the friend asked.

I came around to that side of his bed to help him. Within seconds his face became dark red, his eyes watering, the veins in his neck bulging as he clenched his jaw shut and struggled to breathe. His entire body was spastic, jerking around wildly.

Since his initial collapse in Spain, he hadn't had a visible seizure, but I knew he was having one now. A massive seizure. For four months, I had worked to block that horrifying image from my mind, and in an instant, it came rushing back. In Spain, I hadn't known it was a seizure. I had thought he was dying. Now I knew what a seizure looked like, but I couldn't believe it was happening again, less than twenty-four hours before I was scheduled to leave town. Maybe it was a ridiculous thought, but I wondered if Greg was sending me a signal not to go.

Our friend ran from the room, screaming towards the nurse's station for help. I stood helpless, listening to the code blue announcement repeating over the PA system. Staff ran into the room. A team of doctors and nurses worked on Greg while the doctor in charge explained to me what was happening. A quick dose of Ativan would shut down the seizure. An IV dose of Keppra would keep it from reoccurring. His blood pressure and oxygen levels had been monitored and were okay. He was fine, for now.

The seizure had been short, only about a minute. Greg drifted into a deep, drug-induced sleep while another doctor discussed next steps. "Greg hasn't been monitored for seizures in months, and it's possible he's still having small seizures," he said. "Seizures are exhausting, and this might be why he sleeps all the time." The doctors had been frustrated, as was I, that they couldn't pinpoint the reason for Greg's overall lack of responsiveness. Every time he slept for days on end, I panicked that he was slipping away from me, that he'd never be able to recover. I hoped they'd soon find an answer, hopefully something treatable like controlling seizures.

After an examination to confirm that he was stable enough to transport, the ambulance prepared to take him to UC Health for the planned tests. As they wheeled him past, the friend turned to me and asked, "Are you okay?"

"No," I said, collapsing into his arms, in need of both a good cry and a strong hug.

Although I rarely got headaches, my head was pounding as I left the hospital. I could only imagine what Greg's head felt like after so much trauma. After starting the car, I called Cindy, as I had every day since she left Madrid, hoping for insight and reassurance. As a doctor, she could help me unravel what was happening, and as my best friend, she would be honest with me. Peter was home from work and got on the phone with us. I explained to them what had happened, still struggling with the decision to leave the next day.

When Peter said he thought I needed a rest after the agonizing past four months, I cracked. "I'm just so tired," I said. "I know I need a break." I blew my nose before continuing. "I've noticed it all week—I'm sleeping poorly, waking too early, walking in circles, forgetting what I'm doing, and I've been spacing out commitments I've made." I wiped my eyes and blew my nose again. "I'm losing it."

"Mic," Cindy said, "the doctors are going to do everything necessary for Greg's care whether you're there or not. You should go—you need a break."

Late in the day, the neurologist from UC Health called to report on Greg's tests. The shunt was functioning, and they were adding new epilepsy drugs to prevent more seizures. "Go on your trip and don't worry," the doctor said. Like that was possible.

Even though I was still not fully convinced I should leave, I began packing. It would be the first time in four months I hadn't been by Greg's side every single day, comforting him and advocating for him. But we were far from the end of the journey, and I knew I needed to recharge for the next phase. I was both relieved to get away and terrified to leave.

The morning after Greg's seizure, I woke early, immediately struggling to dismiss my worry and guilt. I had to get busy or I'd lose my resolve. I stripped the sheets on my bed. I sent some last-minute emails before shutting down my computer for the week. My travel tote was sitting on my desk and as I packed it for the flight, I couldn't stop thinking about the last time I had packed this tote before our trip to Spain. I could see myself standing in the hallway of Ramón y Cajal with both Greg's and my suitcases and totes, and I could hear the nurses yelling *"Gregorio!"* I shivered and quickly zipped the tote shut.

I stood under the hot water in my shower trying to relax, reminding myself what the liaison from the rehab hospital had said. Things would get harder, not easier, when Greg moved to rehab. His recovery would require hours of my time each day while he was in the rehab hospital, and almost all of my time when he eventually came home, because he would be wheelchair bound and incontinent. I would need to transport him to outpatient rehab each day. "You know those friends who insist on bringing you casseroles you don't want?" she asked. "Tell them to save it for the rehab stage, when you're going to need all the help you can get." Her blunt words were terrifying. Did I have what it would take to help Greg rehab? She had encouraged me to take a rest while I had the opportunity, and I was grateful for the nudge.

The kids were at the house, ready to help with Greg while I was away, and they were all awake to say goodbye when Susan and her husband picked me up. I hugged the kids briefly, not wanting to linger and lose my resolve, while reminding them to keep me informed. I wasn't sure how I felt. Nervous? Scared? Guilty? Exhausted? Mostly, I just wanted a time-out from my life.

On the first morning of the cruise, I awoke exhausted, despite sleeping nine hours, and blamed it on the nightmares I couldn't seem to shake. I had always been a vivid dreamer, but now when I briefly woke up from a scary dream, my mind started piecing my dream together with my life. Instead of some abstract scene, the images were all too real—Greg trying to talk, Greg in a wheelchair, blood, doctors, me struggling to reach Greg, Greg stumbling—which caused me to spiral with worry. What if something happened to Greg? Would I be able

POCO A POCO

to receive the call for help? I couldn't dismiss my guilt, and I wondered if I would feel better if I got off the ship at the next port, went home, and returned to my job of caring for Greg.

Other dreams were convoluted amalgams of our life. One vivid dream included two couples we knew in a strange montage with another old neighbor and a bunch of babies. In the dream, Greg was rejecting me and saying he was leaving me. It was easy to dissect the dream into parts. Our cruise was in the Caribbean, with pretty turquoise waters surrounding our ship and palm trees blowing in the warm breeze. Greg and I had recently sailed in the Caribbean with the two couples from my dream, so that made sense. The neighbor from the dream had recently helped me assess how to install a first-floor shower for Greg, so I understood why he had crept into my dreams. And the babies were obvious: we were soon becoming grandparents.

I had often dreamt about Greg rejecting me when I missed him. While I had only been gone two days, and while I hoped it would be liberating to be temporarily relieved of the caregiver role, I already missed him. I missed seeing him each day, missed knowing whether he was okay or sick, and missed the reassurances from his nurses and doctors that he was making progress toward recovery. Did he wonder why I wasn't showing up to visit? Did he think I had abandoned him? Was he even alert enough to know I wasn't there? I might never know, I thought, struggling to settle into the spirit of a vacation.

When I had returned from Spain and was enveloped by the love and support of my kids and best friends, I'd slept fifteen hours a night for what felt like days, eventually catching up on much needed sleep and recovering from the inevitable jet lag. But the two months since our return had left me depleted, and now I just wanted to close my eyes. I wanted to block out the reality of my life through sleep and cry with abandon for the sadness of Greg's situation and what it had done to our life together. I tried to balance the need to sleep and cry with what I knew intellectually might help me feel better: spending time laughing with friends and relaxing in the warm sun on a sandy beach. But I was operating in slow motion, and after dinner each evening, I didn't have the energy to stay up late or close down the bars the way Susan and I had done on our last cruise. I knew she understood, but I felt bad about abandoning her.

For the first few days while I was gone, Jon and Keely visited Greg daily; Jenny and Ben would spend time with him later in the week. Chris took the lead in his care. From the moment Greg had collapsed, I'd had trouble seeing our kids as the adults they really were. I'd sheltered them from the gory details while we were in Spain. Then, in Colorado, even though the kids visited Greg regularly and we discussed his care as a family, I was the one managing that care with the broad medical team. The kids saw him weekly; I visited him as many as three times a day. They asked me questions; I was responsible for negotiating his care plan with the doctors. Yes, we were a team, everyone taking part in caring for Greg, but I had held tightly to my role as captain of that team.

Although I had been anxious about leaving Greg for a week, I had sent an email with the kids' contact information to friends and family who were helping, telling them Chris would be in charge while I was away. Chris had replied to the group email, copying everyone. "We've got this," he said. What he really was saying was *he* had this, that he not only could, but wanted to step up to this role.

I wasn't sure if it was a bigger step for me or for Chris that I left town after four months of caregiving and asked him to

POCO A POCO

take charge. At thirty, married, with a child on the way, he was no longer a kid. He could do this, friends reassured me. I sensed he both wanted and needed to step into the role. Yes, Jon, Keely, Jenny, Ben, and Katie would all help, but Chris had taken the lead.

One September afternoon in 2007, when I was playing golf, Chris called my cell phone. I stood to the side of the tee box to take the call, my heart racing, and braced for more bad news. It seemed every time the phone rang, it was news that Chris had gotten himself into some sort of trouble—run-ins with the law, financial messes, and more. He was nearly twenty-one, but Greg and I worried his life was spinning out of control.

"I owe money to a drug dealer—if I don't pay him I don't know what's going to happen," he said.

"I can't do this now Chris. I'll call you in a few hours," I said. Damnit, I thought as I hung up the phone and put my golf glove back on, when was this going to stop? I was running out of ideas of how to help this kid. He had a heart of gold, but he kept making bad decisions. Counselors thought we should adopt a tough-love approach, but because of his diabetes, I didn't feel I could throw him to the streets. How would he survive without a refrigerator to store his insulin?

I was driving home, angry, when Melanie called, and I erupted. "I can't fucking believe I'm dealing with this," I said. "When is he going to get his shit together?" She'd had family challenges of her own, so I knew she understood my frustration.

"You should call Jay Zink," she suggested. Jay was a counselor who had figured out a great way to make a living: for a hefty price, he took private calls from his boat in San Diego to help parents straighten out family messes. It seemed cushy to me, like he was taking advantage of people with money, but I knew he had a good reputation.

I called him as soon as I got home and conferenced in Greg from work. We quickly explained Chris's history—he'd struggled in school, had been diagnosed with juvenile diabetes at fourteen, dropped out of high school, incurred lots of minor run-ins with the police, suffered from attention problems, and now he wanted us to pay off a drug dealer. Jay listened silently as we summarized the issues.

"You need to stop everything you're doing and send him to rehab," Jay said. It was something we hadn't even considered. "I'll call a place I usually recommend to see if they'll admit him tomorrow."

Our heads were spinning. Did Chris really need inpatient rehab? What would that cost, and would insurance cover any of it? Would he go, or would he fight us on this as he had on seemingly everything so far? We knew Jay had helped many of our friends when their kids had been in crisis, so we agreed.

Greg came home and we drove to Chris's condo. "How should we do this?" Greg asked as I drove.

"Let's keep it simple like Jay suggested," I said. "We don't give him a choice. He's either going to rehab tomorrow or we're cutting him off." It sounded so easy, but as we pulled up in front of Chris's place, my heart was racing and my mouth was dry. I always had trouble sticking to a script with Chris, but I knew we couldn't continue enabling him.

Chris thought we had come over to give him money to pay off the dealer. We asked him to sit down and talk. The condo was a modest two-bedroom unit that we had purchased, using money we had saved for him for college as a down payment. We had hoped he would develop some pride of ownership, but it was littered with liquor bottles and smelled of cigarettes, telltale signs of what had been going on here. "Chris, your life is spinning out of control," Greg said, using the words Jay had scripted for us. "You're in danger and we can't keep doing this."

"I have flights booked tomorrow for you and me," I said. "I'm taking you to rehab in Tucson so you can get help." I still wasn't convinced he needed rehab, but I needed to put an end to the insanity.

"That's ridiculous!" He glanced nervously at us both. "I don't need to go to rehab!"

"You don't have a choice," Greg continued. "You get on that plane tomorrow with mom or we're done. We'll take your car and stop giving you money. And you won't be in our lives anymore." This was incredibly hard for Greg—his kids were everything to him—and my heart ached as he made our demands.

Chris relented. "Okay, I'll go, but I have to pay that dealer first."

What if something goes wrong with this drug dealer today, I wondered? What if we never get the chance to help him?

Greg handed him two hundred dollars. "This is it—you understand?"

Chris nodded.

"I'll be here at seven-thirty in the morning to head to the airport," I said. "Pack some clothes and be ready."

Greg and I hugged Chris, left his condo, and cried all the way home. Nothing we did was as important to either one of us as raising our kids. Just keep loving them, Greg always said, and things would work out, but despite our love and good intentions, this felt like a monumental failure of parenting.

A few days later, Chris sent us a letter to thank us for sending him to rehab and promising to make something of his life. It was my birthday, and it was the best gift I could have hoped for that year. "We're a good team," Greg said, as he read the letter, wiping away his tears. "He's going to be okay."

While I was away, Chris visited Greg, called Cindy to discuss his medical progress when he needed a second opinion, coordinated pet care for my dogs, and managed household issues. He sent me encouraging notes and text updates, checking to be sure I was holding up okay. He sheltered me, I would learn later, by keeping difficult news and friends' concerns about Greg's lack of progress to himself. Greg had been right all those years ago. Nearly a decade later, Chris was more than okay. I had never been prouder of the man he had become or more grateful for his support.

I normally signed up for excursions on cruises, but before our departure, nothing had captured my interest—or maybe I had been simply unable to make one more decision. At the last minute I had committed to an excursion to make chocolate in Cozumel. It was chocolate, so how demanding could it be?

The morning got off to a rough start. Our departure from the previous port had been delayed the night before because of rough seas. During the night, our captain had put the ship at full throttle in an effort to reach Cozumel on time, but the speed of the ship through rough waters had left us all bouncing in our beds, barely able to sleep and fighting off queasiness.

By six in the morning I knew if I didn't see the horizon I was going to be sick, so I quietly snuck out to the back deck. I snuggled into a lounge chair, pulling my robe around me against the whipping winds in the early gray dawn of morning. I gazed at the horizon, then watched the many stages of sunrise, in complete solitude, over the next ninety minutes. I kept thinking about Greg. He loved sunrises and sunsets, and adored being out on the water. As I looked at the orange ball of fire rising from the sea and passing through the low clouds, I felt his presence.

We arrived at Cozumel only thirty minutes late, but it was enough to turn the ship's entire schedule upside down. I had purposefully signed up for an early and short excursion, so I could return to the ship to rest and read. My early excursion had been rescheduled for twelve forty-five; it would cut right through the middle of the day, which meant I would miss the opportunity to sit in quiet solitude by the pool that afternoon. Had another woman in our group not planned to go with me, I would have ditched it. I felt guilty abandoning her, so I waited for the departure, trading texts with family and friends about their visits with Greg.

When it was time, I hustled off the ship to the meet the guide and boarded a bus for the short ride to the facility for our chocolate making and tasting. As soon as I entered the room, I softened. My friend and I sat together behind a cocoa bean grinder, and I could feel a small piece of my prior life creeping back to me. I had spent ten years attending every food event or cooking class I could, in locales all over the world, before launching my business in 2006. This was familiar; this felt comforting.

The young Mexican woman teaching the class spoke with an easy, soft accent, welcoming us with a small chocolate martini. I pushed my worry and sadness aside so I could enjoy the experience. As I sipped my martini, she began to explain the history behind chocolate making in Mexico. Within a few moments I found myself taking notes and snapping photos, inspired to write a blog post about the experience. I had hardly taken any food photos or blogged since before we left for Spain, and I missed my work.

The class was taught in an open-air pavilion with spectacular views of the azure Caribbean lapping at the shores a few yards away. With the water sparkling in the distance, my friend and I worked together to grind the cocoa beans and sugar. We added vanilla and shaped the mixture into a mold. Then we tasted eight different varieties of chocolate paired with wines.

After the tasting, we ate a lunch of small, handmade chicken mole tortillas with a mug of steaming cinnamon hot chocolate. I was tipsy and full, both physically and emotionally, from the experience. Standing in line to purchase some chocolate, I thought: this is what I love, this is my life in food and wine that I have put on hold for four months to take care of Greg. I hadn't been cooking, had only taught one cooking class, and had all but abandoned my blog. I missed these things, for the simple reason that I loved my work, but also for the bigger reason that I missed the life I'd had before tragedy struck.

I had never been particularly homesick when I traveled and never missed Greg much when we were apart. I had always been fiercely independent. I traveled well by myself, and for the past thirty years, I'd loved our annual girlfriend trips. But on this trip, I was really homesick. I didn't just miss Greg; I missed the life he and I had built together over the past forty years.

Not the momentous events, but the simple moments of our life together. Laughing at a sitcom. Drinking wine on the deck. Planning a trip together. Retelling the day's events to each other. Hugging our dogs. Sharing news of friends. Talking about the kids. Listening to music. Going out to dinner.

I had a bad habit of perseverating on things out of my control, and I'd had moments during the past few months when only a "tell-it-like-it-is" friend from New York like Susan had been able to stop me from spiraling. I knew it could be a while until I got another break from caregiving. As I paid for my chocolate, I scolded myself for overanalyzing everything and reminded myself to relax.

It proved difficult, however, to either relax or stop obsessing. Over the final two days of my week away from Greg, I battled tears and homesickness constantly. The week had been restorative, but it was a long time to be gone after having spent every day for the last four months at his bedside. I kept grabbing my phone, logging onto the ship's Wi-Fi, checking for a text or email from anyone who might have seen Greg and have news to report that would lift my spirits. The short updates were teasers.

"He almost touched his nose with his hand twice."

"He said he felt better and was smiling at us a lot."

"He said hello clear as day—it was probably the loudest I've heard him speak yet."

"Best and longest visit yet—kept asking him if I should leave and he shook his head no."

And from Jenny: "He asked Ben what's new with the house,

and he asked for an ice pack for his shoulder. His voice is getting a little louder."

The updates all sounded like Greg had progressed miraculously in the week I had been away. Before I'd left he hadn't initiated any conversation, yet from the reports it sounded as though he was now asking people questions. I wanted to be thrilled, but I had a nagging feeling people weren't telling me the full story. Everyone at home was intent on helping me enjoy this week. Were they exaggerating for my benefit? What had happened that they weren't mentioning?

On the last night aboard the ship, I sat on the deck outside our stateroom sipping a glass of champagne while everyone got ready for dinner. As I relaxed into the warm Caribbean breeze, Jenny sent me a text that read, "He'll be happy to see you—we told him today that you get back tomorrow and he opened his eyes wide."

They had told Greg I would be coming back with a tan, she said, and Greg had responded, "She likes that." I chuckled to myself, thinking of how he always slathered himself with sunscreen on our sailing trips while I lay on the deck tanning myself.

Looking out over the vast ocean, I finally grasped what had been nagging at me all week. Did Greg know that I had been away, and if he did, did he care? Did he know how much I had grieved for the past four months about his illness and how that had obliterated the life we had shared? Would he understand I had rediscovered how deep my love for him was? Would he feel relieved to come home with me when the time came? My deepest worry stemmed from my lack of understanding about what parts of his brain would never recover and what damage would cause permanent losses, in both abilities and memories. Would he remember that he used to love me? Would he love me still?

The next morning, before we left the ship, Gail and I started crying instantly as we hugged goodbye. She was a special friend who had been incredible to me during the past four months; not a day had passed when I hadn't reflected on how very lucky I was to be surrounded by the gentle love and strong support of friends like her during this difficult journey. They had been the ones who had brought me hope, peace, and comfort during the past months. I believed in them and had faith in them—they were, in a way that I didn't expect most people to understand, my religion.

Over the months since Greg's collapse, more than one person had framed a message to me on CaringBridge in terms of their own faith, and I had struggled to relate. They were praying to a God I didn't believe in. They were expecting miracles I didn't have faith could happen. They believed a higher power controlled the outcome of this journey while I did not. Their well-intentioned comments just didn't resonate with me. When people tried to tell me "God has a plan" or "It's all in God's hands" or said that "God would not have handed me this burden if he didn't think I could handle it," I balked. I simply didn't believe in a God like that.

When I was younger, I had tried to understand if the doctrine of any organized religion spoke to me, but in the end, I identified myself as an atheist. Although some people "find religion" as they age or when faced with a difficult life challenge, that hadn't happened with me. I'd held firmly to my beliefs in science, rational problem solving, and evolution. I firmly believed all humans were responsible for their own actions. I believed people should do the right thing because it was the right thing to do—not because of the threat of hell or the promise of heaven.

What I now understood after so much reflection during the weeklong cruise was that although I didn't share the faith of some of these friends, I was holding tightly to *my* faith—faith in the strangers I had met during the past months who had shown me incredible kindness; faith in our many friends who had showered us with love and support to help us through this journey; faith in the skilled medical professionals who worked tirelessly and were doing everything in their power to heal Greg; and faith in Greg himself, who was fighting the fight of his life. Despite what others might have thought about me, I had abundant faith: I had faith in the goodness and kindness of people.

CHAPTER FIFTEEN

STARTING OVER

I PUSHED MY way through the crowds in the Denver airport, anxious to get to the hospital to see Greg. As I exited, I saw Jenny in a heated argument with the security guard. They were arguing about stopping in a no-waiting zone. "My mom is right there!" Jenny yelled at the woman, pointing towards me. Although she could be hot tempered, she looked too fired up. Instantly I thought something must be wrong. I threw my bag in the back and quickly jumped in the car, turning towards her for understanding. "We need to go to UC Health," she said. "Dad fell out of his chair and they've taken him to the ER."

I had been fantasizing about my reunion with Greg the entire week I was away. Bolstered by the upbeat reports from friends and desperate for him to interact with me, I had pictured him smiling when he saw me, happy to have me home. But the trip to the ER had exhausted him, and when I finally saw him, he was agitated and sleepy. He didn't smile at me, and he certainly didn't say any of things I longed to hear: "I missed you" or "glad you're back" or "nice tan" or even just "hi." My disappointment overshadowed my anger about the incident, and I left in tears. Welcome home, I thought.

The next morning, I arrived at Kindred early. I needed the staff to explain how they could have let Greg fall, and I was anxious to see if he had any residual problems from the incident. He was sleepy when the doctor examined him, which worried me, but he opened his eyes for me as soon as the doctor left the room. Classic Greg, I thought once again. He's going to decide whom he interacts with and whom he ignores.

"I missed you while I was away," I said. "I love you."

Greg was moving his arm around more than I had seen before and he kept holding onto my thigh right above the knee, squeezing it ever so gently in what felt like a familiar touch between the two of us. "Love you too," he said back to me in a whisper. I had been worried the reports from friends during the week I was away had been exaggerated, but this looked like real recovery to me.

The orderly arrived with breakfast—until this point Greg had only been tube fed—and Greg looked excited to eat real food. I shared his excitement because it felt like measurable progress. The therapist showed me how to put a little yogurt on the spoon to feed him, and he swallowed. "What flavor?" he asked. This was the first thing he'd eaten since our lunch in the Frankfurt airport on the way to Spain. Although Greg didn't care much about food—he ate to live rather than lived to eat—I couldn't imagine going four months without eating real food.

He was talking rapidly, sometimes making sense and sometimes not, but talking nonetheless. I knew his words meant something to him, knew he was trying to get something out, but his brain was still so jumbled. I tried not to worry and focused instead on how he kept rubbing my leg. It had been four months since he had held me in any way whatsoever. I sat next to him for three full hours, not wanting him to let go.

He didn't appear to have any injuries from his fall, and in fact, this was the most interactive I had seen him since his collapse. Could he finally be turning the corner? Could he at last be ready to start rehabbing instead of constantly fighting to recover from one medical setback after another?

My euphoria was short lived. Despite that encouraging visit, he slept for most of the day on both Tuesday and Wednesday. Was he having more seizures? Was he sick again? Would he be able to recover or not? Was he simply giving up, too tired to keep fighting?

I was slipping back into the funk I had felt when he had been facing life or death every day in Spain. Wednesday night I didn't go back to the hospital as I had been doing each night. Instead, I texted Susan asking for "permission" to stay home and cry. I needed reassurance that I wasn't a bad person for not being able to handle the strain every minute of every single day. I needed her to say she understood and that it was natural. I needed her to say everything would be okay. Of course neither of us knew if it would.

Earlier that day, when Greg briefly opened his eyes, I had cried in front of him, then hadn't been able to stop crying, wiping away my tears while I held his hand. As he watched me, I couldn't tell if he understood that tears were an expression of sadness. I didn't know if he had any idea why I was crying. I looked deep into his eyes, but the way he just stared at me left me wondering if he knew it was me.

Just the day before, one of his nurses asked him who was coming to visit that day and he had said, "My wife, Michele," though I was standing right there. Did he not know I was there? Did he not recognize me? I couldn't stop testing him, trying to see what he knew or understood. I asked him what my last name was, and he said, "Fugere," my maiden name. So his long-term memories might be intact, but did he remember he had married me?

In an attempt to cope with the uncertainty of Greg's condition, I had been seeing a therapist and reading about Buddhism. Both suggested I should let go of worry, which was easy to understand—there was nothing to be gained by worrying about how well Greg would eventually recover, because there was nothing I could do to control the recovery process. I advocated for his care and worked with him, I followed the doctors' instructions, and I relayed the information to friends who visited, but worrying wouldn't control the outcome; it would only rob me of today's joy.

The Buddhist teachings I read also advocated letting go of hope, which was harder for me to understand. If I did, did it mean I had given up? I had been hoping Greg would magically have a complete recovery, but after four months of this journey, I had little confidence. I wasn't sure he would ever walk again or recover fully mentally. A couple weeks after his collapse, a doctor in Denver had explained to me the many things that affect the brain's ability to recover. We wouldn't know how far he could recover until much later, he had said, maybe not for a year or more.

After much introspection, I began to understand that holding onto hope for a complete recovery was a giant setup for disappointment. Every time I saw Greg, I yearned for him to engage with me; when he didn't I left disappointed and sad. I needed to approach each day with zero expectations: what was going to happen was going to happen.

Understanding these concepts didn't mean it was at all easy to do. So, when I woke up again at four in the morning, unable to sleep, my mind whirling, I stared at the tattoo on my right arm and said the words out loud to myself, *"Poco a poco."* I needed to live in the moment and follow the journey as it happened, one day at a time.

By Thursday, just four days after returning from my vacation, I was procrastinating, making pizza dough instead of heading to the hospital, subconsciously afraid to go. I'd had this fear every day in Spain. Greg's condition was so tenuous, at times hour-to-hour, that I'd had a pit in my stomach as the taxi pulled up to the hospital each day, not knowing what I'd encounter. While his condition was no longer life-threatening, I still experienced that same dread when I went to see him. I wanted to find him awake and doing well, but if I didn't, if I found him sleeping steadily like he had been for the past two days, it was a gut punch. So much for letting go of worry and hope.

That Thursday, I was bracing for the worst when I arrived

but was pleasantly surprised to see Greg working with his physical therapist. She went to get some bicycle pedals for him—pedals anchored to wheels that she could roll under his feet while he sat securely belted in his hospital chair. When she returned, she and I worked together to strap his feet into the pedals.

Greg looked as if he didn't know what to do. I said, "It's like the exercise bike at home." He never used the exercise equipment, or spent much time working out. He was blessed genetically with "thin genes," I always said, and over the years it had frustrated me that I'd had to exercise so much to stay at a healthy weight. We had added the bike to our exercise room—my exercise room—for rehab after my first knee replacement. I hoped he at least remembered how a bike worked.

He looked at me briefly and then started pedaling. I had been worried he might not regain the use of the left side of his body. It had been paralyzed from the damage to the right side his brain, but the doctors had explained that another part of his brain could take over those functions. As he pedaled, I could see that he was using both legs to push the pedals around, giving me hope he might one day walk again. He didn't break any speed or distance records, but after a few rotations he looked pleased with himself. The therapist joked that he might need a massage after his big workout and Greg laughed. I smiled, not at the joke, but because Greg loved getting massages and his laughing at her comment showed me he understood the context.

Speech therapy had started with skills that seemed to have nothing to do with speech. Greg had needed to relearn how to use the muscles in his throat first—how to swallow and cough, handle ice chips and water, and eat food. He had successfully

POCO A POCO

passed those hurdles, and now the therapist was ready to work on actual speech. I watched expectantly.

"Greg, say 'OW,'" she began.

He said it, softly.

"Now say 'OH.'"

He repeated the sound, his voice still uncertain.

She continued for a while, working on his enunciation and pronunciation while guiding him through number and letter patterns and encouraging him to project a stronger voice. Greg did better than either of us expected. He worked for about fifteen minutes before closing his eyes, the only way he could signal that he'd had enough and needed to rest. I was so proud of him.

That day, I floated out of the hospital, excited to call the kids and tell them about the bicycle pedals and the speech progress. "Riding a bike?!" they all exclaimed. Although it seemed impossible at times, although we were trying not to hang onto hope, we all needed to believe Greg could recover.

When I arrived in Greg's room the next morning I sensed instantly that something was wrong. He looked like he was hallucinating, his eyes weren't tracking, and his mouth was stuck in an open, downward frown. He was moaning and unable to speak at all, not even a simple "hi" or "no," or his name. I called for his nurse, but after five minutes, nobody had come. I missed the ICU, where the dedicated nurses had responded instantaneously. Angrily, I ripped off my gown and gloves and found Greg's nurse near the elevator.

"The doctor gave Greg a new muscle relaxant to help with

his rigidity," he explained," and the dose was probably too high, so we're backing it off some." He seemed confident the medication would level out, though I wasn't convinced this was the cause of Greg's condition. It didn't seem consistent with the great display of progress I had seen the day before.

After a few more minutes trying to interact with Greg, I felt sure something serious was happening. I impatiently pulled off my gown and gloves again, and ran down the hall to the nursing station where Greg's neurologist was doing chart work. "Something's wrong with Greg. Please come right away," I pleaded.

As soon as the doctor saw Greg he concluded he was having another seizure, just not a massive seizure like he'd had before I left for vacation. In the span of five minutes the attitude of the staff changed from calm to crisis mode, as they filled his room to treat the seizure. What if I hadn't been there? What if I hadn't pressed the doctor to see him? And why, every time we made forward progress, did we have to endure a setback?

Since the seizure meds would make Greg sleep for the rest of the day, I went home. I photographed food, blogged about food, ate potato chips and ice cream, and made pizza, trying to pass the time without making myself crazy with worry. He would sleep off the meds, I told myself, and be ready to interact with me the next morning like he had the day before.

But on Saturday he was still unresponsive. I asked all day to see a doctor, but nobody ever came—it was the weekend, and very little happened over the weekend. I lashed out, sending text messages filled with frustration to anyone who would read them, before giving up and heading home late in the day.

I slept horribly.

Sunday morning, crazed with worry, I went back to the hospital early, marched into Greg's room, and, when I found him still unresponsive, I called the hospital's head doctor on his cell phone—he had given me the number strictly for an emergency—and asked him to come immediately. Upon examining Greg, he wasn't convinced something critical was happening, but I pressed him, reminding him of everything Greg had been doing just days before. He humored me by contacting Greg's neurologist at home, using FaceTime from his phone to show Greg's altered state.

The neurologist quickly responded, "I agree with the wife."

I felt validated. Something was wrong—Greg's state was clearly altered from a few days before. But why had it taken three days to reach this conclusion? What would have happened if Greg hadn't had someone like me to push the system? And now what? What would happen next?

By ten-thirty on Sunday morning, Greg was in an ambulance headed back to UC Health; we spent all day in the emergency room while they ran a battery of tests. "We don't see signs of more bleeding or stroke on his brain scans," the ER doctor said. I relaxed ever so slightly. Ever since Greg's collapse I'd worried that further brain bleeds or strokes would lead to further brain damage. They suspected an infection in his cerebral spinal fluid was making him unresponsive. We had been down this path once already in December, and I fully understood the implications: spinal meningitis would be difficult to battle. Given the highly antibiotic resistant bacteria he was carrying in his system, it could be even be fatal. It would take a few days for the test results, so they would start broad-spectrum, heavy hitting antibiotic and antiviral drugs immediately to attack any infection he might be carrying.

I had spent most of February fighting to convince rehab hospitals in Denver to admit Greg. My first choice had been the world-class Craig Hospital, which was only a couple of miles from our home. They had rejected him early because of the antibiotic resistant bacteria he carried, and from everything I'd read, I knew that the bacteria colony wasn't likely to clear his system until he had been out of a hospital setting for months or even years. I tried calling in favors from connections Greg had at the executive levels of the hospital, but they refused to change their policies.

My second choice had been Spalding Hospital, who'd had the same fears about introducing the bacteria into their facility. I had worked every angle possible, even enlisting the help of a friend on the board. In the end, I had convinced them to rewrite their procedure manuals to safely admit Greg. After his success with the bike pedals, speech therapy, and eating the week before, he had finally been cleared for rehab. He was scheduled to be admitted on Monday. I had toured the rehab facility, talked to the doctors, and had even seen his room, just days before.

Now instead of starting rehab, he was admitted back to the ICU, with an entire team of doctors—neurologists, epilepsy specialists, pulmonary intensivists, nephrologists, hematologists, and the head of infectious diseases for the entire hospital system—working together to diagnose and treat him.

While they worked, Greg slept.

I had been home from my cruise for one week. Any sense of rest or rejuvenation I felt had already been stripped from me.

Rollercoaster. Ordeal. Nightmare. Experience. Challenge. Situation. Horror. Difficulty. Struggle. I had used all of these words to describe what Greg and I and our family had been going through for twenty weeks, but the word that I used most often, that really resonated with me, was journey. A journey has a beginning and an end, but the road meanders, and it forces you sometimes to take an alternate route. While you might plan a journey, you don't control how the journey will unfold. That was what I had felt every day since Greg's collapse.

Now, for the first time since our journey had started, I was at a complete loss. Greg was back in ICU and I was home—unable to do anything other than binge on comfort food and lie on the couch. I tried to watch TV but couldn't focus. I stared at my dogs for hours but didn't have the energy to walk them. I had a pile of ironing that might distract me, but no enthusiasm to tackle it.

My mind was working overtime to decipher how Greg's condition could have spiraled from such an upbeat day on Thursday, when he had been ready to move to the rehab stage of this journey. I couldn't fully grasp that after twenty weeks I was still facing the possibility he might not make it. His vitals were stable, and he was breathing on his own, yet he couldn't wake up, focus his eyes, track a conversation, speak, or answer with a nod of his head. He wouldn't squeeze my hand or pick up his arm, and he most certainly wasn't eating, drinking, smiling, or pedaling a bike.

It felt like starting all over again, and it was crushing. UC Health had treated Greg for a month in the neuro ICU when he had returned from Spain, and with no definitive explanation for his lack of response, they had sent him to Kindred.

At Kindred, they had started waking up his brain with neuro stimulants, and it seemed the approach had been starting to work. But playing with brain chemicals could be tricky, I was told. Anytime Greg became unresponsive, it was because his brain wasn't strong enough to wake up on its own. He needed the help of stimulants to come out of this catatonic state, but giving more medication might backfire, his brain too damaged to cope. Neuroscience didn't feel like science at all. It felt like a crap shoot.

While the medical team had many patients to look after, Greg was my only patient, and I had become finely attuned to his condition. Five days after he had been readmitted to UC Health, I heard my phone ping while driving to the hospital and became agitated instantly. I waited impatiently to stop at a red light before checking my email. The hospital's electronic medical record system provided instantaneous results of all Greg's tests, which was great when there was good news. But I had become a slave to the reports, rushing to open them so I could research every single test and reach my own conclusions about best next steps. As soon as I saw that a blood test had been performed, followed by a chest X-ray, I knew bad news was waiting.

I linked to the blood test first—white count up to 17,000. Shit, he's got an infection again. I linked to the chest X-ray results next, and there it was—*left lower lobe atelectasis and consolidation, suspicious for superimposed aspiration in the setting of leukocytosis. Small left and small right pleural effusions.* Pneumonia. How could someone who had been on heavy-hitting antibiotics in a world-class hospital for the past five days contract pneumonia?

I had just come from an hour with my therapist in which I had tried to calm myself. Now my blood pressure was rising and my heart was pounding. When I got to the hospital, I quickly dumped the car with the valet, rushed up to Greg's room, and put on my gown and gloves. I looked at his frail body. His breathing was so rattled by chest congestion that I immediately requested a respiratory therapist to suction his lungs.

What followed was a predictable set of interactions with doctors and nurses:

"Yes, we're as stumped as you are because his white count started rising only yesterday even though he's been on massive antibiotics."

"No, we don't know for sure it's an infection because he doesn't have a fever, but we'll treat him aggressively anyway."

"Yes, we need to culture the sputum to see what bacteria might be in there—and yes, we're worried about a possible antibiotic-resistant bacterial infection."

"Yes, we did have limited success before with some specific antibiotics."

The art of practicing medicine, I thought. They were trying everything they could think of but were still stumped. I wished desperately I had a better answer.

As I watched Greg sleep, wheezing despite the humidified oxygen being pushed into his lungs, I wondered, is this it? Is this how it ends? After nearly five months of fighting is he going to lose to pneumonia? I was wracked with sadness and felt sucked under, drowning from fear that the end was near. For the first time since Greg's collapse, his doctor used the word "if" to talk about next steps. As in *if* he could survive the pneumonia, *if* they could stabilize him, and *if* he would be able to have a meaningful recovery.

I was terrified but asked the hard question I knew I had to ask. "Is it possible, even though two weeks ago he was showing such positive steps forward in his recovery, that now, with this setback, he might not be able to recover enough to enjoy a decent quality of life?"

I longed to hear the kind Spanish doctor's reassuring voice tell me, "*Poco a poco*, there have been many cases far worse than Greg's where the patient has recovered nicely." Instead, the neurologist explained how Alzheimer's patients never fully regain the cognitive functioning they lose after a medical setback. He had purposefully side-stepped the question, but I knew what he was trying to tell me—this was bad. This had been my nightmare since Greg's collapse in Madrid. Would we work so very hard to save his life only to have him end up hating his life? Unable to walk, incontinent, tube-fed through his stomach, barely able to speak, sleeping most of the time: it was a life he would never want and yet here we were, trapped between possible outcomes. He could die from this setback, and our family would be filled with anger and frustration that the heroic measures taken hadn't saved him. Or he could live, and the ongoing sadness of his situation would crush our family. Nobody on the medical team said what they had previously been saying: there was reason to hope, he had a good shot at a good recovery, it would just take time. Nobody said anything now except they were sorry, and those words were both telling and terrifying.

My head was constantly throbbing from lack of sleep, worry, anxiety, and depression. My stomach hurt so badly I couldn't tell if I was famished or ready to vomit. Being around people would provide moral support, but I couldn't face anyone, especially my kids. They would instantly see the terror in my eyes. The medical team told me to go home and rest. I wasn't sure what was worse: sitting in that hospital room in the stifling gown and gloves watching Greg struggle to breathe, or sitting in my quiet, lonely house trying to imagine how I would ever live without him. Although I had been on this journey with Greg for nearly five months, I kept thinking it was just that—a journey, from point A to point B, from his collapse in Spain to his eventual return to our life together. But our future now seemed out of reach, and my heart ached with the inevitability of his illness and what it meant for our marriage.

I spent the next two days in a state of shock. Just like the early days after Greg's collapse, it felt impossible that this setback was happening, that it must be a bad dream. I couldn't tell: was Greg was ready to stop fighting? Or was he just sidelined because he was sick? I didn't know how we'd help him start his recovery all over again. I was unraveling.

Jenny was as distraught as I was when we talked on the phone, but she said to me through her tears, "He did it before, and he'll do it again. He's a fighter." That became our mantra. If we didn't hold on to that belief, then why had we done all we had for the past five months?

There had been three distinct times when I feared I was losing Greg: October 21, when he collapsed; day seventeen—Black Monday as my kids came to call it—when we thought we had run out of treatment options; and at the end of 2016, when many of his vital organs were failing. But he had survived all of this and had gone on to begin his recovery. Now, five months into the journey, as he lay sick and unresponsive, I once again thought: we're losing him.

Then, astonishingly, after two weeks in ICU, after 125 different lab tests, after subclinical or focal/partial seizures, neuroleptic malignant syndrome, viral and bacterial meningitis, bleeding in the brain, stroke damage, hydrocephalus, encephalitis, lung infections, blood and urine infections, and drug toxicity reactions had all been ruled out, Greg began to recover.

He started breathing over the ventilator again.

He opened his eyes again.

He moved his eyes to look at me again.

He squeezed my hand again.

He nodded in response again.

And with those baby steps, I regained some small hope he might actually be able to recover after all.

I hadn't posted on CaringBridge the entire time Greg was back in ICU, too scared to voice my fears publicly. But March 21 marked the five-month mark of Greg's journey; I decided to acknowledge the milestone publicly with a post.

I wrote that I was in disbelief that Greg was still lying in a hospital bed largely unresponsive. Early conservative predictions had suggested he'd be discharged and coming home around April 1, yet after five months, he wasn't even ready to start rehab. I tried to sound upbeat about the little progress he was making, like going the night without breathing assistance from the vent. I lamented that he still slept for me but showed off more for others. I shared that he would be starting over at

Kindred soon, starting the process of weaning from the vent again, learning to eat ice chips again, and rebooting physical therapy since he hadn't moved in ten days.

Reading the post, it would have been impossible not to feel my anguish and understand my heartbreak. Over a hundred people left a note of encouragement on that post. If only their love and support could have made Greg well.

After I finished the post, for reasons I couldn't express then and don't fully understand still, I printed off every single CaringBridge post and private journal entry I had written over five months and started reading from the beginning. I started crying immediately—on the first page when I mentioned picking Greg up from work to leave for vacation—and I didn't stop crying the entire time I read. I sat on a stool at the kitchen counter for hours—four? eight?—and completely lost track of time. When I finished with the final page, that "Five Month" update I had just shared, I punched holes in the pages, put them in a thick binder, printed an image of a dragonfly from the internet for the binder cover, and set the binder on a shelf in my office.

I was completely drained.

But I had also gained perspective. I would no longer keep comparing each day to the day before, or even the week before. That was a setup for disappointment. Greg's recovery would never be straightforward, I now fully understood. I resolved that day to compare every day to the beginning, when he was bleeding out in the UCI with teams of neurosurgeons working frantically to save his life. Any responsiveness now would feel like a massive step forward compared to that day.

That night I slept soundly for the first time in a very long time.

Three days later, Greg was out of ICU and settled back into the care of the Kindred team. I still wondered if he would ever wake up and recover.

When I walked into his room a few days later, the physical therapist had him seated on the side of the bed, helping him remember how to hold himself upright. His back was to me, his gown hanging from his bony shoulders, open in the back to reveal every vertebra in his spine. "Guess who's here to see you," she said to Greg.

"Michele," Greg said in a soft voice without turning to look at me, sounding almost bored.

"Say her name nice and loud, Greg."

"Michele!" he yelled, and then laughed because he realized he was shouting. It reminded me of how he always yelled for me from downstairs when I was upstairs at our house instead of coming to find me. It used to annoy me; what I'd give to have him home yelling for me now.

She finished her work and settled him into his chair so I could sit beside him. When she left the room, I pulled a chair close. "You have to keep working hard like that, so you can come home with me," I said.

Then Greg said the most lucid thing he had said since his collapse. "What happened to me?"

Holy shit! He knows something happened. But how much does he know? I didn't know how to explain such a complicated illness when I didn't know yet to what level his brain could comprehend basic cognitive thinking. And I certainly didn't want to scare him.

"Do you remember anything that happened?" I asked. Greg scrunched up his eyes and shook his head no, so I kissed him and said, "Someday I'll tell you the whole story." I thought I had plenty of time to explain.

Cindy was in Denver in early April for a medical conference, so I invited the hand-holders who were in Colorado— Rob and Lee, Rod and Melanie, Susan and Scott—to a dinner of gratitude. These people were not just my support system, they were some of Greg's and my dearest friends, and they had grieved alongside me for months. During dinner, there were tears—at times a lot of them—but we all needed the catharsis of remembering the terror and celebrating Greg's progress together.

At the end of the evening, Melanie asked Cindy what she, as a doctor, thought about Greg's recovery. She had visited him just that afternoon before we came home to cook dinner. "Greg has defied all odds, but he's not doing great," she shared. "He's had so many setbacks it's mind-boggling, but he continues to fight, and we just have to keep taking it one day at a time and work to get him as well as we can." Her comments were sobering. I knew what she was saying: he might not get all the way better. He might not even get "well enough."

Then, as if Greg had heard Cindy and was intent on proving her wrong, he started improving. He got stronger when sitting, engaging his back and head to pull himself up straight when he was falling over. He began working with his therapists in a prone position and learning to flip himself over. He showed anticipation of something being put into his mouth and began eating ice chips again. And, finally, he began talking to me again, even though his brain often struggled to make his tongue say the right words.

When I gave him some ice chips one day, not wanting him to choke, I reminded him to chew. Because he didn't look as though he was chewing or swallowing, I said, "Chew it," and showed him a chewing motion with my own mouth to make sure he understood.

He grinned lopsidedly and started laughing. "I know how," he said.

I regretted talking to him as if he were a child. "Sorry, but honestly I don't know what you understand or not at this point," I said as I took his hand. Greg nodded his understanding, and we smiled at each other. We'll get through this together, I thought.

CHAPTER SIXTEEN

REHAB

ON APRIL 14, Greg was finally ready for rehab. I would have liked the move to have happened mid-week during the daytime, knowing the complete team would be at the new facility when we arrived. Instead, by the time a rehab bed was secured, and the discharge paperwork had been completed by Kindred, it was four-thirty on Friday afternoon. I watched from the curb as the EMTs loaded Greg into the ambulance, then I threw his belongings into my car to follow them.

We drove across town during rush hour before getting on the highway that wraps around the west side of Denver, and as I drove, I pulled out my phone and snapped a photo of the ambulance in front of me. I knew I shouldn't use my phone while driving, but I posted to Instagram anyway:

Greg's 15th ambulance ride—finally left the LTAC and he's on to rehab. #pocoapoco #hopeful #grateful.

It was spring, the season of new beginnings. I was upbeat that Greg would soon start making progress with the additional focus the rehab team would provide.

Because we didn't arrive until after five o'clock, the front door was already locked for the evening. The EMTs wheeled Greg's gurney up the sidewalk while I pressed the buzzer. Then we waited. It wasn't yet dark, the setting sun casting a glow across the parking lot to the ornamental grasses swaying lightly in the warm breeze. I was holding Greg's hand. When I looked at him, his eyes were wide open, surveying everything around him, and it dawned on me he hadn't been outside, other than going in and out of an ambulance, for nearly six months. "It's nice to be outside, isn't it?" I asked. He nodded, watching me. It felt nice to me also, to be out of a hospital room with him, even if just for these few minutes.

I had been discussing Greg's eventual move to rehab for months and had been working with his team to facilitate the move to Spalding, but his setback in March had taken a toll on him. In early April, the Kindred case manager had stopped me in the hall, and said, "We don't think he's strong enough to go to Spalding. I want you to take a look at Care Meridian, a nursing home in Littleton. They accept patients who aren't ready for rehab."

I bristled. Were they giving up before we even started? After all of my negotiations to get him cleared for rehab at Spalding, after these many months of work, how could he end up in a nursing home?

I didn't want to admit it, but she was right. Rehab hospitals required the patient to participate in at least three hours of rehab a day. Greg wasn't even awake for three hours a day, and on his best days had only done about thirty minutes of therapy. Still, I feared if we took this route—a nursing home—he would never recover.

She saw my hesitation. "It's not what you think. They're licensed as a nursing home, but they're really a rehab facility for patients not strong enough for Craig or Spalding. Go visit, you'll see for yourself." She handed me a card with the liaison's contact information.

Jenny went with me to tour Care Meridian. It certainly didn't look like most nursing homes, and the facilities seemed exceptional: pools, rehab gyms, and more. It was new and clean, and the rooms had a homey feel to them. Plus, it wasn't filled with old people who looked ready to die. There were young people who had suffered injuries during military service along with a wide variety of other patients working to get stronger. I asked the liaison if Greg would eventually go to Spalding.

"That's up to you," he said. "Some patients start here then go to another rehab hospital, but many do so well here that they decide to complete their rehab here." He pointed to the grassy area outside of his office where a young man was kicking a soccer ball with his therapist. This patient would go home the next day, he said, which was encouraging. I tried to shake the feeling that we had failed because Greg hadn't made it to Spalding.

After a short wait, someone let us in the building and I followed the nurse to the room assigned to Greg. The EMTs transferred him from the gurney to his new bed. I surveyed the room—private bathroom, nice cushioned bench beside his bed, and far less machinery than at any of the previous hospitals. Yes, this felt like a step forward.

Unfortunately, it was already Friday evening, the lead doctor long gone for the weekend. I delivered a rapid-fire debrief on Greg's care needs to the night nurse. Most pressing was my concern that they suction his airway frequently to prevent another round of pneumonia and ward off another setback. She was kind and enthusiastic, as were the physical therapist and speech therapist who popped in to introduce themselves. I was anxious to get started, but it had been a long day and I was worn out. When I was convinced they had enough of a handle on the basics to care for Greg through the night, I headed home.

Set in the southwestern foothills of a Denver suburb, Care Meridian was a long drive to my house—but a lot closer than Madrid, I thought, turning out of the parking lot. While driving, I realized I would pass right by the house of one of Greg's brokers, the same broker who had been with me when Greg had the massive seizure before my trip. I called him as I drove, and his wife insisted I stop for a glass of wine. Well, it would certainly make my commute easier each day, I thought, knowing I had friends with an open door on the way home.

I collapsed onto their patio loveseat, drained not only from the transfer day, but from everything that had happened in the past six months. His wife handed me a glass of wine. "I feel good about this place. I think he's going to make progress," I said, hoping it was true. "You should come see him tomorrow." We agreed to meet at Care Meridian in the morning, and I drove home to my waiting dogs.

The next day when Greg's broker visited, Greg was awake and animated. He smiled at the nurse as she told him a story, laughed along with her, and even answered a question his friend asked him, correctly naming the broker's youngest son. He's on his way, I thought, he can do this. It was refreshing to be in this new facility, and I wasn't carrying the same worry I'd had before when he'd changed hospitals, the worry about transitioning care when he was critically ill. I kept thinking of the kid kicking the soccer ball from the day before and wondering how long it would take for Greg to make that kind of progress.

CHAPTER SEVENTEEN

FAILING

THAT WAS THE last time I saw Greg alert, the last time he interacted with me, the last time he spoke. For the next two days, he mostly slept.

On Tuesday of that week, Chris helped me bring one of our dogs to see Greg. She hadn't seen him in six months, but her sense of smell was strong, and she nearly dragged Chris across the bed in his room to reach Greg in his chair and launch herself into his lap. Greg never woke up.

On Wednesday, although he was barely awake, they put Greg in a standing harness for therapy. Throughout the therapy, he was unable to track to our conversation, his head turned away from the therapist, staring at the wall. He didn't respond in any way to questions.

Greg was so small and frail; he was only fifty-nine yet looked twenty years older. I couldn't believe how much he looked like his father near the end of his battle with pancreatic cancer at the age of seventy-nine. The therapist decided the standing therapy was too difficult and sat him in a special wheelchair for quadriplegics. Before wheeling him back to his room, I took him to the back patio of the building, hoping he'd enjoy the fresh air. He didn't seem to know where he was or care about a change of scenery, so I wheeled him to his room, put the chair into the safe resting position, kissed him goodbye, and left for the night.

Something's wrong, I thought as I drove home. I had been on this journey for six months and had become hyper-intuitive about Greg's condition. I had called seizures before nurses recognized them. I had advocated for changes in treatment plans based on my research. I had become the head of the team caring for him, and my mind spun out of control with worry that night.

The next day was our thirty-second anniversary. Greg never woke up to celebrate. He didn't look well, and I called the nurse. "He's sick again," I told her. "I'm pretty sure he has another infection in his lungs." She was skeptical—none of his vital signs indicated an infection—but after six months I knew by looking at him, by his lack of responsiveness, that he was sick. Every time he had spiraled, there had been an underlying infection, even when it had been hard to diagnose. He had been treated for pneumonia five times already in the past six months, and I feared the new nurses' inexperience with his suctioning needs had led to pneumonia again.

I was having dinner with Jenny and Ben at Ben's parents' house that evening when the call came: "Greg has another lung infection. We're putting him on antibiotics, so we'll get this handled." I hated that I had been right and wasn't at all convinced they would get it handled. They had only been treating Greg for a week.

The next morning the nurse called to say Greg needed a blood transfusion, so they would be transferring him to a nearby hospital. "Over my dead body is he going there," I wanted to say, knowing they didn't have the advanced facilities or medical team that UC Health had, but I reined in my frustration. "No, he needs to go to UC Health where his neuro team is," I said.

"But our doctor does rounds at this other hospital," she pressed. "He'd like Greg there, so he can follow him. Plus, it's a longer ambulance ride to UC Health."

"Your doctor has only seen Greg for a week. The neuro team at UC Health has been following his case since he collapsed in Spain," I said. "He's going back to UC Health so please order the ambulance right away and I'll meet them there."

After six months of advocating for Greg's care, I didn't hesitate for one second to push back and demand what I thought was best for him. But none of my strength, grit, or determination mattered, because here we were, on the way to the ER once again.

At UC Health, I pressed the doctors for answers. Why did Greg need blood transfusions? They had again ruled out any bleeding in his brain, and he wasn't bleeding externally. So where, exactly, was his blood going?

"We draw blood from him each day, so that could be part of the cause," the doctor said.

I could tell even he wasn't convinced that was a plausible explanation for Greg needing multiple pints of blood. Something was happening to him, something ominous.

"I don't know what we're doing anymore," I said. "He keeps getting sick and never seems to make any forward progress.

Each time he recovers from a setback, he's less responsive—I feel like he's losing cognitive function." I was at the edge of the cliff, and I could feel I was about to jump, fall, or be pushed off. Greg wasn't recovering, and the burden would fall to me to decide what to do next. The doctor had a clear mission—try to save lives. I had a very different job—try to do what I thought would be best for Greg—and the weight of that responsibility was unbearable.

"I understand what you're saying," the doctor said. "Let's run a few tests tomorrow—nothing invasive, just some things that will give you a clearer picture so you know what you are dealing with." He wasn't arguing with me. He wasn't telling me Greg was getting better. I knew by what he wasn't saying exactly what he was saying: he didn't think Greg could recover. By not countering my concerns, he was pushing me frighteningly closer to that cliff.

The nurse brought paperwork for me to sign. I stared at the form asking whether they should resuscitate Greg. I had signed this form seven times already: when Greg was admitted to the hospital in Spain; before the air ambulance ride; twice when he was admitted to UC Health; twice when he was admitted to Kindred; and, most recently, when he was admitted to Care Meridian. On every single form, I had checked the box to resuscitate—yes, please try everything you can to save my husband, my life partner, the father of my children, the love of my life. Now, for the first time in six months, I looked at my frail and sick husband and thought no, enough is enough.

I had long since released any guilt that I was the one keeping Greg alive. It was obvious to me and everyone else that he had been fighting for his life for six months. Now it looked like he no longer had the strength or will to keep going, and I would not make him. I shakily checked the box marked "no" and handed her the papers, then watched guiltily as she placed the card with a big bold letter N over Greg's bed. Who was I to be making this decision? But if not me, then who would make sure that Greg's wishes were followed?

I sat by his bed that evening and sent texts to some of his best friends. "He's not doing well. He's back in ICU at UC Health. I don't feel good about this. If you want to see him, come soon."

I put my phone away and looked at Greg, once again struggling to breathe. I stroked his arm, my tears dripping onto his sheets. "I'm so sorry baby. Is it too much? Are you tired?" I so wanted him to tell me what to do. I wiped away my tears and kissed him goodbye for the night before going home and crying myself to sleep.

On Saturday, a few of Greg's best friends came to see him. I fell sobbing into the arms of each new person coming into his room. How could it possibly be that I was losing him after such a long and difficult fight?

It was gut-wrenching to watch his friends who were essentially saying goodbye to Greg. His breathing got more ragged throughout the day, and each time the nurses suctioned his airway the tubing was full of blood. One friend nearly vomited as she watched. I now guessed why he needed transfusions—it looked like he was bleeding inside his lungs.

This has to stop, it's too hard on him.

But how can I stop now?

We're torturing him.

But I'm not ready to lose him.

I was stepping across a line, my mind and my heart trying to come to grips with the question I'd likely need to answer very soon—was it time to stop treating Greg? But I was frozen, unable to make the next move on my own. I sent a text to the kids. "Dad is not doing great this morning—he's very sick and nonresponsive. They are going to run a few more tests and then we need to make some decisions as a family."

While I had protected the kids from the harsh realities of Greg's critical condition while we had been in Spain, we were now in this together as a family. Jenny and Ben were visiting Jon and Keely in New York for the weekend, and I hated what this text was going to do to their weekend.

"I'm sorry I'm sending this by text instead of calling," I typed, "but it's hard for me to talk right now." My tongue felt swollen in my throat, and I knew it would be impossible to speak, but I needed the family behind me. I needed to know they would support me and that it would be our decision together, not mine alone. They sent their love and support back in rapid fire texts, and I could feel their devastation as I read each text.

For six months, it had been my pattern to update the kids first, then my hand-holders. These friends not only had come to Spain to help me, but also had been my support system, my rock, throughout this ordeal. I sent them a group text with the same message I had sent the kids. They responded with the same support the kids had. We had become so close I could read through their words to their thoughts: they too were worried it was time to stop fighting.

I had made the first move. I had told the kids and my hand-holders that we were facing a decision. I was both horrified and relieved.

It was now early afternoon and there was nothing more I could do. I couldn't bear watching Greg suffer any longer, watching the invasive suctioning process every time he struggled to breathe, so I hugged him hard and kissed his warm, soft cheek before leaving the hospital.

Around six in the evening I sent a text to the kids and the hand-holders to tell them the hospital would perform a test that night to see what was causing so much bleeding in Greg's lungs: "If it's as 'simple' as the blood thinners are causing bleeding and he has an infection from aspirating that can be 'easily' treated, they will treat and hope for a good outcome. If it's more complex or it's not easy to treat, then we'll have a different discussion. I'm home for the night and resting."

I put my phone down and threw myself onto the couch to cry. With my outpouring of tears came the deep pain and frustration that had built up over the past six months. I still couldn't believe Greg had collapsed in Spain. Then, given the multiple times we had thought we were losing him, I couldn't believe he had survived. More than anything I couldn't believe we'd endured six months of such a difficult journey only to have it end like this.

The dogs hovered next to me, sensing my pain as dogs are keen to do, and I stroked their soft heads. I knew what the next day was going to bring. I would need to be at the hospital early to meet with the doctors, and the calls I would need to have with the kids would be agonizing. As I sat crying, I noticed the painting on the wall across from the couch from our twenty-fifth anniversary trip to Italy. I couldn't fathom that Greg would never be with me in Italy again and that our life together was ending. He would never come home to me, I knew, and it cut through my heart like a knife.

CHAPTER EIGHTEEN

THE END

IMAGES OF GREG and his care swirled in my head all night. I didn't sleep more than two hours. At five-thirty, unable to settle my racing mind, I slipped into the hot tub with a cup of coffee. When I realized it was the two-year anniversary of my mom's death, I started to sob as I soaked in the steaming water. The sun rose through the sparse cloud cover, casting a warm orange glow over the backyard, and I thought: please let me have clarity today.

I arrived at the hospital before seven, knowing if I wanted to catch the doctors as they rounded, I needed to show up early and wait. I gowned up and entered Greg's room. The day before, they had put him back on a ventilator to assist his breathing. I had listened to his ragged, uneven breaths all day as he battled his sixth round of pneumonia. Now, his breathing was perfectly synchronized. He was no longer breathing on his own; the ventilator was doing all the work as his body continued to fail. I sat beside Greg and gently held his hand while he slept, listening to the relentless swish of the ventilator.

Every time the nurse came to suction massive bloody secretions out of his lungs, his eyes bulged and his face contorted, and I wanted to scream. Two paths were possible. We could aggressively treat this pneumonia, as tortuous as it seemed, get him back to Kindred, and give him another chance at rehab. Or we could allow this setback to take him peacefully. I had become increasingly concerned about two things: he had been getting less alert, less verbal, less responsive, and seemingly more confused with every infection, and the infections were now coming closer and closer together. I feared even if we treated the pneumonia, he'd soon spiral right back to the ICU.

This was the moment of clarity I had hoped for while soaking in the hot tub: it was time to stop treating Greg. Still, I couldn't believe I was being forced to make this decision. My heart pounded, my head ached, and my mouth was dry. I felt dizzy. I ripped off my scarf and sipped some water.

Later that morning, the doctor came into the room with a group of medical students. I hadn't met him before, which ordinarily would have triggered worry about transitioning Greg's care to someone new. Those details were now unimportant. I sat quietly in the small chair beside Greg's bed as he asked one of the students to present Greg's case.

"Mr. Morris is a fifty-nine-year-old male who suffered a ruptured aneurysm on October twenty-first in Madrid, resulting in a level IV subarachnoid hemorrhage," the student began. I was silent as he continued to explain the evolution of Greg's case, all the way up to this latest bout of pneumonia.

UC Health is a teaching hospital, and the eager young

students were quick to suggest treatments. I squeezed Greg's hand, biting my tongue to stay silent and not interrupt the teaching process. They suggested one possible intervention after another that might prolong Greg's life just a tiny bit longer. When they finished, the attending physician asked if I had any questions.

"Just one," I said. "What if we don't do any of those things? Can we talk about not doing anything more?" I exhaled deeply. The words were finally out, the end-of-life conversation finally started. I knew in my heart it was time. I had made a commitment to the man I loved—I would not let them continue the efforts that now looked like torture. That would not be his choice, and the life he was facing with nursing care would not be what he'd want.

I had talked with Cindy and Peter by phone the day before, wanting to make sure my decision making was sound before stating my wishes to the medical team. I needed their support and approval, the burden of making this decision for my family too great to handle on my own. "From the very beginning I worried this wouldn't be what he wanted," I'd said through my tears. "At best he'll live out his days in nursing care. He would hate that. It's not the life I want for him."

"Mic, Greg would hate a nursing home," Peter began. "We all agree that's not a life he'd ever want. But it's more than that. I told Cindy if this were happening to us, if I were in the shape Greg is in, I wouldn't want *her* to have that life either. You're young, Mic, and have a lot of life ahead of you. I'm certain Greg wouldn't want you to spend every day caring for him in a nursing home. He'd want you to let him go and go on living." Cindy agreed.

I wailed on the phone, a guttural cry that came from deep

inside my psyche. They had known Greg for as long as I had, and I knew they were right. I was so grateful they were helping to carry some of the burden of making the decision.

By raising the question, I had put the wheels in motion with the medical team. "I'd like to talk to you more," the doctor said. "Let me finish rounds and come back."

It wasn't yet noon. I might have to wait a long time to talk to the doctor. I pulled my hand away from Greg and found my cell phone in my bag, dreading the calls I was about to make. I sucked in a giant gulp of air. Then I pushed my heartbreak aside.

I had a job to do now.

I called Chris. We had spent the past two months tip-toeing around what we both feared: Greg wasn't recovering well and maybe we shouldn't prolong his life any further. "I think it's time to let your dad be at peace," I said. I was terrified he would be angry that I was giving up. I could hear him crying gently. "Am I doing the right thing?" I asked, desperate for his support. "Should we keep trying to fight?"

"Mom, I've been preparing myself for this since the day Dad collapsed," Chris said.

Over the months, I had seen Chris continue to ratchet down his expectations for Greg's recovery, just as I had. Back when Greg and I had still been in Spain, Chris had been the first to ask me to put a stake in the ground, and I had told him six months for Greg to recover. Over these past six months, we'd had many conversations about what Greg's deficits would look like. Chris had been doing the same analysis I had been doing: how much is too much? With so much damage to his brain, would Greg have enough functioning left to enjoy any sort of a life at all?

"He wouldn't want to live like this," Chris said. "We need to let him go."

We were both gulping back sobs.

Given the blood transfusions Greg had required on Friday, the amount of blood being suctioned every hour from his lungs, and his dependence on the ventilator, he would likely die quickly once we removed life support. Jenny and Ben were in New York visiting Jon and Keely. I needed to get them all home, so I hung up with Chris and called Jon. When he answered, the four of them were walking in Central Park. As I told Jon it was time to say goodbye to their dad, that they needed to come home, I could hear Jenny weeping in the background.

Later she would tell me she was happy she had been in New York when they got the call because Jon, the only member of the family not living in Colorado, had had to endure the pain of this journey without the rest of the family close by for support. Jon would later tell me how grateful he was to have been there to comfort his sister at such a painful time. Much later, I understood how our tragedy had brought the kids closer to each other, how it pulled our entire extended family into a tight, close circle.

Jenny and Ben were already scheduled to fly home that afternoon. Jon and Keely booked flights for the next morning. I called Greg's younger brother in St. Louis—they wanted to be there also and booked flights for the next day. I called my sister. Greg had been a father figure to her son since their move to Colorado fifteen years before; they would come say their goodbyes to Greg the next morning. I talked with Greg's older brother and his wife. Yes, they said, they would be with us on Monday when the rest of the family arrived. I called a few of

THE END

our closest friends who might want to see him one more time that afternoon.

Calmly and methodically, I worked through the list of people while I waited for the doctor to return to Greg's room to discuss options. When I finished with these calls, I lowered the safety bar on the side of Greg's bed so that I could be closer to him. I scooted my chair as close as I could and wrapped my arm in his arm, so small and frail after all these months. "I love you so much Greg," I said to him, "but I think it's time to let you be at peace." I dropped my head onto his arm and breathed in the smell of him.

It was nearly four in the afternoon by the time the doctor finished rounds and came back to meet with me, this time accompanied by only a single resident. I pulled myself away from Greg and we sat down in the chairs in the corner of the room.

"I'd like to know what you're thinking," the doctor said.

"I've been watching Greg's progress," I said. "He keeps having setbacks. This is his sixth round of pneumonia, and every time he recovers, he's less responsive. In February, when I asked him about our children, he could name them all. Now, when I show him a picture of them, he just stares at it blankly. It seems like there's little chance he can recover to a meaningful life." I was speaking too rapidly, but I had an uncontrollable need to get everything out now that I had made my decision.

He looked me directly in the eye. "You have incredible clarity about the situation," he said. He was an older doctor who traveled between hospitals to teach, and I knew he must have had this same conversation many times before. How do doctors do this, I wondered?

"This is all I've done for six months, so yes, I have clarity," I said. "He keeps bouncing around between hospitals, and in and out of ICU, but he's not recovering."

"I agree with you. While Greg might recover from this current round of infection, it's unlikely he will ever recover fully. Odds are he'll go back and forth between this hospital and another, and he'll eventually die somewhere in between."

As I listened to his prognosis, the finality hit me: Greg will not recover. He won't ever come home. For his sake, for my sake, and for the sake of our family, I needed to let this end. I needed to let him go.

The doctor could see the burden of the decision I was about to make. "I know you're struggling because you believe you're making the decision to let Greg go," he said. "But it's not your decision at all. Look at him—he's dying, and we need to let him be at peace."

I slumped in the chair, the pain too much to bear. The doctor was right. In fact, the decision had never been mine, despite my earlier fears that I was keeping Greg alive against his will. It had been his decision—and strength and courage—that kept him fighting for six months so that he would have that extra time with me, the kids, and the rest of his family and friends. Now he was ready to go, having done what I could only guess he had needed to do before leaving us. For the first time in this six-month journey, I believed I was doing the right thing.

The doctor took my hand. "We'll talk about the next steps, but first, I'd like to know about the two of you, about your family. How did you meet?"

It was too much. His kindness and empathy cracked wide open the hard shell I had surrounded myself with all day in order to accomplish the biggest task I had ever faced in my life. I began to cry, and I told him our story. "We met at college. Bucknell. I was eighteen. We have three kids. We're having a

grandbaby. He wouldn't want to live like this. I know Greg."
I was speaking in short bursts, trying to sum up a forty-year
life together in a few words between sobs, and I hoped he
understood.

As I wept, the doctor, continued to hold my hand, continued to comfort me. He looked to the resident and asked
him if he had anything to add. Yes, this is a teaching hospital,
I remembered, and I pitied this young doctor who would be
assigned to see this case through.

I watched the resident through my tears, as he said, "I only
want to add, we can keep him alive, but we can't give him a
life."

For six months I had wondered if I was keeping Greg alive
only to have him hate me for doing so. This young resident had
summed it up in one sentence: *we can't give him a life.*

That night, with the wheels in motion, family flying in,
and the medical team getting ready to, as they said, transition
Greg's care plan, I sat home alone, feeling oddly serene and at
peace, for the first time in a very long time. I knew it was the
right thing to let Greg escape this misery. It would be the last
thing I could do for the man I had loved for forty years.

Adrenaline coursed through me on Monday morning as
we got ready to go to the hospital. I wandered around the yard
cleaning up dog mess, took the trash out, and emptied the dish-
washer in an almost manic fashion. I went to the liquor store
as soon as they opened, stocking the plastic shopping cart with
bourbon, beer, and cava. If anyone I knew had seen me, they
would have thought I'd finally cracked, finally lost my mind.

While I wasn't consciously thinking it, I was preparing for the wake that would be happening in my house sometime soon.

Jenny and Ben and I stopped for bagels, hoping heavy carbs in our bellies would curb our nausea, but I was unable to eat. I drove Ben to get Jenny's car at his parents' house, so he could pick up Jon and Keely when they landed that afternoon. Everyone else had a plan for getting to the hospital, so Jenny and I went to Greg's room to wait for family to gather.

During the day, a steady stream of people came and went. My sister, her son, and her boyfriend came first and huddled quietly around Greg. Ben arrived with Jon and Keely from the airport; Chris and Katie came soon after. My sister, her son, and her boyfriend left to give the kids and me time alone with Greg before other family arrived. Greg's younger brother and his wife arrived about the same time as his older brother and his wife. Throughout the long day, I alternated between reclining in a chair trying to calm myself, holding Greg's hand and kissing him, and sobbing. I had requested they stop suctioning Greg because it was too difficult for him, but shortly after the request, he regurgitated the feeding from his stomach tube. I asked the nurse to remove the feeding tube and suction his stomach out fully to ease his pain. The only other treatment administered was a heavy sedative anytime we worried he was in pain.

By four o'clock that afternoon, our family had gathered. The nurse came into Greg's room and glanced towards me briefly. Her eyes softened as she saw my face. "Are you ready?" she asked us.

The day before, the doctor had said, "Michele, you've done all you can. Greg is ready." He hadn't asked me if *I* was ready. Would I *ever* be ready for this?

THE END   273

I blinked and tried to look away, unsure of what to say, afraid to open my mouth, afraid my grief would come pouring out.

The nurse reached out to touch my shoulder, because she could see I was near collapse. I was heartbroken, crestfallen I couldn't save Greg, that his long six-month journey from Madrid to today, despite heroic efforts by the medical teams and a heroic battle on his part, would end this way. I stared at the polished linoleum floor and nodded my head decisively yes. But I couldn't look the nurse in the eye, knowing what would happen next. There was pain and torment on the kids' faces, and I ached that I could not protect them from this loss and grief. I clenched my teeth; I had been clenching my teeth to prevent a meltdown ever since this nightmare had started.

I stared at Greg. Please let him be at peace.

Then, just as quickly: I'm not ready to lose him.

"I'll explain what's going to happen next," the nurse said.

For six months, everyone had been telling me how I strong I was; now I needed to draw on that strength. I needed to help Greg let go, and I needed to help my family through this, even though my own grief was asphyxiating. I walked towards the bed and stood right next to the nurse, our family silently surrounding Greg, tears rolling down our cheeks, waiting for her to make a move. In the silence, the ventilator and monitors around us sounded louder than before. The room was too warm. It felt suffocating and oppressive. There were still so many things hooked up to Greg. Ventilator. Feeding tube. Catheter. IV. Central line. Blood pressure. Pulse ox. The machines were crowded together—too many of them. The nurse had explained she would be removing everything except an IV to administer pain meds and a monitor to track Greg's breathing. If I was going to lose Greg, then I ached for it to happen quickly and for him to die peacefully. Turn it all off immediately, I willed. Then I scolded myself: stop rushing this. He's going to die when it's time, and nothing I do, or think, will speed up or slow down that process. For six months, this battle had been Greg's, not mine, and I could no more control how or when he died than I could anything else these past six months.

The kids were all crying. I don't remember any of them saying goodbye to their dad, only I love you. Chris and Katie and Jon and Keely had told me earlier they didn't want to witness Greg's death, so I hugged them hard before telling them to go home and be together, choking back my own tears.

After they left, I looked at everyone around Greg's bed—his brothers and their wives on one side, Jenny and Ben with me on the other. Nobody was breathing.

Without saying a word, the nurse began to turn off the machines as we watched. Suddenly it was completely silent except for Greg's ragged breaths. One breath. A longer breath. A still longer breath. Then several seconds of no breath. I held my own breath, counting in my head. One, two, three, four, five....

"Is this it?" I asked the nurse

But then Greg began the ragged breathing pattern once again. One breath. A longer breath. A still longer breath. Then several seconds of no breath. One, two, three, four, five....

"It could take time," she said, before slipping out the door quietly, to give us privacy.

After thirty minutes of watching Greg and listening to every one of his ragged breaths, Jenny was near breaking. Ben gathered her into his arms, where she looked more like a wounded child than a woman. "Let's go home to be with your brothers," he said gently. Tears streamed down her face as she left with him. I collapsed into the chair in the corner, allowing myself to finally cry with abandon now that the kids were gone.

After another hour, as Greg continued his shallow breaths, the nurse came into the room. "We don't know when he'll die," she said. "It might not be until tomorrow." With that news, Greg's older brother and his wife said their final goodbyes to him and went home for the night, promising to return in the morning if he was still alive. His younger brother went to my house to be with the kids. My sister-in-law Lynn, who had come to Spain in December, stayed so I wouldn't be left alone to watch Greg die.

"There have been so many people here all day," she said. "You need some time alone with him. I'm going to the cafeteria for a few minutes."

"It's okay baby, you can go," I said to him quietly after she left the room. I caressed his face while he struggled for each breath. The nurse had turned off the display in the room to make it more peaceful for our family, monitoring his progress instead from the nursing station, but I hated not knowing where things stood, so I turned the monitor back on. I couldn't believe how Greg was continuing to fight to breathe, and I needed to see for myself on the monitor what was happening, fearing we had made a mistake, that we shouldn't be doing this. His oxygen levels were far below what was considered necessary for sustaining life, yet his heart continued its strong, even beating. Unbelievably, each time I wrapped my arms around Greg and talked to him, his oxygen levels actually improved slightly.

He's fighting to stay with me, I realized. Everything he had done these past six months, his heroic fight to survive, he had done for me, for our family. Although they had given him plenty of morphine and he didn't look as if he was in pain, I worried he was suffering; it was excruciating to watch. "You don't have to do this anymore," I said. "I'm going to be okay."

Lynn returned to the room, and I sat down to give her a chance to try to help Greg transition. "We love you," she said, rubbing his arm. Then to me: "Maybe he isn't going to die if he thinks we are still here." Although the nurse had assured us he wasn't in pain, I still worried about that as we listened to each scratchy inhale and exhale.

Please let him be at peace, I thought again.

And again, just as quickly: I'm not ready to lose him.

It was now ten at night, six hours after we began the process of withdrawing life support and twelve hours after I had arrived at the hospital. My head felt disconnected from my body: I am going to lose my husband. I couldn't believe it or accept it.

My cell phone buzzed, and when I saw it was Chris, I answered.

"How are you holding up?" he asked. In the six months since Greg's collapse, our relationship had transformed. He was no longer an uncertain young adult needing guidance and direction. He had become a strong and supportive man, and a nurturing caregiver.

"I'm okay," I told him.

"What's happening there?"

"I don't know. It doesn't seem like he's ready to die."

"It's ten o'clock, Mom. You aren't planning to spend the night there, are you? Are you going to stay until he dies?"

"Don't you think I should?" I whispered, barely able to speak. How could I leave the man I had loved for my entire adulthood to die alone? This sense of obligation was something I didn't understand—I hadn't felt the need to be with my parents or Greg's when they had passed. But this was different. This was my husband, the love of my life. I had been bedside for the last six months, so shouldn't I see it through and stay until he died? Would it be selfish to let him die alone?

"It's time to come home, Mom. You're exhausted. You haven't eaten all day. You've done everything you could for Dad." Chris paused for a few seconds. "We need you here more than Dad needs you there. Just come home, okay?"

"Okay." I exhaled. Later I understood: Chris had given me the permission I needed to leave, helping me realize that while Greg was dying, my kids were very much alive. They were hurting, and they needed me.

I hung up. Lynn looked at me, and we both started crying.

"The kids want me to come home," I told her. "And I don't think Greg wants to die with me here." Did I believe that or was I just looking for a way past the suffocating guilt?

For six months, I had agonized that I was fighting to keep Greg alive, possibly to endure a miserable life with painful deficits. I feared he would hate me for what I had done, for not letting him die in Madrid. Now I understood: I hadn't been keeping him alive at all. For one hundred and eighty-five days, he had been fighting to live. He had needed to come home from Spain and see his kids. He had needed time with his best friends. He had needed to laugh with his colleagues. He had needed to hear he was going to be a grandfather. He had needed to know Jon and Keely were getting married. I believed he had wanted to kiss me, to hold my hand, to tell me he loved me, for just a little longer before he was ready to go. Had he died in Spain, none of that would have happened. I knew how very lucky we were to have had the past six months with him, and I was overwhelmed with gratitude that he had fought so hard. What an incredible final gift he had given me.

I turned to him, my face an inch from his, and whispered, "I will always love you. It's okay for you to stop fighting now. We're going to be okay. The kids and I will take care of each other, I promise." I kissed him one last time and then buried my face in his neck as I wept.

Lynn and I walked down the long, quiet corridor of the empty hospital and out into the night air. It didn't seem possible I would never see or touch my husband again.

I walked into the kitchen through the back door from the garage, and I heard Greg's voice immediately, stopping me in my tracks. Had it all been a dream?

The kids were playing family movies on the TV in the family room. Instantly I felt grateful for the many videos Greg had narrated, even though it was impossible to believe this would be the only way I could ever hear his voice again. The kids had ordered pizza and were drinking, half toasting to memories of their dad, half anesthetizing themselves. The wake, it seemed, had already begun.

"The nurse said it could take time," I told them. "I don't know how he's still breathing. He just keeps fighting. I don't think he was going to let himself die if I had stayed." I was still trying to dismiss the oppressive guilt I felt for leaving Greg.

The kids had music playing over the sound from the video, and they alternated between laughing at home movies and crying manically. We were all too exhausted to function well, but too filled with adrenaline to relax. Jenny poured me a glass of cava. "Here Mom. I love you." I wrapped my arms around her and held her for a while as she cried.

Thirty minutes later the nurse called. "Greg's breathing is changing. I think he's close to the end."

"Thank you." I hung up. The kids hovered close to me. How would they survive without their dad? How could I possibly parent them solo? "He's transitioning," I told them.

Ten minutes later the phone rang again. We all knew what it meant.

"Hello?"

"Hello. I'm calling from University Hospital," the doctor said. "Is this Michele?"

"Yes."

"How are you?" he asked.

What a bizarre thing to ask. How am I? How am I supposed to be when you are about to tell me my husband has died? "I'm fine," I lied.

"Greg has taken his last breath. He died peacefully a few moments ago," the doctor said. "Be with your family. The hospital will call you tomorrow to discuss arrangements. I'm very sorry for your loss."

I hung up the phone and let out a guttural wail as the kids threw their arms around me.

The love of my life was gone.

CHAPTER NINETEEN

A YEAR OF GRIEVING

THREE WEEKS BEFORE Greg died I told my writing coach I wanted to write this book, but it felt wrong to start it before Greg recovered. I envisioned telling a story that began with our tragedy abroad and ended with Greg's miraculous homecoming. My private fantasy was that we'd go on a book tour together where everyone would applaud his recovery as I retold the harrowing story.

It wasn't until after he died that I understood. *Poco a Poco* was never meant to be about Greg's journey. This book is about *my* journey—my heartbreak, my grief, and my quest to survive the tragic loss of the only man I ever loved.

There is no prescribed way to travel through grief after a significant loss. If anyone says they know what the journey is like, at best, they know what *their* experience was like. Everyone handles loss differently—what follows is how

I traversed my very personal grief journey in the year after Greg's death.

For the first days after Greg's death, I was unable to do anything. Sleep eluded me, my mind continually replaying scenes from our six-month journey. I had a constant headache. I was sick to my stomach and unable to eat. I cried hysterically, then stopped abruptly. I had never understood that grief actually hurt physically. In those early, tender days, my grief came in waves, sometimes so gentle I could easily skip over the wave, sometimes so strong the pain literally knocked me to my knees. This is what experts call acute grief.

I have little memory of what I did during the first few weeks, but my calendar shows a steady stream of activity. Friends took me to lunch or dinner. I bought a new condo, desperate to escape the ghosts of our old house. I helped Chris and Katie pick a crib. I went for a massage. I cleaned out my house in preparation for a neighborhood garage sale. I went to Pilates classes. I rode my bike with Susan. I played golf with friends. I had a physical. I took the dogs for grooming. I had my windows cleaned.

On paper it looks completely normal, but in between all of these routine calendar entries are clues that it wasn't. Appointments with my therapist. Meetings with financial planners. A visit to the lawyer to revise my estate documents. A tour of Greg's company's new office space, which he never saw completed. A new tattoo of a Celtic friendship knot to symbolize the phrase *Anam Cara*—which means friend of the soul—to remind me of the friends who had been unwavering during our difficult journey.

It was hard for me to find meaning early after Greg's death. Religious scholars have written that religions formed over the years largely around each civilization's need to find peace and comfort through their difficulties. Gods of plenty were imagined by people who were hungry. Gods of peace were created to soothe victims of war. And heaven was imagined because people needed to believe their loved ones were "in a better place." In contrast, my pragmatic and rational beliefs offered little to soothe me now.

I so wanted to believe Greg was with my dad and his dad, golfing and telling jokes. I wanted to believe he was with old friends, laughing and having a beer. But I simply didn't. I knew a little about the laws surrounding the conservation of energy in the universe. While energy might change forms—a spark to fire to heat, for example—in the end, the universe is believed to be a closed system and the energy remains constant. When someone dies, it then stands to reason, the energy from their body must be absorbed somewhere in the universe.

The day after Greg died, I sat in the hot tub early in the morning, gently crying. I listened to a bird chirping—one Greg had loved, with a two-tone chirp: *WHEEE-whooo*. I was mesmerized for a moment, then realized I was trying to attach meaning to the sound. *WHEEE-whooo, WHEEE-whooo, WHEEE-whooo*.

Suddenly the bird sounded different to me: *THANK-you, THANK-you, THANK-you*. Was Greg telling me I had done the right thing in letting him die in peace? It was the first time—but most certainly not the last—I felt Greg's energy and presence surround me after his death.

Without the daily demands of Greg's care, I understandably

felt relief—and then, predictably, suffered from survivor's guilt. For months I questioned decisions I had made along the way, struggling to accept that it was okay to be relieved it was over. If I enjoyed my life in any way after Greg died, did it mean I didn't love him after all? Of course not. But in times of grief, our thoughts aren't always rational.

I became highly attuned to signs and symbols. A mug from Cherry Hills Country Club (Greg's golf club) strangely showing up in a restaurant fifteen miles away. A new friend who had also lost a spouse to a ruptured brain aneurysm. A store full of dragonfly items right next to quotes from Winston Churchill (Greg's middle name was Winston, named for Churchill). A chance encounter with a doctor from Denver who had been in Madrid the day Greg collapsed. Another full moon.

I made a conscious decision very early to accept any invitation to be with friends, as difficult as it was. Some people hugged me too long and hard—it was suffocating, and I thought I would break. Some people had no idea what to do or say. I wasn't sure what felt worse—when people didn't acknowledge that Greg has passed, or when people wouldn't stop talking about it. I needed an escape line: "I'm sorry, I know you mean well, but I can't do this right now." Instead, I tolerated their good intentions and tried to smile.

When someone seemed to be sadder than I somehow felt they should be, I reacted angrily, lashing out to close friends and my therapist. I had trouble understanding how other people's relationships with Greg affected them and how they were grieving. I struggled with the irrational thought: how dare anyone steal my grief?

I came as close as I ever had to full blown panic attacks, struggling to accept that Greg was gone, in disbelief that our life together was over. Some nights I couldn't wait to go to sleep, hoping I would see him, hear him, touch him in my dreams. When I didn't, I woke up depressed. The first time I scattered some of his ashes—in San Francisco Bay with Cindy in early May—the thought that he would never be coming back hit me so hard it felt like a lightning strike. When I inevitably saw photos of him in our home, I couldn't believe he was gone.

I had never understood funerals as a child, thinking them morbid and pointless, but at Greg's memorial, I finally got it. I scheduled the celebration of his life to coincide with his sixtieth birthday in June, but I began writing his eulogy within days of his death. I needed time to think about what I wanted to say about him. I needed to shed the acute disabling grief that was smacking me down every day, and I needed to be able to see friends without instantly bursting into tears. I didn't want a funeral with mourners because that wasn't what Greg would have wanted. I wanted a party that truly celebrated him—as a man, as a father, as a husband, as a friend, as a boss, and as a leader in our community. Two months after his death, this seemed manageable.

During our journey, I had been continually surprised by the kindness of both friends and strangers, but nothing over-whelmed me as much as the friends who sponsored Greg's cel-ebration of life. I wanted to hold the celebration at Greg's golf club, but I had resigned from the club six months before, so I called our good friends Michael and Teresa to see if they would sponsor the event—in name only, because I fully intended to pay for the party. We had been friends since our kids had played lacrosse in high school; we'd traveled with them and had shared parenting challenges, and Michael and Greg were golf buddies. They kindly agreed to sponsor the celebration, then added they wouldn't let me pay for anything.

I objected instantly. The attendance would likely be huge, possibly hundreds of people, and I knew how expensive the party would be.

But Michael pushed back. "Michele, it's the least we can do. It's been difficult for many of us to assist you during the last six months, and this small gesture would be helpful for us."

I was only beginning to understand how it helped our friends who were also grieving to help me and my family.

In the end, thirty-three couples stepped forward to sponsor Greg's celebration of life. As I marveled at this tremendous show of support for our family, it occurred to me that one of the gifts of Greg's dying so young was that most of his friends were still around. They were there to rally around me and my family, they were there to honor Greg and tell us how much he had meant to them, and they all gathered—an incredible 550 people from near and far—to celebrate Greg's life.

I knew it would be difficult to speak at the celebration, but I had been "speaking" to our friends through CaringBridge for months. This felt like my final entry. I wanted to be the first at the celebration to honor Greg. I wanted to set the tone by describing the man I loved so that people understood what he meant to me. And I wanted to publicly express my gratitude for the doctors who had given us just a little more time with Greg.

As the three kids stood to speak next, I reached for my tissues, overwhelmed to see them as both strong adults and vulnerable children in one single moment. Jon spoke about funny camping trips that had always ended with some mishap for Greg and the boys. Jenny had hoped the lightness of his words would make it easier for her to speak next. It didn't. When she opened up her piece of paper to speak, her face instantly contorted in grief, and she began to cry. Chris, who hadn't intended to speak, stepped up to the podium, took the paper from Jenny, and began to read. He had never seen what she had written, but he read the entire thing without stumbling. Jenny ended her tribute with, "In this life and all the rest, Namaste, Dad." Greg had always gently poked fun at her slightly hippy tendencies and her tattoos of Buddhist symbols, and this was both a joke back to him, as well as her heartfelt wish for him to find peace after death. I was so proud of all three of them and proud that Greg and I together had raised such incredible young adults.

Cindy and Peter, Greg's brothers, and various friends and colleagues spoke next, everyone smiling and laughing at the stories and memories they shared. The celebration was exactly what I had hoped for, and the party continued for hours. Greg had never wanted any party to end—perhaps that was why he had fought so hard for six months—and the celebration of his life was exactly the party he would have wanted.

During the three months following the celebration of Greg's life, as if I had learned nothing from the six months of his hospitalization, I attacked my days with intent, purpose, and a strong will to direct and control every aspect of my grief journey. I overfilled my time; if I was busy, I wouldn't wallow in the sadness. Because I'd decided to accept every invitation for a lunch, coffee, drink, dinner, party or trip that was offered, I was rarely home and rarely alone. It was easier to smile and remain stoic in a public place than alone in my house. So I kept running.

I went to my niece's wedding in Asheville and explored the Biltmore estate, art galleries, and botanic gardens.

I began working again, accepting catering jobs for large parties, teaching cooking classes, and blogging.

A week before Greg died, I had begun looking for a new home that could meet his needs. But within days, when it became clear he would not survive, my search shifted to looking for a home that would meet *my* needs. I didn't want to stay in our home any longer, too sad that Greg wasn't there with me. I needed a fresh start, and knew I would need a project to fill my days.

Remodeling a condo provided the perfect distraction during the first months after his death. I picked out cabinets, designed a teaching kitchen, chose lighting, met with plumbers, directed the placement of light switches, picked paint and stain colors, chose tile, designed my master bathroom, and bought appliances. It was a fun diversion that helped fill my time each day.

I marched through the closing of Greg's estate, advocating for life insurance benefits, negotiating contracts to transfer assets, conferring with lawyers and financial planners, and reconciling medical bills.

For three solid months, I used busyness as a way to control my grief. Although I couldn't escape my sadness entirely, I had created an alternative reality where I controlled my grief instead of my grief controlling me. And as long as I kept doing things, kept overly busy every day, I was able to stay in control.

I even said to Susan one day, "I think I'm doing quite well managing my grief," as if it were some contest or competition.

Towards the end of September, I felt an emotional shift. Carter Winston Morris was born late in the month, carrying the middle name of the grandfather he would never meet. Despite the tremendous joy I experienced witnessing the miracle of my first grandchild's birth, I cried all the way home from the hospital. Greg would never be a grandfather; I would be entering this wonderful stage of life alone. I tried tamping down these feelings to concentrate on the sheer joy I felt of being a grandmother, but the shift was already under way, my carefully crafted control starting to crack.

A few days later, it was time to move into my renovated condo. Eight women rallied to help me carry the entire contents of my kitchen in tubs from my house to the condo to save time packing and unpacking. I had pictured the day like this: we'd pack up my old house in the morning. I'd pull out the chicken salad I had made, and we would have lunch together. After lunch we'd drive to the condo and place everything in the specific cabinets, drawers or closets I had mentally assigned for things, finishing in the late afternoon. Then we'd sit on the back patio and sip the cava I had refrigerated while we ate pizza.

That's not at all how it went.

Everyone had different schedules, so some came earlier than I had planned, and some arrived later. The work felt haphazard, not orderly. I hadn't gauged how chaotic it would be having so many people emptying the kitchen and loading cars, bumping into each other as they moved in and out of the house. If anyone ate the chicken salad, I don't remember it. We packed up the old house more quickly than I had anticipated, and by mid-day we were descending on the new house like the front line of an army. The builder wasn't expecting a crew like this—the house was still full of dust and noise as workers were frantically trying to finish things before my movers showed up with furniture the next day. As the women carried the contents of my kitchen in from their cars, they tracked construction dirt onto the shiny new wood floors. Everything was happening so fast, I barely had time to direct traffic:

"Yes, china in that closet over there."

"No, not there—put the silverware in that drawer left of the stove."

"I don't know, can you give me a sec?"

I couldn't keep up. I felt the snap. I was no longer in control—not just of arranging my kitchen, but of my grief journey. I turned away from everyone, collapsing into a massive meltdown, and my friends bundled me into a big group hug.

In hindsight, it was a textbook reaction. All of that busyness for the prior three months had, on most days, barely kept me one step ahead of my grief. Now, with the remodel project over and the move underway, the finality of Greg's death was unavoidable. While I was still living in the old house, I now realized, I had carried some tiny fantasy that I might wake up one day and he'd be there. As I let go of the fantasy, I also let go of any efforts to control my grief.

I grieved hard for most of October, crying more and obsessing more about my loss than I had at any point in the journey. The grief had been festering. It was time to surrender to it. Although Greg died in April, I felt like I had really lost him when he collapsed in Spain. October 21 marked that anniversary, and I sobbed to my hand-holders about my loss. I had now been without my husband for a full year.

As I worked on this book with my writing coach, I delved deeper into the emotions of the experience. Through that work, I became almost addicted to writing, to the process of assessing and rehashing everything that had happened. On some days I cried so violently as the story came pouring out that I couldn't even see the computer screen. But as I continued to write, as I talked with friends, and as I processed the entire journey and loss with my family, I slowly began to heal.

On September 30, just two days after I had moved, my kids and best friends brought a potluck feast to my new home for my birthday—the first one I would celebrate without Greg.

On October 28, I had a housewarming party, attended by a hundred friends.

On November 1, I went to a cooking school in Italy for two weeks to relax and recharge.

I hosted Thanksgiving at my condo, surrounded by my entire family.

I decorated my house for Christmas, attended holiday parties, and made a feast for Christmas Eve dinner with my family.

I hosted a New Year's Eve party with close friends.

I spent time every week with my sweet grandson.

I often felt joyful and found much to celebrate, but in between those days and moments, I continued to grieve that Greg was no longer a part of my everyday life. Too often, I sought comfort in potato chips and cava. Sometimes my sadness was more pronounced if I had been drinking—that maudlin response to alcohol. Sometimes I drank because I wanted—needed—to cry. I was raw. I relinquished all need to control my grief and submitted to it fully.

Throughout those final months of 2017, although I had moved into my new house, I felt more like I was preparing to live here than actually living here. It was difficult to find my rhythm, in a new house, alone, when none of the rituals of my prior life carried over. I spent more time organizing, decorating, unpacking, hanging art, and furnishing the condo than I did living in it. I had trouble finding a routine for the normal activities of daily living: cooking, cleaning, laundry, caring for the dogs, shopping. I rarely sat still.

I also found myself doing things that were out of character: playing music while I was alone in the house, lighting candles, watching football, and adding a television in my bedroom. It wasn't until later, as I continued to write about this journey, that I understood these were things Greg would have done. The music, the candles, the football, and the TV in my bedroom all made it feel like Greg were here with me.

As the year came to an end, my grief softened. The jagged edges smoothed over and no longer felt as sharp or painful. I was emerging from grief. New Year's has always been my favorite holiday, representing new beginnings and a chance for a fresh start, and January 1, 2018, was no different.

Early in 2018 I discovered that being able to say "My husband died last year"—instead of last month, or this year—put the loss at a bit of a distance. With that distance, I gained a newfound sense of peace and acceptance that helped me develop new routines. My life wasn't over, just different. Instead of either running from the loss of my old life or preparing for my new life, I began to simply live my life.

My schedule was still full, but not because I felt the need to be busy all the time in order to hide from my sadness. I began relishing a quiet weekend at home with the dogs to relax and unwind, something I had been terrified of during the months of intense grieving in late 2017. My new house began feeling like my home. I added houseplants and new artwork. I created a wall of family photos. I was comforted by talking to Greg's photo in my closet each morning as I dressed. I discovered the spot on the couch I liked for watching television. I resumed making dinner for myself, learning how to shop and cook for one. I began living my single life and enjoying my work, my friends, travel, dinner parties, family visits, my grandson, food photography, and my volunteer work. I still had times when I broke down about my loss—I sobbed daily during the two weeks leading up to the anniversary of his death, rehashing every single thing that had happened. But more often I smiled and laughed at the memories I cherished from Greg's and my forty years together.

I was with some of our very best friends—Cindy and Peter and Rob and Lee—exactly one year after Greg's death. We smiled and laughed at our shared memories, toasting Greg as we set off together on a trip to explore the Kentucky Bourbon Trail—an adventure Greg would have loved. At only one point during the trip did I look around at these good friends and collapse into tears, thinking Greg would never be with us again.

Instead of my grief overwhelming me daily, I now carry my grief beside me. I will always miss Greg, but know that I can, and will, survive without him, because he will always be with me, in my heart.

Love never dies.

Epilogue

IT'S NO SURPRISE that, because of this experience, I carry a deeper understanding that life is short, or that I cherish every moment with those people I love, but I've changed in other ways as well. While I still like to organize and direct, I catch myself when trying to control things I know I can't. I didn't find Jesus or join a church or start believing in heaven or hell when Greg died, but I no longer have the need to make rational sense of or produce a scientific explanation for everything; some things are simply beyond explanation. I believe the universe sends signs every day, and I slow down and take time to notice—something I rarely did before Greg's collapse. While I still don't believe in a God who controls our world, certain events I experienced were too uncanny to be dismissed as coincidence. I learned, from my sister, to call these synchronicities, and they give me strength during difficult times.

Perhaps as a natural extension of those aspects of spirituality, I now attach quite strongly to many symbols, but none so much as the dragonfly. I know dragonflies were here before Greg collapsed, but the way they have presented themselves to me, my family, and our friends since has been nothing short of spectacular—landing on friends' hands, showing up at precise moments that are just too uncanny, or hovering in front of my face when I'm dealing with a crucial decision.

When Colorado inevitably settled into winter, the sightings of live dragonflies stopped, but they continued to arrive in many other forms from friends near and far. A framed card, a tissue box cover, twinkly dragonfly lights, a garden ornament, a door-stop, three dragonfly necklaces, a crystal dragonfly, cards, a small frame with a jeweled dragonfly, a candle, a kitchen towel, a charm, a vase, and a gorgeous six-inch glass dragonfly.

I don't know what happened to Greg after he died, but it comforts me to think that maybe he was reincarnated as thousands of dragonflies who have been sent on a mission to remind us all of his life, bring us joy, and make us smile. I feel his presence every time I see one.

Many people over the six months of Greg's hospitalization and the months following his death told me, "You're amazing." Every time, I flinched, feeling as if I had been slapped. It was meant to be a compliment, but it never felt that way, and it was months before I understood my vehement reaction:

If I was so amazing, why hadn't I been able to save Greg?

It wasn't a rational thought. Teams of the very best doctors in both Spain and Colorado, along with millions of dollars of medical care, had been unable to save Greg. In no way should I have borne this responsibility. Yet I did. For four full months after Greg's death, I wasn't willing to release my grip on that guilt. I played it back often to my best friends, hoping they could talk me down before I spiraled completely out of control. When his autopsy report arrived in August, I scanned the first paragraph, my eyes locking on the final sentence:

Ultimately, the chances for meaningful recovery were deemed nonexistent.

From the day of his collapse, I'd worried that Greg would never recover; here was a definitive report telling me I had been right. The report confirmed I had done the compassionate thing in letting him die, and I finally released that massive burden of guilt. It wasn't surprising that he had died; rather, it was shocking to realize how hard he had fought to live for six months even though his body was so frail. Months earlier, I had told my therapist I would be furious if he died after we had worked so hard to keep him alive, but with the autopsy report in my hands, I felt nothing but gratitude to Greg for the heroic effort he had made for us.

Nine months after he died, when a friend asked how I was doing, I said what I always said: "I'm so grateful I have a full life. I have a career, I have kids, I have a grandson, I have lots of friends, I volunteer with three nonprofits, I golf, I ride my bike, and I'm comfortable traveling alone. That doesn't mean I don't miss Greg every day, but I'm doing well." In the beginning, it felt like if I said it enough times, I'd start to actually believe it. After nine months, I think I did.

"Greg would be proud of you," my friend said.

That was when I finally understood: I had endured the long and painful journey without Greg telling me I had done a good job, without him thanking me, without him saying he was proud of me.

Oddly, he had always needed praise and recognition for his accomplishments much more than I did. Seeing results from my hard work had usually been enough for me, and I had never needed others to acknowledge my success to feel successful. But this time, despite all of my efforts, I hadn't succeeded; Greg hadn't survived. I had failed at the most challenging task I had ever faced, and although I knew Greg would have said thank you if he had been able, I ached to hear him tell me he knew I had done the very best I could.

I would not have reached this understanding without the reflection and introspection required to write this book; telling the story of my journey has been extremely cathartic. While I had written either on CaringBridge or in my private journal every day Greg was sick, taking the time to reflect on the experience in the year after his death helped me "unpack" everything for a clearer understanding of what it meant to me and how it shaped me. I am stronger, healthier, and more at peace because of this book. Writing about my journey gave me a powerful gift: I forgave myself for not being able to save Greg, a burden I hadn't even known I was shouldering until I started writing.

I hope my story provides inspiration for others who suffer the unfathomable pain of grief and loss.

ACKNOWLEDGMENTS

THIS BOOK WOULD not have been possible without the guidance of my writing coach Shari Caudron. I am deeply grateful for her education, coaching, and emotional support. I also owe thanks to my fellow writers who provided feedback on drafts of my manuscript: Melanie Buscher, Carol Grever, Rachel Kodanaz, Tanja Pajevic, and Sandra Windsor. Rebecca Berg, your edits were invaluable. Susan, thank you for proofreading, "just one more time."

To the many medical professionals, both in Spain and in Colorado, thank you for giving my family and our friends just a little more time with Greg. I could not have navigated the complexities of Greg's care without the gentle guidance and steadfast commitment of these special doctors: Dr. Susana, Dr. Eduardo, Dr. Gabriela, Dr. Mariana, Dr. Case, Dr. Cava, and Dr. Neumann. I was humbled by the gentle care every nurse, orderly, and therapist provided to Greg—thank you all.

Everyone who is suffering should have a group of hand-holders—words cannot express my gratitude to these special friends: Cindy, Peter, Melanie, Susan, Rob, Lee, Lynn, and Gail. Cindy was there for me every single day—or night—during this journey, whether I needed medical advice or just a shoulder from my oldest friend. Thank you for your love and support, your honesty, and for making me laugh.

To Greg's close friends who visited him regularly to help with his recovery—Don, Doug, Michael, RC, Rob, Rod, Pete, Scott, and Tim—Greg lit up when you were with him. Thank you for helping him—and my family—smile and laugh in a dark time.

To every friend who helped by taking over a task, bringing food, walking my dogs, cleaning up my yard, writing a note of encouragement, sending me a dragonfly, or any other act of kindness, thank you for your tremendous generosity and car-ing. My sister Janine gently encouraged me to accept the help of friends, and I am deeply grateful she took on the daunting role of managing the care calendar.

To the hundreds of friends in Denver and across the coun-try who helped us celebrate Greg's life, thank you. Special thanks to Michael and Teresa and our other friends who gener-ously hosted the event at Greg's beloved golf club.

To the many strangers in Madrid who stepped forward to help after tragedy struck—especially my friends Clodagh and Pedro—I will never forget your kindness.

Thank you to my entire extended family, who helped to carry me through this most difficult journey, and who con-tinue to uplift and support me. I love you all.

Chris, Jon, and Jenny: your dad will always be with you, cheering you on, celebrating your successes, and carrying you through life's difficult times. You meant the world to him, and he was so proud of you. He loved you fiercely, and he will live in your hearts forever.

CPSIA information can be obtained
at www.ICGtesting.com
Printed in the USA
FSHW01n1804220818
51550FS